Endorsements for *Modelling Paralanguage Using Systemic Functional Semiotics*

This innovative theorizing of meaning-making via the facial expression, gesture, posture, body movement and vocal qualities such as loudness, pitch level and tension provides new analytic frameworks to enhance research in social interaction in multiple disciplinary contexts. An indispensable resource for social semiotic research.

Len Unsworth
Professor of English and Literacies Education
Australian Catholic University, Australia

A highly relevant and necessary book for researchers interested in expanding Halliday's multifunctional theory to the study of meaning of the semiotic resources embodied in our voices, gestures, facial expressions and postures in order to enact social relations.

Teresa Oteíza
Associate Professor of Linguistics
Pontifical Catholic University of Chile, Chile

A timely and welcome addition to the field demonstrating robust developments in systemic functional theory and its application. It draws together leading experts in this domain, offering critical insights and various pathways for further exploration. A must-read for linguists and specialists in non-verbal communication alike.

Luke A. Rudge
Senior Lecturer of Linguistics
University of the West of England, UK

Modelling Paralanguage Using Systemic Functional Semiotics

Bloomsbury Studies in Systemic Functional Linguistics

Series Editors:
David Caldwell, University of South Australia, Australia
John S. Knox, Macquarie University, Australia
J. R. Martin, University of Sydney, Australia

Advisory Board:
Thomas Andersen (The Danish Language Council, Denmark)
Chang Chenguang (Sun Yat-Sen University, Guangzhou, China)
Priscilla Cruz (Ateneo de Manila University, Philippines)
Meg Gebhard (University of Massachusetts Amherst, USA)
Isaac Mwinlaaru (University of Cape Coast, Ghana)
Teresa Oteíza (Pontifical University of Chile, Chile)
Mary Schleppegrell (University of Michigan, USA)
Akila Sellami Baklouti (University of Sfax, Tunisia)
Miriam Taverniers (University of Ghent, Belgium)
Orlando Vian (Federal University of Sao Paulo, Brazil)
Li Zhanzi (National University of Defence Technology, Nanjing, China)

Among functional approaches to language and related semiotic systems, Systemic Functional theory stands out as an evolving paradigm, constantly developing new systems to accommodate descriptive challenges. Bloomsbury Studies in Systemic Functional Linguistics responds to this ever-developing field, speaking to instances of evolution at the frontier of the discipline.

Publishing contemporary, cutting-edge research in Systemic Functional Linguistics, this cohesive series unites complementary developments into an integrated multiperspectival whole. Titles focus on specific themes to explore emerging new fields of research in Systemic Functional theory alongside innovations within long established areas of SFL research. Placing emphasis on new voices and directions, Bloomsbury Studies in Systemic Functional Linguistics demonstrates how a disciplinary singular like SFL continues to evolve and subsume its past into possible futures.

Modelling Paralanguage Using Systemic Functional Semiotics

Theory and Application

Thu Ngo, Susan Hood, J. R. Martin, Clare Painter,
Bradley A. Smith and Michele Zappavigna

BLOOMSBURY ACADEMIC
LONDON • NEW YORK • OXFORD • NEW DELHI • SYDNEY

BLOOMSBURY ACADEMIC
Bloomsbury Publishing Plc
50 Bedford Square, London, WC1B 3DP, UK
1385 Broadway, New York, NY 10018, USA
29 Earlsfort Terrace, Dublin 2, Ireland

BLOOMSBURY, BLOOMSBURY ACADEMIC and the Diana logo are
trademarks of Bloomsbury Publishing Plc

First published in Great Britain 2022
This paperback edition published 2023

Copyright © Thu Ngo, Susan Hood, J. R. Martin, Clare Painter,
Bradley A. Smith and Michele Zappavigna, 2022

Thu Ngo, Susan Hood, J. R. Martin, Clare Painter, Bradley A. Smith and
Michele Zappavigna have asserted their right under the Copyright, Designs
and Patents Act, 1988, to be identified as Authors of this work.

Series Design by Toby Way
Cover illustration © Magnia / Shutterstock

All rights reserved. No part of this publication may be reproduced or transmitted in
any form or by any means, electronic or mechanical, including photocopying,
recording, or any information storage or retrieval system, without prior
permission in writing from the publishers.

Bloomsbury Publishing Plc does not have any control over, or responsibility for, any
third-party websites referred to or in this book. All internet addresses given in this
book were correct at the time of going to press. The author and publisher regret
any inconvenience caused if addresses have changed or sites have ceased
to exist, but can accept no responsibility for any such changes.

A catalogue record for this book is available from the British Library.

Library of Congress Cataloging-in-Publication Data

Names: Ngo, Thu, author. | Hood, Susan, 1952-author. | Martin, J. R., 1950-author. |
Painter, Clare, 1947-author. | Smith, Bradley A. (Research assistant), author. |
Zappavigna, Michele, author.
Title: Modelling paralanguage using systemic functional semiotics: theory and application / Thu Ngo,
Susan Hood, James R. Martin, Clare Painter, Bradley A. Smith and Michele Zappavigna.
Description: London; New York: Bloomsbury Academic, [2022] |
Series: Bloomsbury studies in systemic functional linguistics |
Includes bibliographical references and index. | Summary: "This book is the first
comprehensive account of 'body language' as 'paralanguage' informed by
Systemic Functional Semiotics (SFS). It brings together the collaborative work of internationally
renowned academics and emerging scholars to offer a fresh linguistic perspective on gesture, body
orientation, body movement, facial expression and voice quality resources that support all spoken language.
The authors create a framework for distinguishing non-semiotic behaviour from paralanguage,
and provide a comprehensive modelling of paralanguage in each of the three metafunctions of meaning
(ideational, interpersonal and textual). Illustrations of the application of this new model for multimodal
discourse analysis draw on a range of contexts, from social media vlogs, to animated children's narratives,
to face-to-face teaching. Modelling Paralanguage Using Systemic Functional Semiotics offers an innovative
way for dealing with culture-specific and context specific paralanguage"– Provided by publisher.
Identifiers: LCCN 2021025523 (print) | LCCN 2021025524 (ebook) |
ISBN 9781350074903 (hardback) | ISBN 9781350074910 (ebook) | ISBN 9781350074927 (epub)
Subjects: LCSH: Paralinguistics. | Systemic grammar. | Functionalism (Linguistics) | Body language.
Classification: LCC P95.5.N46 2022 (print) | LCC P95.5 (ebook) | DDC 410.1/833–dc23/eng/20211012
LC record available at https://lccn.loc.gov/2021025523
LC ebook record available at https://lccn.loc.gov/2021025524

ISBN: HB: 978-1-3500-7490-3
PB: 978-1-3502-7758-8
ePDF: 978-1-3500-7491-0
eBook: 978-1-3500-7492-7

Series: Bloomsbury Studies in Systemic Functional Linguistics

Typeset by Newgen KnowledgeWorks Pvt. Ltd., Chennai, India

To find out more about our authors and books visit www.bloomsbury.com
and sign up for our newsletters.

For Theo

Contents

List of Figures	x
List of Tables	xii
Preface	xiii
Phonological transcription conventions	xiv

1	Embodied meaning: A systemic functional perspective on paralanguage	1
2	An ontogenetic perspective on paralanguage	45
3	The semiotic voice: Intonation, rhythm and other vocal features	67
4	Ideational semovergence: Approaching paralanguage from the perspective of field	91
5	Interpersonal paralanguage: Approaching paralanguage from the perspective of social relations	115
6	Textual convergence: Approaching paralanguage from the perspective of information flow	161
7	Afterword: Modelling paralanguage	197

Appendices	213
Notes	231
References	241
Index	257

Figures

1.1	Kendon's Continuum	2
1.2	English MOOD systems	6
1.3	Metafunctions: A trinocular spectrum of meaning	9
1.4	Stratification: A trinocular perspective on realization	11
1.5	Basic organization of IDEATION	12
1.6	Discourse semantic systems	18
1.7	A model of behaviour	20
1.8	Somasis and semiosis	21
1.9	Sonovergent and semovergent paralanguage	41
1.10	Alternative realizations of expression form in language	43
1.11	Emblems as gestural signs	43
2.1	Early somasis	48
2.2	Hal's protolanguage at ten-and-a-half months shown as a system of affect	53
3.1	Praat visualization (with annotated Praat functions) showing RHYTHM and SALIENCE	71
3.2	Praat visualization showing RHYTHM and SALIENCE	72
3.3	Praat visualization showing rhythmic pauses	73
3.4	Praat visualization showing tone 1	75
3.5	Praat visualization showing super-salience	81
3.6	Praat visualization showing pitch range	82
4.1	Paralinguistic entity network	95
4.2	Paralinguistic figure network	101
4.3	Paralinguistic state figures	103
4.4	Paralinguistic occurrence figures	105
4.5	Paralinguistic entitied occurrence figures	105
4.6	Iterating occurrence figures	108
4.7	The system of FLOW and DIRECTION in occurrence figures	110
4.8	A system network for paralinguistic figures	111
5.1	The system of APPRAISAL in English	118
5.2	Oppositions in the system of AFFECT in language	119
5.3	The system of FACIAL AFFECT	121

5.4	The system of FACIAL AFFECT and PARALINGUISTIC FORCE	124
5.5	Perceptual channels for identifying ideational triggers	126
5.6	The system of VOICE QUALITY	130
5.7	The system of VOICE AFFECT	131
5.8	VOICE AFFECT as [spirit:down] with opposing features of [misery] from [ennui]	133
5.9	Voice qualities realizing features of [fear], [anxiety] and [anger]	135
5.10	Voice quality realizing [surprise]	138
5.11	The system of BONDING	141
5.12	The system of ENGAGEMENT in language	144
5.13	The system of PARALINGUISTIC ENGAGEMENT	144
5.14	The system of PARALINGUISTIC (body) GRADUATION	145
5.15	The system of PARALINGUISTIC PROXIMITY	148
5.16	The system of PARALINGUISTIC ORIENTATION	150
5.17	The system of PARALINGUISTIC POWER	151
6.1	Taxonomy of recoverability strategies triggered by presuming reference	163
6.2	A partial system of PARALINGUISTIC DEIXIS	166
6.3	An extended system of PARALINGUISTIC DEIXIS	169
6.4	Modelling the hierarchy of periodicity in language	185
6.5	The circuit of body movement synchronous with four-figure sequence	189
6.6	Extended circuit of body movement, beginning with hyper-Theme	191
6.7	Circuit of body movement convergent with macro-Theme, hyper-Theme and four-figure sequence	192
6.8	Body position and movement synchronous with hyper-New	194
7.1	Semiotic versus somatic behaviour	198
7.2	Sonovergent versus semovergent paralanguage	199
7.3	Paralanguage in relation to metafunction	199
7.4	The place of emblems in our model of language and paralanguage	204
7.5	Approaches to multi/modality (ontic vs discursive relations)	206
C.1	Praat visualization showing time, frequency and energy (or intensity)	226
C.2	Visual representation of harmonics showing voice 'tenseness'	227
C.3	Visual representation of rough and smooth voice quality	227
C.4	Visual representation of breathy and clear voice qualities	228
C.5	Visual representation of vibrato and plain voice qualities	228

Tables

1.1	SFL metafunctions	3
1.2	Discourse semantic systems	12
1.3	Convergent verbiage/image relations in children's picture books	21
1.4	Sonovergent and semovergent paralanguage	22
1.5	Sonovergent paralinguistic systems	23
1.6	Converging discourse semantic and paralinguistic systems	29
1.7	Concurrent construals of entities in examples (66)–(69)	29
2.1	Somasis contrasted with Nigel's gestural signs at nine months	49
2.2	Microfunctions of protolanguage: Active and reflective	52
2.3	Emotions underlying early microfunctions	52
2.4	Categories of 'body language'	60
4.1	Terminology for describing ideation at each stratum of language	92
4.2	Concurrent construals of entities	94
5.1	The linguistic system of AFFECT and opposing features	119
7.1	Sonovergence – language and paralanguage	207
7.2	Semovergence – language and paralanguage	208

Preface

This book is based on a series of workshops involving the authors held at the University of Sydney, beginning in January 2016. Their goal was to further develop the work on paralanguage, which was developed as part of the research on Youth Justice Conferencing consolidated in Zappavigna & Martin (2018). Chris Cleírigh, who worked as a research assistant on that project, was a key figure in developing the model deployed in that work.

During the workshops Brad Smith led the discussions on prosodic phonology (intonation and rhythm) and Clare Painter the discussion of language development. Jim Martin concentrated on general modelling issues. Their contributions are reflected in Chapters 1 to 3 and Chapter 7 of this book. The group as a whole worked on the development of ideational, interpersonal and textual resources – Michele Zappavigna drawing on her interest in social networking, Thu Ngo on her research on animated films and Susan Hood on her focus on academic discourse. The results of these discussions are documented in Chapters 4 to 6.

We are deeply indebted to our functional linguistic colleagues around the world for their feedback during presentations of one or another aspect of this material over the past three years. In particular, we would like to thank Lorenzo Logi for his painstaking editing of a challenging manuscript into its current form.

We would like to dedicate this book to our colleague Theo van Leeuwen for his undaunted and ever-inspiring work drawing attention to the meaning-making resources that abound in all dimensions of human culture. He has opened a pathway for our research and for many multimodality scholars around the world.

Phonological transcription conventions

[numerals]	choice in TONE
//	tone unit boundary (always also foot boundary)
/	foot boundary within tone unit (always also syllable boundary)
[**bold**]	tonic syllable
[*italic*]	salient syllable
^	silent Ictus
↑, ↓	significant jump up or down in pitch which does not involve a choice of tone, signalling pronounced salience
::	stretched sound
+	high falling tonic
_	low tonic (underscore)
–	restart (dash)
[…]	non-verbal happenings

Note: This list has been adapted from Halliday and Greaves (2008: 210–11).

1

Embodied meaning: A systemic functional perspective on paralanguage

1.1 Embodied meaning

Commenting on a pivotal moment in his career, Australia's legendary Indigenous singer Archie Roach speaks about his wife's reaction to his reluctance to take up a recording offer as follows:

> 'Even if I live to be a thousand years old, I'll never forget what happened', Roach recalls about the moment. 'Ruby seemed to gather herself up taller than I'd ever seen her before, put her hands on her hips (then) she turned sharply and went about her day, leaving me with a lot to think about.' (Roach, 2019: 215)[1]

No words were spoken; but life-changing meaning was exchanged.

In this chapter we introduce our social semiotic framework for analysing paralanguage that accompanies spoken English discourse. Our approach draws on the New South Wales Youth Justice Conferencing research consolidated in Zappavigna and Martin (2018).[2] The foundational unpublished paper is titled 'Gestural and Postural Semiosis: A Systemic-Functional Linguistic Approach to "Body Language"' (by Chris Cléirigh); this model informs work published by Zappavigna et al. (2010), Hood (2011), Martin (2011b), Martin and Zappavigna (2013) and Zappavigna and Martin (2018). Cléirigh's work drew in part on Matthiessen's synopses (2004, 2007, 2009) of work on early child language development informed by systemic functional linguistics (hereafter SFL). Following Matthiessen (2009), we use the term 'paralanguage' to include

- gestural resources arranged along what McNeill (1992) formulated as 'Kendon's Continuum' (including gesticulation, pantomime and emblems, but not sign language);
- facial expression, posture and body movement; and

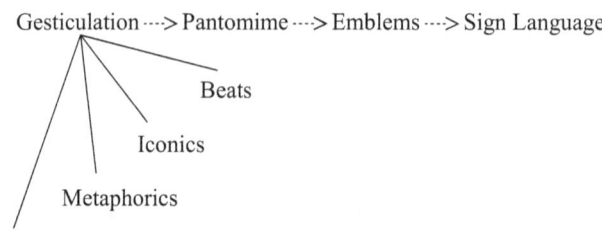

Figure 1.1 Kendon's Continuum (as rendered in Sekine et al., 2013).

- the vocalizations outlined in van Leeuwen (1999) which are not usually included in linguistic descriptions of the segmental and prosodic phonology of spoken language (timbre, tempo, tension, pitch range etc.).

There are of course many ways to classify gestural resources. Kendon (2004: Chapter 6) provides a thorough historical survey. The most useful vantage point from which to compare classifications is what has come to be known, following McNeill, as Kendon's Continuum. The introductory chapters in McNeill (2000, 2012) include clear presentations of the model outlined in Figure 1.1 (taken from Sekine et al., 2013). The basic idea is that as we move from left to right across the continuum the gestures noted have less need to accompany spoken language and share more properties with language proper. We will cross-reference our work to this model as we present our framework in this book, setting aside the sign languages of deaf communities (ASL, BSL, Auslan, Amaslan, LSF etc.)[3] since these are languages in their own right (themselves involving paralanguage; Johnston, 2018).

Following on from groundbreaking SFL-inspired studies by Martinec (1998, 2000a,b, 2001, 2004, 2008) and Muntigl (2004), we will organize our description of paralanguage around the kinds of meaning being made – in SFL terms the trilogy of ideational, interpersonal and textual meaning.[4] Ideational meaning involves resources for construing reality, interpersonal meaning involves resources for enacting social relations and textual meaning involves resources for composing information flow. Textual meaning corresponds roughly to the beats and pointing/deictics shown in Figure 1.1; ideational and interpersonal meaning involve what are labelled as iconic and metaphoric gestures on that continuum. The correspondences with Kendon's distinction between representational and pragmatic functions of gestures are outlined in Table 1.1. Ideational gestures would be representational in his terms; and his pragmatic gestures (defined as not involving referential or propositional content) include both interpersonal

Table 1.1 SFL metafunctions (ideational, interpersonal and textual meaning)

SFL metafunctions	'Function'	Kendon (2004: 158–9)
Ideational	Construing reality	Representational
Interpersonal	Enacting social relations	Pragmatic (modal, interactive, performative)
Textual	Composing information flow	Pragmatic (parsing)

and textual functions. We clarify the place of metafunctions in SFL theory in Section 1.2.

In this chapter we proceed as follows: In Section 1.2 we present an introduction to the SFL theory and descriptions informing our work; readers familiar with SFL may wish to skip over this review. In Section 1.3 we touch briefly on SFL research on early child language development – work which will be more fully developed in Chapter 2. We then move on to draw a distinction between behaviour (somasis) and meaning (semiosis), and introduce our current paralanguage framework in Sections 1.4 and 1.5, respectively. We close with a note on emblems. As noted earlier, for this framework we adopt the term 'paralanguage' to refer to semiosis dependent on language and realized through both voice quality and body language (including facial expression, gesture, posture and body movement).

1.2 Systemic functional linguistics

There are a number of reasons why our SFL-informed interpretation of paralanguage is timely. One has to do with the explosion of SFL-inspired work on modalities other than language triggered by Kress and van Leeuwen (1990, 1996), who focused on single static images. As reviewed in Martinec (2005), Taylor (2017) and O'Halloran et al. (2019) this work has now been extended to the study of diagrams, PowerPoint slides, webpages, comics, picture books, animations, film, sound and music, architecture, sculpture, toys and behaviour. Since so many texts involve one or more of these modalities, it is advantageous when studying intermodal relations to be able to draw on descriptions informed by the same theoretical principles. The concept of metafunction introduced earlier, for example, allows us to compare like with like as far as convergence and divergence of meaning across modalities is concerned (Painter et al., 2013).

Paralanguage is so closely coordinated with spoken language and so regularly implicated in intermodal texts of several kinds that the usefulness of a common metalanguage is clear.

Alongside theoretical integration, SFL is particularly well-suited to the study of paralanguage in a number of ways. One is that it provides a linguistically informed model of prosodic phonology (Halliday, 1967; Halliday, 1970a; van Leeuwen, 1992; Martinec, 2002; Halliday and Greaves, 2008; Smith and Greaves, 2015) which can be used to make explicit the coordination of rhythm and intonation in spoken language with beats and strokes in gesture. This facilitated Martinec's development of Kendon's (1972) early work in this area, taking into account later work by Tuite (1993). We will in fact suggest that what SFL refers to as a tone group, analysed for rhythm and intonation, provides an essential unit of analysis for work on paralanguage as far as questions of synchronicity across modalities are concerned.[5] SFL's description of English rhythm and intonation is the focus of Chapter 3.

Another advantage of SFL is the clear distinction it draws between paradigmatic and syntagmatic relations (system vs structure in SFL terminology). As is well-attested, there is more variation in the language structures realizing systemic options than in the underlying systems themselves (Caffarel et al., 2004). This is even truer when comparing the structural realization of systems from one modality with another. Kendon's (2004: 186–7) well-known example of the different trajectories of the gestures accompanying *sliced the wolf's head off* versus *sliced the wolf's stomach open* illustrates this point. The swinging arm motions are very different structurally from the clause structures in play; but from the perspective of system, the oppositions in meaning are comparable.[6] Systematically separating system from structure is crucial when comparing and contrasting modalities.

We also feel that further development of Martinec's pioneering modelling is timely in light of theoretical and descriptive developments in SFL since his work. This has mainly to do with proposals for the stratification of language as levels of phonology, lexicogrammar and discourse semantics (e.g. Martin, 2010, 2011b; Martin and Rose, [2003] 2007); this model of stratification is the one adopted for this book. Martinec's work draws largely on Halliday's lexicogrammatical systems (those proposed in Halliday, 1985), the same systems which inspired Kress and van Leeuwen's (1990) breakthrough. We have found it illuminating to further develop this work by drawing on ideational, interpersonal and textual systems at the level of discourse semantics (IDEATION, APPRAISAL, IDENTIFICATION and PERIODICITY in particular).[7] Work on APPRAISAL (the language of evaluation)

(Martin and White, 2005) has a number of ramifications for models of paralanguage, especially in relation to the relative marginalization of these resources in canonical work by Calbris (2011), Kendon (1997) and McNeill (2006). These discourse semantic systems will be introduced in Section 1.2.

1.2.1 SFL: Theoretical parameters

In this section we introduce the three main theoretical parameters which have shaped our model of paralanguage: axis (the complementarity of paradigmatic and syntagmatic relations), metafunction (kinds of meaning) and stratification (levels of semiosis).

Systemic functional linguistics, as the name of the theory implies, distinguishes itself from other linguistic theories by foregrounding systems as the foundational organizing principle for description. Drawing on Saussure's notion of valeur, it conceives of language (and semiosis in general) as a network of systems (Martin, 2016; Martin et al., 2013a). Each system involves choices (usually two or three) which have structural consequences shaping anything we mean. The relationship between system and structure is referred to technically as axis. By way of illustration, consider the following examples – taking note in particular of the segments highlighted in bold and the effect they have on meaning:[8]

(1) Because **I would** be talking to the people in the comments…
(2) **Can we** talk about it?
(3) **What else** can we talk about?
(4) **Talk** about it.

In the first example the sequence *I would* indicates that the clause is giving information. In the second and third the sequence *Can we* indicates that the clauses are asking for information. In the third *What else* specifies the kind of information being asked for. And in the fourth example the absence of these indicators and the tenseless verb *talk* (which comes first in its clause) indicate that we are asking someone to do something. These grammatical oppositions are formalized in Figure 1.2. The square brackets therein mean 'or' (e.g. a clause can be either indicative or imperative, an indicative clause can be either declarative or interrogative); and the downward slanting arrow links the different choices to their structural consequences (i.e. realization statements organizing the structures we contrasted informally earlier).[9]

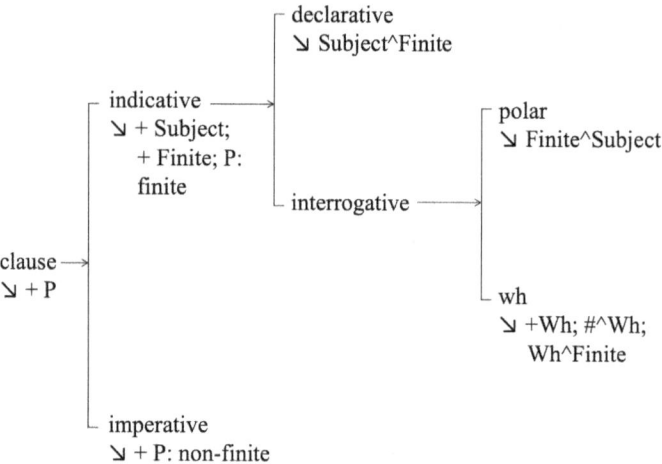

Figure 1.2 English MOOD systems.

We will not go into detail about this kind of formalization here; detailed accounts can be found in Matthiessen and Halliday (2009) and Martin et al. (2013a). We introduce the system network in Figure 1.2 at this point to clarify what it means to say that SFL involves a relational theory of meaning (rather than a representational one). This means that SFL treats language (and semiosis) as a resource for meaning (rather than a set of rules about what one can say or not). What matters are the relationships among choices, as they are formalized in system networks. The basic organizing principle for descriptions is thus paradigmatic, rather than syntagmatic. Note however that for a paradigmatic choice to be meaningful, it must have structural consequences; system depends on and is motivated by structure (Martin et al., 2020). In Chapters 4, 5 and 6 we will use system networks to model paralanguage as a resource for meaning.

Over the past five decades of research (Martin, 2016), SFL has generalized a number of key parameters concerning the way paradigmatic relations are organized in language. One is **metafunction**. Consider now the choices in (5)–(8). In (5) the speaker hears something happening; in (6) she predicts the children will ask for food; in (7) she notes that she has in fact just fed them; and in (8) she comments on a state of affairs.

(5) I hear children coming.
(6) They're going to ask for more food.
(7) I just gave them Chex Mix and applesauce squeezes.
(8) Something's up.

What matters here are choices about what is going on (sensing, speaking, acting or describing). At the same time we need to take into account that each one of these clauses is related to alternatives reflecting the oppositions in (1)–(4). We illustrate this for just clause (6).

(6') They're going to ask for more food.
(9)   Are they going to ask for more food?
(10) What are they going to ask for?
(11) Ask for more food.

Contrast now clauses (12) and (13). Both clauses are like (1) earlier – they are giving information. And in another respect both clauses are like (7) earlier – they are about something happening. But they differ from each other with respect to whether the temporal circumstance *next time* comes first or last.

(12) I will get my hair colour back **next time**.
(13) **Next time** I will get my hair colour back.

If we put (13) back into the text from which it comes, we can see how putting *next time* early makes sense – since in that position it contrasts nicely with *for now*, which comes first in the ensuing clause (where it also could have come last).

(14) So hopefully **next time** I will get my hair colour back;
(15) but **for now** this will do.

Putting *next time* and *for now* early in the clause also has implications for the way these clauses are spoken, with both phrases naturally given phonological prominence in a separate intonation contour from the remainder of the clause. We present the details of this analysis in Chapter 3; key elements of the notation are outlined here (adapted from Halliday (1967, 1970a) and Greaves (2007)).

'//' marks a tone group boundary
'/' marks a foot boundary
italics indicates a salient syllable
bold indicates a tonic syllable (i.e. the salient syllable carrying the major pitch movement in the tone group)
the numeral (1, 2, 3, 4, 5, 13, 53) indicates the tone choice

What matters for the current discussion is the phonological prominence encouraged by the sequencing (marked in bold in the examples that follow).

(14')
// ... so
//3 *hope*fully next / ***time*** I will
//1 *get* my / ***hair*** colour / *back* //

(15')
//3 [handclap] / *um* / *but* for / ***now***
//3 *this* will / ***do*** //

Our focus here is on the way that information is organized – as clauses which are alike in terms of the oppositions in (1)–(4) and (5)–(8) enter into further oppositions (e.g. (12)–(13)) so they can fit coherently into a text as it unfolds.

In SFL the oppositions in (1)–(4), (5)–(8) and (12)–(13) and oppositions closely associated with them are generalized as metafunctions (Halliday, 1970b) – interpersonal, ideational and textual (respectively). Interpersonal resources are concerned with enacting social relations, ideational resources with construing what is going on and textual resources with composing the flow of information in discourse. The basic idea here is that we almost always mean three things at the same time and that in order to understand language (and semiosis) we have to analyse it from three points of view (one kind of 'trinocular' vision in SFL). In this respect SFL is very different from models of language which distinguish form and meaning, treat meaning as representational (semantics) and then ask questions about how representational meanings are used (pragmatics).[10] SFL's paradigmatic perspective on meaning suggests on the other hand that the oppositions in (1)–(4), (5)–(8) and (12)–(13) are not stacked up in layers – from form to meaning to use. Rather the sets of oppositions are seen as complementary kinds of meaning, generalized as metafunctions and manifested simultaneously in everything we speak, write or sign. A model of this spectrum of meaning is presented as Figure 1.3.

Metafunctions have been SFL's most influential parameter as far as multimodal discourse analysis is concerned. Kress and van Leeuwen's (1990) groundbreaking publication and its better-known reworking (Kress and van Leeuwen, 1996) are both organized around the spectrum of meaning SFL calls metafunctions (Kress and van Leeuwen's interaction, representation and composition). It is crucial to keep in mind that metafunctions are generalizations about bundles of oppositions. Kress and van Leeuwen's breakthrough depended on their paradigmatic perspective on how images make meaning – formalized as system networks and tables in Kress and van

Embodied Meaning

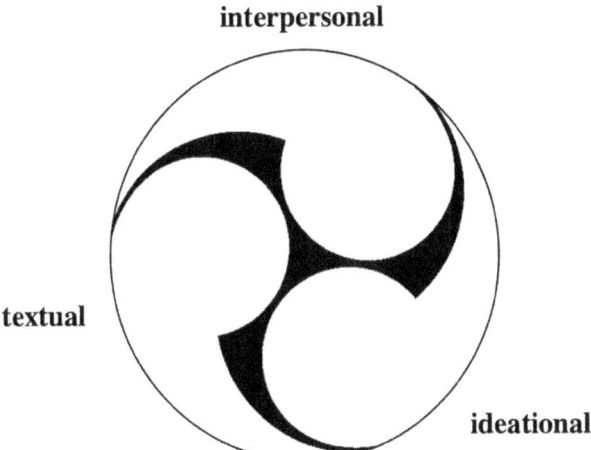

Figure 1.3 Metafunctions: A trinocular spectrum of meaning.

Leeuwen (1990: 49, 61, 86, 108).[11] This relational approach enabled them to bypass the pseudo-problems arising when scholars searched for syntagmatic units in semiotic systems that realize systems in structure very differently from the way language does. As critiqued in Martin (2011b), very little of the work inspired by Kress and van Leeuwen has proceeded along similar lines – unfortunately relying instead on notional definitions of ideational, interpersonal and textual meaning to explore modalities of communication other than language.

Another key parameter we need to consider here is **stratification**. When introducing the textual metafunction earlier we talked about the way in which the sequence of elements in a clause encouraged different kinds of intonational phrasing. Although not made explicit, we were discussing grammatical oppositions in relation to phonological ones. In (12)–(13), for example, we were contrasting structures realizing grammatical oppositions.

(12')   I will get my hair colour back **next time**.
(13')   **Next time** I will get my hair colour back.

And in (14)–(15) we brought rhythm and intonation into the picture.

(14")
// ... so
//3 *hope*fully next / ***time*** I will
//1 *get* my / ***hair*** colour / *back* //

(15")
//3 [handclap] / *um* / *but* for / ***now***
//3 *this* will / ***do*** //

It should be clear from the examples that the choices about sequencing in a clause and those about rhythm and intonational prominence are different oppositions. In SFL the terms 'lexicogrammar' and 'phonology' are used to refer to these distinctive bundles of oppositions. The lexicogrammar of English comprises oppositions distinguishing morphemes, words, groups and phrases and clauses; the phonology of English comprises oppositions distinguishing phonemes and syllables and managing rhythm and intonation.[12] SFL uses the term 'lexicogrammar' because it models lexis as delicate grammar – with more general options in system networks realized by structures and the more specific options realized by lexical items. Phonology and lexicogrammar are treated as different levels of abstraction, with phonological oppositions realizing lexicogrammatical ones.[13] The Danish linguist Hjelmslev (1961) referred to these levels of languages as the expression plane and content plane, respectively.

In the model of stratification assumed here, Hjelmlsev's content plane is itself modelled as a stratified system, with discourse semantics realized through lexicogrammar. This makes it possible to entertain the possibility that (14) earlier was in fact negotiated in conversation as a request for goods and services rather that an offer of information. This is exemplified in the exchange that follows. What is significant here is that even though the first move is grammatically declarative, its speech function is negotiated as one we might normally associate with an imperative clause (a clause such as *Get some of my hair dye from Target for me, will you?*, for example).

(16)
So hopefully next time I will get my hair colour back.
- OK, I'll go to Target for you.

The process whereby the content plane makes meaning on two levels, one symbolizing the other, is referred to in SFL as grammatical metaphor (Halliday, 1985). The grammatical metaphor in (16) is an interpersonal one, with declarative MOOD symbolizing a command. Ideational grammatical metaphors can be interpreted along similar lines. In (19), for example, what is construed verbally in (17) and (18) is construed nominally as *her desire for restoration of her hair colour* and *her visit to Target*. The nominal groups in (19) thus encode occurrences as if they were entities.

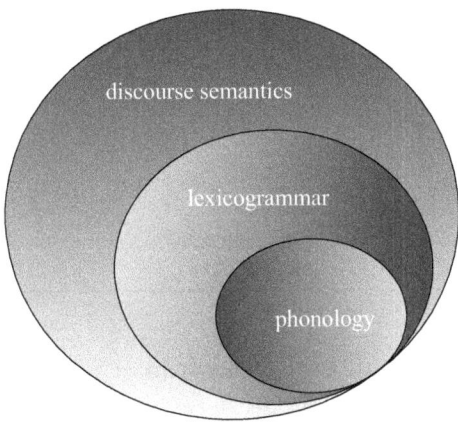

Figure 1.4 Stratification: A trinocular perspective on realization.

(17) She wanted to get her hair colour back,
(18) so she headed to Target.
(19) Her desire for restoration of her hair colour prompted her visit to Target.

The second major advantage of stratifying the content plane has to do with meaning beyond the clause. This allows SFL to move beyond a lexicogrammatical conception of text as a bag of clauses and set up systems and structures dealing with cohesive relations of indefinite extent (Martin, 2015b). These discourse semantic systems will be introduced in Section 2.2. They are crucial to our work on paralanguage since in our model it is these systems rather than lexicogrammatical ones that converge with paralanguage in spoken discourse.

A model of this trinocular perspective on levels of language is presented in Figure 1.4. In SFL the co-tangential circles of increasing diameter have been designed to capture what is technically referred to as metaredundancy – the 'pattern of patterns' principle whereby discourse semantics is conceived as a pattern of lexicogrammatical patterns and lexicogrammar is in turn conceived as a pattern of phonological ones (Matthiessen and Halliday, 2009).

1.2.2 Discourse semantics

We will briefly introduce six discourse semantic systems here, organized by metafunction as per Table 1.2. For a detailed presentation of these systems, see Martin (1992), Martin and White (2005) and Martin and Rose ([2003] 2007); useful introductory overviews include Butler (2003), Martin (2009, 2014,

Table 1.2 Discourse semantic systems (organized by metafunction)

Metafunction	Discourse semantic systems
Ideational	IDEATION
	CONNEXION
Interpersonal	NEGOTIATION
	APPRAISAL
Textual	IDENTIFICATION
	PERIODICITY

2015a, 2019) and Tann (2017). For each system we will note the diversification of grammatical systems realizing discourse semantic ones, including where relevant what we will refer to as metaphorical realizations; and we will exemplify what we mean by co-textual relations between units of discourse that are not grammatically related to one another (i.e. meaning beyond the clause). As will be introduced later, in our model paralanguage converges with discourse semantic systems in language, not lexicogrammatical ones – IDEATION, APPRAISAL, IDENTIFICATION and PERIODICITY in particular.

1.2.2.1 Ideational discourse semantics

The key ideational discourse semantic systems are IDEATION and CONNEXION.[14] IDEATION comprises resources for construing experience as goings-on and relationships. The basic framework for analysing IDEATION adopted here is based on Halliday and Matthiessen (1999), Hao (2015, 2020a) and Doran and Martin (2021). As flagged in Figure 1.5, it deals with sequences consisting of one or more figures and figures consisting of one or more elements; and the main types of element are occurrences, entities and qualities – which in various combinations constitute figures. In simple terms, occurrences realize activity, entities realize items participating in activity and qualities realize associated

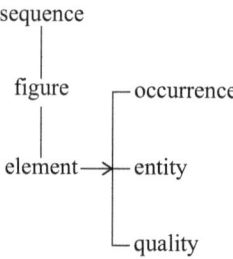

Figure 1.5 Basic organization of IDEATION.

properties. Figures including an occurrence are referred to as occurrence figures (e.g. *she headed to Target*); figures not including an occurrence are referred to as state figures (e.g. *her hair dye wasn't there*).

In terms of diversification IDEATION allows us, for example, to position[15] figures lexicogrammatically through a range of clause types (Halliday and Matthiessen, 1999; Hao, 2015, 2020a,b):

(20) (behavioural clause realizing the positioning of a state Figure)
'It will be kind of fun', **she smiled**.

(21) (mental clause realizing the positioning of a state Figure)
She thought it would be kind of fun.

(22) (relational clause realizing the positioning of a state Figure)
She was sure it would be kind of fun.

In terms of grammatical metaphor IDEATION allows us to formalize the difference between an occurrence figure realized congruently in grammar as a clause or metaphorically as a nominal group (Hao, 2020b):

(23) (congruent realization of an occurrence Figure)[16]
Her granuloma was spreading.

(24) (metaphorical realization of an occurrence Figure)
The spread of her granuloma was upsetting her.

In terms of meaning beyond the clause, IDEATION allows us, for example, to anticipate activity – using one figure to name what's to come (*another thing that has been really annoying* in (25)) and others to spell it out:

(25)
Oh another thing that has been really annoying this summer is –
⇓
you know when you go to a parking lot and it's a busy place. You get in your car and you don't necessarily want to leave immediately. Like you might want to - I might want to have Henry test his blood sugar, give the kids snacks. Or if we were at the pool, like change or look at my phone or send a text message or whatever. It drives me crazy when a car is like sitting there following you and then they just wait for you to leave.

CONNEXION comprises resources for relating discourse semantic figures (both occurrence figures and state figures) to one another in sequences (via additive, comparative, temporal and causal relations). In terms of lexicogrammatical diversification it allows us to connect figures to one another in a variety of ways:

(26) **Due to** him harassing her, she left the parking lot.
(27) **Because** he was harassing her, she left the parking lot.
(28) He harassed her, **so** she left the parking lot.
(29) He harassed her. **Consequently** she left the parking lot.

In terms of grammatical metaphor CONNEXION allows us to formalize relations between figures realized congruently between clauses or metaphorically as single clauses:

(30) (congruent clause complex construing a causal sequence)
Because he was harassing her,
she left the parking lot.
(31) (metaphorical cause in the clause)
His harassment **led to** her departure.

In terms of meaning beyond the clause CONNEXION allows us to connect indefinitely long phases of discourse to one another (viz. the long explanation of why subscribers are watching a random chatty vlog rather than a prepared video below):

(32)
Hi everybody it is August first and I'm going to do just a random chatty vlog for you guys.
⇓ (implicit cause)
I had a video for today. I filmed it and I was going to edit it. It was a type one Tuesday. I was showing all the diabetes supplies – like the extra supplies we brought on vacation but I had bent down like before I started filming and my shirt got caught in my bra so it was like sitting – it just – it's all I could see the whole time so I was like 'I'm not posting this video 'cause that's all people would be looking at.'
⇑ (explicit cause)
So this is what you get today.

1.2.2.2 Interpersonal discourse semantic resources

The key interpersonal systems are NEGOTIATION and APPRAISAL. NEGOTIATION comprises resources for enacting social relations in dialogue. In terms of diversification it allows us, for example, to realize greeting moves through a range of more and less lexicalized structures:

(33) Hi everybody.
(34) Good morning.

(35) How's it going?
(36) What a surprise!
(37) Lovely to see you!
(38) Didn't know you were back in town.

In terms of grammatical metaphor NEGOTIATION allows us to realize moves directly, or metaphorically through so-called indirect speech acts:

(39)
What's his name? (congruent interrogative clause requesting information)
- Andy.

(40)
Tell me his name. (metaphorical imperative clause requesting information)
- Andy.

(41)
His name is…? (metaphorical declarative clause requesting information)
- Andy.

In terms of meaning beyond the clause NEGOTIATION allows us to relate moves in conversation, including moves comprising several clauses (as in the following request and compliance sequence):

(42)
Tell us why you left the parking lot.
⇓⇑
- I had just got in my car, got my phone and as I was doing that some guy was sitting there and there was cars behind him and he was like [mimics man's gesture and expression] like waving me out.

APPRAISAL comprises resources for enacting social relations by sharing attitudes (Martin and White 2005). In terms of diversification it allows us, for example, to realize affect across a range of grammatical structures:

(43) **Regrettably** she left the parking lot.
(44) She **regretfully** left the parking lot.
(45) She's **regretful** because she left the parking lot.
(46) Our **regretful** vlogger swore not to do it again.
(47) She **regretted** her behaviour.

In terms of grammatical metaphor APPRAISAL allows us to realize feelings as if they were things and deploy them accordingly.

(48) He was **angry** because she was sitting in her car. (congruent adjectival feeling)

(49) His **anger** prompted her departure. (metaphorical nominalized feeling)

In terms of meaning beyond the clause APPRAISAL allows us, for example, to evaluate indefinitely long phases of discourse. The extended connexion example we used as (25) earlier does more than elaborate a proposition; it also positions viewers to bond attitudinally in a specific way around a recurring parking lot event.

(25')

Oh another thing that has been **really annoying** this summer is –

⇊

you know when you go to a parking lot and it's a busy place. You get in your car and you don't necessarily want to leave immediately. Like you might want to – I might want to have Henry test his blood sugar, give the kids snacks. Or if we were at the pool, like change or look at my phone or send a text message or whatever. It drives me crazy when a car is like sitting there following you and then they just wait for you to leave.

1.2.2.3 *Textual discourse semantics*

The key textual systems are IDENTIFICATION and PERIODICITY. IDENTIFICATION comprises resources for composing discourse with respect to introducing and then tracking entities. In terms of diversification it allows us, for example, to track entities through a range of nominal resources.

(50) **Andy** went and got it yesterday at the store.
(51) **He** said not to film it.
(52) **Our** neighbourhood gathers together.
(53) **Amy's husband** did Q-and-As with her.

In terms of meaning beyond the clause IDENTIFICATION allows us to identify and track indefinitely long phases of discourse; the demonstrative *that* is used in this way in (54) to reference the 'national night out' activities that were soon to get underway.[17]

(54)

It is two twenty and I just got out of the shower and I just put some makeup on because it is national night out – and I put a fancy shirt on. I like never wear this. I think I have worn this one time since I got it. I'm usually in like a tank top with sports bra with these like yoga pants. So. But it is National Night Out like I said and our neighbourhood gathers together and we have like a potluck and the police come and the fire truck come and there are neighbours that I see like once a year and I wanted to look – I wanted to look presentable. Different than they normally probably see me every single day walking with the kids. I wanted to look nice.

⇑

So **that**'s kind of exciting.

PERIODICITY comprises resources for composing text as waves of information. The basic idea here is that there is a hierarchy of periodicity, extending from the small wavelengths of tone group and clause up through an indefinite number of indefinitely long phases of discourse. In the example that follows we have a topic sentence introducing what has been happening to the vlogger in parking lots and a retrospective comment on the frequency of this annoying behaviour. A wide range of resources, including text reference (in bold) and generalized ideation (in italics), along with internal conjunction and ideational grammatical metaphor in more abstract registers, cooperate with one another to scaffold information flow along these lines.

(55)

Oh another *thing* that has been really annoying this summer is

> you know when you go to a parking lot and it's a busy place. You get in your car and you – you don't necessarily want to leave immediately. Like you might wanna – I might want to have Henry test his blood sugar, give the kids snacks. Or if we were at the pool, like change or look at my phone or send a text message or whatever. It drives me crazy when a car is like sitting there following you through the parking lot and then they just wait for you to leave. I cannot stand that.

And **that** has *happened* so many times.

The discourse semantic resources briefly reviewed here are outlined by metafunction in Figure 1.6. Space precludes detailed consideration of the interaction of these systems in the realization of register and genre (for a discussion of which, see Martin, 1992; Martin and Rose, [2003] 2007, 2008).

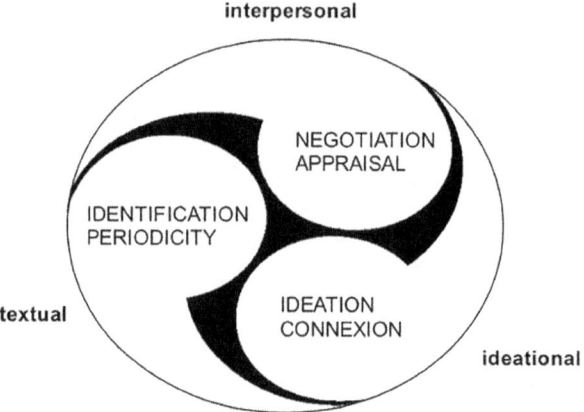

Figure 1.6 Discourse semantic systems (organized by metafunction).

1.3 Language development (ontogenesis)

SFL research on language development in young children has proven a useful starting point for work on paralanguage in two respects. On the one hand, the emergence of the first signs (protolanguage) highlights the issue of what counts as semiosis and what does not. On the other hand, the realization of these first signs is multimodal – linguistic and paralinguistic resources are not differentiated at this stage.

Matthiessen (2004, 2007, 2009) reviews the emergence of language and other semiotic systems based on SFL studies of child language development by Halliday ([1975] 2004), Painter ([1984] 2015) and Torr (1997). These studies show that language develops out of a protolinguistic system in which children draw on sounds, facial expressions and gestures to enact signs. With the emergence of language proper, however, these resources become specialized in distinctive ways. Segmental articulation and prosody (rhythm and intonation) are marshalled as the phonology of spoken language.[18] But vocal resources such as timbre, tempo, tension and loudness (explored in detail in van Leeuwen, 1999, 2009) continue as expressive resources, often referred to as sound quality. And gesture, posture and facial expression develop as resources often referred to as body language. As Matthiessen points out, sound quality and body language are then coordinated with language as texts unfold:

> Certain interpersonal contrasts in language are realized vocally by contrasts in tone (pitch movement) accompanied by facial contrasts involving eyebrow movements; textual contrasts in deicticity are often accompanied by pointing gestures; talking to babies may involve rounding, pouting lips – a feature that

affects the sound but which is also visible; and as detailed studies have shown, there is a complex relationship between addressing somebody in language and gazing at them. (2007: 6–7)

The influence of SFL research on the ontogenesis of language on our model of paralanguage is explored in detail in Chapter 2.

1.4 Non-semiotic behaviour (somasis)

One basic challenge that has to be faced when working on paralanguage is how to distinguish it from behaviour – separating semiosis from non-semiosis in other words.[19] This is of course the challenge faced by specialists in ontogenesis as they track the emergence of protolanguage out of the pre-linguistic interaction, as explored by Trevarthen (2005). We focus in detail on this issue in Chapter 2.

From this point on we will use the term 'somasis' for non-semiotic behaviour (such as sneezing, stretching, scratching an itch and so on) and 'semiosis' for systems of signs. As far as somasis is concerned we have found it useful to draw on Halliday's (1996) proposals for an evolutionary typology of systems. He recognizes four orders of complexity, with semiotic systems evolving out of social systems, social systems out of biological ones and biological ones out of physical ones. We have adapted this framework in our classification of somatic behaviour, distinguishing physical activity, biological behaviour and social communion. Physical activity covers material action involving some change in the relationship of one physical entity to another (walking, running, jumping, throwing, breaking, cutting, digging, pulling etc.). Biological behaviour can be divided into changes that restore comfort (sneezing, coughing, scratching, laughing, adjusting garments or hair etc.) and those that index discomfort (nail biting, fiddling, fidgeting, wriggling, blushing, shivering, crying etc.). Social communion can be divided into mutual perception (sharing gaze, pitch, proximity, touch, smell etc.) and reciprocal attachment (tickling, cradling, holding hands, hugging, stroking, hugging, kissing, mating etc.). These proposals are outlined in Figure 1.7.

Trained as we are as linguists and semioticians we are not ourselves well qualified to further develop this model;[20] it might be that third-generation activity theory could be brought to bear (Cole and Engeström, 1993). For our part we have found it useful to try and compile a range of behaviours that border on semiosis and which can be interpreted by social semiotic animals as indexing purposeful activity. As Halliday and Painter have shown (Halliday 2004; see Chapter 2), early protolinguistic semiosis involves a reconstrual of

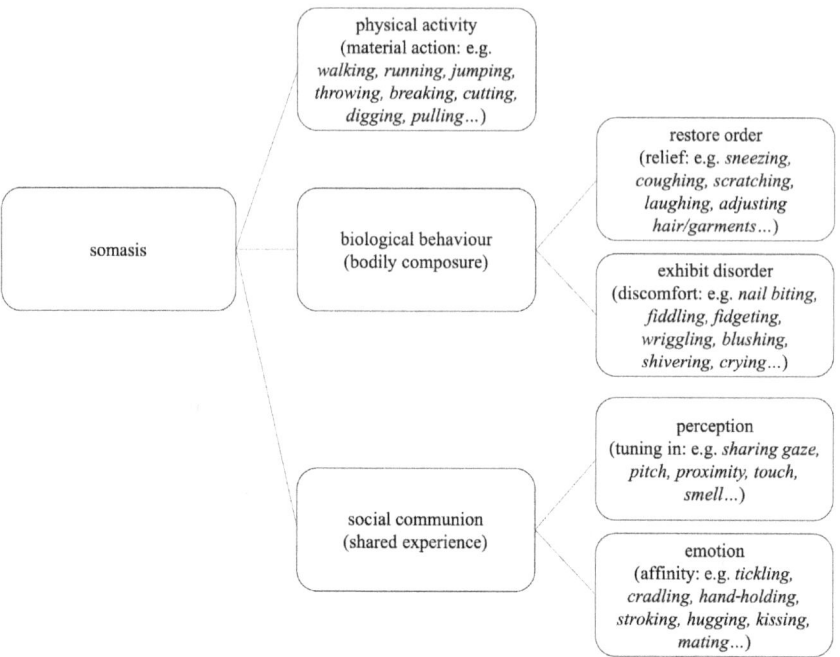

Figure 1.7 A model of behaviour (somasis).

some of these activities as the expression face of signs. And all of the behaviour outlined earlier has the potential to be used as signs – for example, stamping one's foot in frustration, coughing to remind a meeting of one's presence, shivering to indicate one is cold, sniffing to object to an odour, kissing on the cheek as a greeting and so on. In these cases there is some degree of deliberation involved, as manifested in the fact that the behaviour will synchronize with the prosodic phonology (see Chapter 3 for discussion) and turn-taking structure of an interaction and will be responded to as meaningful by co-participants. To put this another way, we are arguing that the behaviours outlined in Figure 1.7 can be treated as paralinguistic or not depending on whether or not they are negotiated as meaningful in interaction.

The model of non-semiotic and semiotic behaviour we have developed to this point is outlined as Figure 1.8.

1.5 Embodied meaning (semiosis)

In their work on intermodal relations in children's picture books (Painter and Martin, 2012; Painter et al., 2013), Painter and her colleagues suggest a model

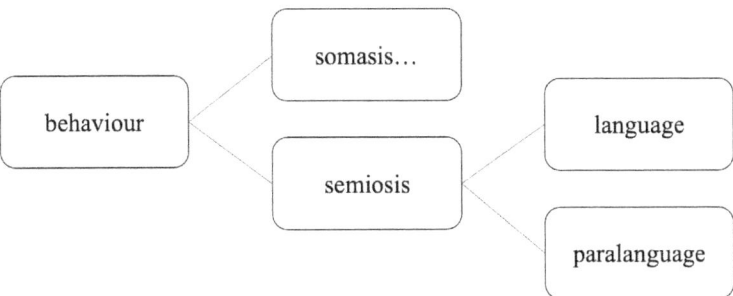

Figure 1.8 Somasis and semiosis.

Table 1.3 Convergent verbiage/image relations in children's picture books

Verbiage	Convergence	Image
Ideational	Concurrence	Ideational
Interpersonal	Resonance	Interpersonal
Textual	Synchronicity	Textual

involving degrees of convergence between verbiage and image. The model is organized by metafunction – degrees of concurrence for ideational meaning, degrees of resonance for interpersonal meaning and degrees of synchronicity for textual meaning (for illustrative text analysis, see Martin 2008; Painter and Martin, 2012). The relevant terminology is presented in Table 1.3.

Painter and her colleagues' main concern in proposing this model was to focus on the way in which the meaning potential of written language and images was taken up in picture books – with language and image sometimes doing comparable work, and other times with language making meaning the images did not, or vice versa. We need to stress once again here that work on semiosis informed by SFL involves a relational theory of meaning. So Painter and her colleagues were asking questions about the meaning potential of language and the meaning potential of images, as formalized in system networks and their uptake in a specific text. As their work makes explicit, the meaning potential of both language and image is organized by metafunction; but the two modalities make different choices available (they have different affordances in Kress and van Leeuwen's (2001) terms). For Painter and her colleagues studying the complementary contribution of language and images in picture books means looking closely at the choices instantiated in a bimodal text in relation to those that could have been manifested and carefully considering the commitment of

Table 1.4 Sonovergent and semovergent paralanguage

Zappavigna and Martin (2018)	Revised terminology
Linguistic body language [expression plane orientation]	*Sonovergent paralanguage* (phonologically convergent)
Epilinguistic body language [content plane orientation]	*Semovergent paralanguage* (semantically convergent)

meaning by one modality or the other. This is the perspective we adopt in this monograph as far as the contribution of language and paralanguage to spoken discourse is concerned. In Chapters 4, 5 and 6 we formalize in system networks the ideational, interpersonal and textual meaning potential of paralanguage and explore its uptake in relation to linguistic resources in terms of the meanings that are and could have been committed.

Table 1.3 also provides us with a model for dealing with two dimensions of the relation between language and paralanguage, treated by Zappavigna and Martin (2018) as 'linguistic body language' and 'epilinguistic body language'.[21] The basic distinction here is between paralanguage that converges with the prosodic phonology (i.e. rhythm and intonation) of spoken language and that which converges with meanings made possible by having language. We propose here a more transparent terminology, with phonologically convergent paralanguage referred to as sonovergent and semantically convergent paralanguage as semovergent. This revised terminology is outlined in Table 1.4.

Sonovergent and semovergent paralinguistic systems will be introduced in general terms in Sections 1.5.1–2, drawing on examples from a YouTube video titled 'Let's Talk. | Random Chatty Vlog', used here with the presenter's permission (https://youtu.be/YRx-zDoPbVw). A 'vlog' (derived from 'blog')[22] is a video in which a user recounts, or presents, some form of personal activity (e.g. a 'day in the life' vlog where the user shows highlights from their activity over a day). The following is the description accompanying the video posted by the vlogger:

> Grab a cup of coffee and a snack. Let's just sit down and talk today. I chat about annoying people who follow me in the parking lot, my kids begging for food all summer, my hair, feet, YouTube … etc. I have no trouble rambling on. If you like this, PLEASE give this video a thumbs up so I know! I want to know what you guys like seeing. Thank you for watching! Subscribe so you don't miss another video. I post every Monday, Tuesday and Thursday at 2pm EST.

A full transcription of the vlog is included as Appendix A of this book. A phonological analysis of the 'Hair dye' phase of this vlog, from which we take most of our examples, is provided as Appendix B3. Sonovergent and semovergent systems will be discussed in more detail in Chapters 4–6; Chapter 4 also draws examples from this vlog.

1.5.1 Paralanguage converging with sound (sonovergent paralanguage)

Sonovergent paralanguage converges with the prosodic phonology of spoken language (Halliday, 1967, 1970a; Halliday and Greaves, 2008; Smith and Greaves, 2015). From an interpersonal perspective, it resonates with tone and involves a body part (e.g. eyebrows or arms) moving up and down in tune with pitch movement in a tone group (TONE and marked salience). From a textual perspective, it involves a body part[23] (e.g. hands, head) moving in sync with the periodicity of speech[24] – which might involve beats aligned with a salient syllable of a foot (which might also be the tonic syllable of a tone group) or a gesture coextensive with a tone group (i.e. in sync with TONALITY, TONICITY or RHYTHM systems). An outline of this sonovergent paralanguage is presented in Table 1.5.

The phonological system of TONE is realized through pitch movement. In example (56) the vlogger's eyebrows move up in tune with the rising tone (tone 2) on the syllable ***prev***.

(56)

phonology[25]	//2 bought	/ previously when I //
paralanguage		eyebrows rise and fall
images		

Table 1.5 Sonovergent paralinguistic systems

Verbiage	Sonovergent	Paralanguage ('prosodic')
Interpersonal: TONE	*Resonance*	Interpersonal: IN TUNE
Textual: TONALITY, TONICITY, RHYTHM	*Synchronicity*	Textual: IN SYNC

As illustrated earlier our strategy for illustrating paralanguage in tables in this chapter involves a top row for relevant verbiage (annotated for relevant rhythm and intonation), above a row or two providing an informal description of the paralanguage (or somasis), above a row with a series of screenshots displaying the relevant embodied meaning.

The phonological system of TONALITY organizes spoken language into waves of information called tone groups, with one salient syllable carrying this tone movement. Gestures may be coextensive with this periodic unit. In examples (57) and (58) the vlogger makes a sweeping right-to-left[26] gesture referencing past time; the gestures unfold in sync with the temporal extent of the tone group.[27]

(57)

phonology	//2 bought	/ *pre*viously when I //
paralanguage	sweeping to past	
images		

(58)

phonology	//3 *loved* the	/ ***first*** time //
paralanguage	sweeping to past	
images		

The phonological system of TONICITY highlights a peak of informational prominence by positioning the major pitch movement of a tone group (its tone) on one or another of its salient syllables (its culminative salient syllable in the unmarked case). In example (59) the vlogger claps on the syllable realizing the tone group's major pitch movement – **hair**.

(59)

phonology	//3 *dyed* my	/ ***hair*** which I //
paralanguage		handclap
image		

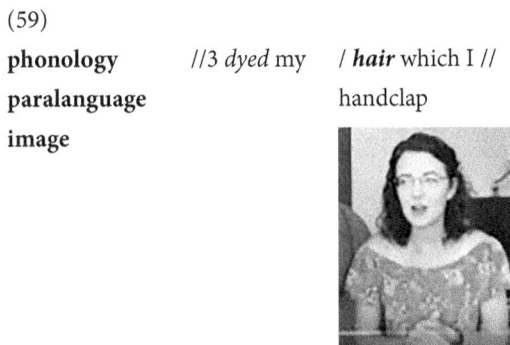

The phonological system of RHYTHM is realized in English through the timing of the salient syllables beginning each foot (relatively equal timing between salient syllables in a stress-timed language like English). In (60), the vlogger beats with her hands in time with the salient syllables of the feet / *not* /, / *find* the / and / ***hair*** dye that I /. The last of these beats in fact syncs with the tonic syllable ***hair***.

(60)

phonology	//4 *but* I could	/ *not*	/ *find* the	/***hair*** dye that I //
paralanguage		down beat	down beat	down beat
images				

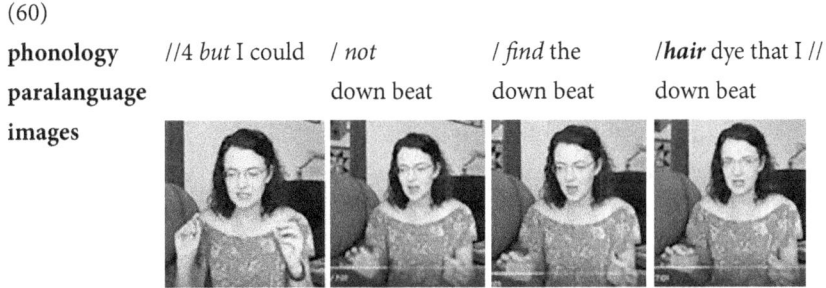

Salient syllables other than the tonic syllable can be given additional prominence (super-salience) through various means. In (14') the vlogger's pitch on the first tone group is unusually high and contrasts with the descending lower pitch of the following tone group (a sing/song effect). We use upward and downward arrows, '↑' and '↓', to signal pronounced salience of this kind.

(14''')

//3 ↑*hope*fully next / ***time*** I will
//1 *get* my / ↓***hair*** colour / *back*

The vlogger's eyebrows move up in tune and in sync with the higher pitch on / *hopefully* /, before lowering again by the end of the following tone group.

(14'''')
phonology   //3 ↑*hope*fully next   / ***time*** I will //
paralanguage eyebrows rise
image

The same sing/song effect follows on and culminates this phase of the vlog, with a high pitch on the tonic syllable / ***now*** // contrasting with the low pitch on / ***do*** //. The vlogger's eyebrows once again move up and down in tune and in sync with the contrasting pitch salience (this time on contrasting tonic syllables).

(15'')
//3 [handclap] / *um* /*but* for / ↑***now***
//3 *This* will / ↓***do*** //

These rhythmic in-tune gestures reinforce the attitudinal import of the RHYTHM and TONICITY (cf. Section 1.5.2.2).

The contribution of sonovergent paralanguage to the vlog is interrupted in tone group 19 of Appendix B3, suspended for tone groups 20–24 and resumes for tone group 25 (examples (61)–(65)) – to allow for a somatic phase during which the vlogger uses her left hand to scratch her right arm. This phase unfolds as follows:

(61)   //3 *light*er than it / *was* a few / ***days*** ago
(62)   //1 ^ but / ***yeah*** it's
(63)   //1 such a / ***bumm***er and then I
(64)   //2 *went* to / ***Targ***et
(65)   //3 ^ like / *two* days / *lat*er and there was a //

The vlogger stops looking at her followers and begins scratching in the final foot of (61').

(61')

phonology   //3 *light*er than it   / *was* a few   / ***days*** ago //
paralanguage   supine hand gesture
somasis   scratching; breaking gaze
images

The scratching and absence of gaze continues for two tone groups ((62')–(63')).

(62')

phonology   //1 ^ but   / ***yeah*** it's //
somasis   scratching; no gaze
image

(63')

phonology   //1 *such* a   / ***bumm***er and then I //
somasis   scratching; no gaze
image

Gaze resumes in the final foot of (64').

(64')
phonology //2 went to / *Targ*et //
somasis   scratching; resuming gaze
image

And the vlogger then resumes gesturing in (65').

(65')
phonology   //3 ^ like / *two* days / *lat*er and there was a //
paralanguage no scratching; resuming gesturing
image

It is interesting to note that the vlogger does not scratch in sync with the RHYTHM, TONICITY and TONALITY of the text; the scratching lasts for two and a half tone groups and does not match the timing of salient and tonic syllables. But the paralanguage remains in sync, stopping precisely at the tonic syllable of (61') (/ *days* ago //), resuming with a smile precisely at the tonic syllable of (64') (/ *Targ*et //) and resuming with gesture precisely at the beginning of (65'). This indicates that synchronicity with prosodic phonology can function as a demarcating criterion for distinguishing somatic from semiotic behaviour.

1.5.2 Paralanguage converging with meaning (semovergent paralanguage)

Semovergent paralanguage is convergent with the lexicogrammar and discourse semantics of spoken language (its content plane). We adopt a discourse semantic

Table 1.6 Converging discourse semantic and paralinguistic systems

Verbiage	*Semovergent*	Paralanguage ('articulatory')
Ideational: IDEATION	*Concurrence*	Ideational: 'mimetic'
Interpersonal: APPRAISAL	*Resonance*	Interpersonal: 'expressive'
Textual: IDENTIFICATION/PERIODICITY	*Synchronicity*	Textual: 'coordinating'

perspective on these meaning-making resources here (Martin and Rose, [2003] 2007). Drawing on terms from Painter et al. (2013) we can position ideational paralanguage as concurring with IDEATION systems (but not CONNEXION, as will be discussed later), interpersonal paralanguage as resonating with APPRAISAL systems (but not NEGOTIATION, as will be discussed later) and textual body language as coordinating information flow alongside IDENTIFICATION and PERIODICITY[28] systems. These convergences are outlined in Table 1.6.[29]

1.5.2.1 Representation (ideational semovergent paralanguage)

From an ideational perspective we need to take into account how spoken language combines entities, occurrences and qualities as figures (IDEATION). Semovergent paralanguage supports these resources with hand shapes, which potentially concur with entities, and hand/arm motion, which potentially concurs with occurrences (Hood and Hao, 2021); the hand/arm motion is optionally directed, potentially concurring with spatiotemporal direction (i.e. to/from here and there in space, to/from now and then in time). We say 'potentially concurring' because ideational paralanguage can be used on its own, without accompanying spoken language; see the discussion of mime in Chapter 7.

By way of illustration we now move to the fifth phase in the vlog, which concerns a visit to the vlogger's dermatologist (for treatment of granuloma). The sequence of events we are interested in unfolds verbally in tone groups as follows (for the complete text of this phase of the vlog, see Appendix B5):

(66) //3 *and* so the / *derm*atologist um / *took* like this / **need**le and

(67) //3 *under* / *each* like / **bump** and in-

(68) //3 *jec*ted this like / **ster**oid and it would like

(69) //3 *all* / **bubb**le up... //

Table 1.7 Concurrent construals of entities in examples (66)–(69)

Language	Needle		Bump
Paralanguage	Holding needle	Holding syringe	Cupped hands
Images	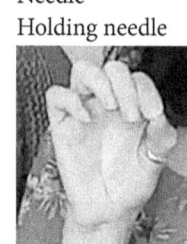	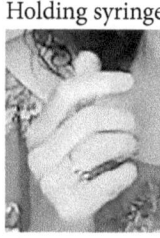	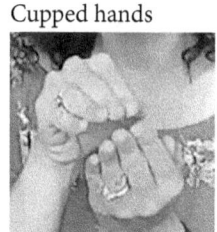

From the perspective of language, the verbiage in this sequence makes explicit four entities (*dermatologist, needle, bump, steroid*). The paralanguage uses hand shape to concur with two of these (*needle* and *bump*). The 'needle' is first rendered as a tiny pointed entity the vlogger holds between thumb and index finger and then with the hand shape used for holding a syringe; the 'bump' is not actually visualized until the fourth tone group, where it renders the shape of the steroid bubbling up (Table 1.7). As we can see, the meanings construed in language and paralanguage can either correspond with or complement one another. In terms of commitment (i.e. the amount of meaning specified across semiotic modes; Martin, 2010; Painter et al., 2013), the 'dermatologist' and 'steroid' are committed in the language but not the paralanguage; but the 'needle' is more delicately committed in the paralanguage as a tiny pointed entity and then as a syringe. And the paralinguistic commitment of the 'bump' convergent with (69) in fact takes place two tone groups after it is committed verbally in (67).

Turning from a static to a dynamic perspective, the language of this sequence makes explicit three occurrences (*took, injected, bubbled*). The paralanguage concurs with these and in addition uses six rapid piercing gestures to make explicit the events implied by the second tone group (67').

(66')

Language	//3 *and* so the / *derma*tologist um / *took* like this / **need**le and //
paralinguistic entity	thumb and index finger together 'holding needle'
paralinguistic occurrence[30]	hand rises as thumb and index finger take hold of 'needle'
Images	 

(67')
Language //3 *under* / each like / ***bump*** and in- //
paralinguistic entity thumb and index finger together 'gripping needle'
paralinguistic occurrence six piercing gestures
Image

In each case the entity indicated by the hand shape is in motion, as the dermatologist picks the needle up, pierces the bumps, injects the steroid and the bump bubbles up.

(68')
Language //3 *ject*ed this like / ***ster***oid and it would like //
paralinguistic entity hand shape 'holding syringe'
paralinguistic occurrence thumb pushes down on 'syringe'
Image

(69')
Language //3 *all* / ***bubb***le up… //
paralinguistic entity cupped hands construing bump
paralinguistic occurrence hands separate as right hand moves up
Images

As with imagic sequences in film, animations, graphic novels, comics, cartoons and picture books, the gesture sequence does not make explicit the conjunctive relations between events (and so cannot support discourse semantic CONNEXION). These relations have to be abduced (Bateman, 2007) from the sequence and concurring language. In the case of the sequence in (66)–(69), conjunctive relations of time and cause are not made explicit in language either; only the additive linker *and* is used. A defeasible reading of the sequence is offered in (66")–(69").

(66") // and so the dermatologist um took like this **needle**
(temporal sequential)

(67") // and under each like **bump**
(temporal overlapping)

(68") // and injected this like **ster**oid
(causal)

(69") // and like it all **bubb**led up //

As noted earlier, for this paralinguistic sequence hand shape and motion are combined. In other cases hand shapes occur on their own. In the following sequence our vlogger concentrates on the size of the snack she has given her children, without setting the bowl in motion:

(70) //3 *then* they had a / ***snack*** I

(71) //4 *gave* them / *each* a / *bowl* - like a *heap*ing / ***bowl***

(72) //3 *full* of / ***Chex*** Mix and an

(73) //4 *app*lesauce / ***squeeze*** and they //

(71')

language	//4 ... *heap*ing / ***bowl*** //	
paralinguistic entity	heap shape vertical	bowl shape horizontal
images		

Motion can also occur on its own, without a hand shape concurring with an entity. For example, the vlogger uses a circular hand motion (two rotations) concurrent with the tone group //1 *tried* washing it / ***out*** it's //.

(74)

language   //1 *tried* washing it / ***out*** it's //

paralinguistic occurrence   circular rotating motion of hands

images

Motion can also be used to support direction in space or time. In Section 1.5.1 we illustrated two examples of hands sweeping right to left towards the past, concurring with the tone groups //2 *bought* / ***prev***iously when I // (57) and // *loved* the / ***first*** time // (58). These contrast with left-to-right movement towards the future, concurrent with // *hopefully next time I will* //. This motion to the right is reinforced by a pointing gesture, which we discuss in Section 1.5.2.3 (as textual semovergence).

(14'''')

language   //3 *hopefully* next / ***time*** I will //

paralinguistic occurrence   hand/arm motion to right

image

As noted earlier, ideationally semovergent paralanguage, as formulated in Chapter 4, does not involve resources for explicitly connecting gestures in terms of addition, comparison, temporality or causality and so does not converge with CONNEXION in spoken language.

1.5.2.2 Evaluation (interpersonal semovergent paralanguage)

From an interpersonal perspective we need to take into account how spoken language inscribes attitudes, grades qualities and positions voices other than the speaker's own (APPRAISAL). Semovergent paralanguage potentially resonates with APPRAISAL resources through facial expression, bodily stance, muscle tension, hand/arm position and motion (Hood, 2011; Ngo, 2018; Hao and Hood,

2019; Ngo, 2019) and voice quality (Caldwell, 2013). Whereas spoken language can make explicit attitudes of different kinds (emotional reactions, judgements of character and appreciation of things), paralanguage can only enact emotion. A further interpersonal restriction, setting aside emblems (e.g. the 'thumbs-up' or 'OK' gestures discussed in Section 1.6; cf. Kendon, 2004; McNeill, 2012), is that semovergent paralanguage cannot be used to support NEGOTIATION by distinguishing move types in dialogic exchanges (although sonovergent paralanguage can of course support TONE choice in relation to these moves).

Paralanguage deploys facial expression and bodily stance to share attitude. In (75) our vlogger nuances her appreciation (*exciting*) of a neighbourhood get-together she has dressed up for with raised eyebrows and a lopsided-mouth expression[31] (which we might read as indicating that some followers might not find it all that exciting).

(75)

language	//3 ^ so / *that's* kind of ex-	/ *cit*ing //
paralinguistic affect	Surprise	
image		

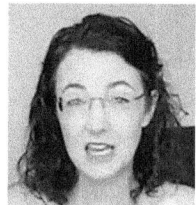

As outlined by Martin and White (2005) attitude may not be explicitly inscribed in language but invoked by ideational choices a speaker expects a reaction to. We introduced an example of this in (64) earlier; a headshot from this image is blown up in (64"), as the vlogger introduces the good news that her hair dye is back in stock at Target. Her smiling face makes explicit the affect that her language does not.

(64")

language	//2 *went* to	/ *Targ*et //
paralinguistic affect	smiling	
image		

A good example of a combined face and body commitment of affect in the vlog we are drawing our examples from comes as the vlogger is complaining about being hassled for her parking spot before she is ready to leave. The relevant tone groups are presented here, and we will return to this example in our discussion of mime in Chapter 7 (for a complete phonological analysis of this phase of the vlog, see Appendix B6). At this point we are simply interested in the way the vlogger's facial expression and arm position are used to express the hassler's exasperation (79).

(76) //3 *some* / ***guy*** was

(77) //3 ***sit****ing there and there was*

(78) //3 *cars* be- / ***hind*** him and he was like

(79) // [mimics man's gesture and expression]

(80) //1 ^ like / *wa*ving me / ***out***… //

(79')

paralinguistic affect   exasperation

image

Turning to GRADUATION, as noted by Hood (2011) the size of hand shapes and the range of hand/arm motion can be used to support graded language. In (81) the sweeping extent of the hand/arm motion resonates with the large quantity of hair dye in stock (*whole stack*).

(81)

language   //1_ *whole* / ***stack*** of them so I //

paralinguistic   right arm sweeping low left to high right
force

images

The most striking example of intensification in the hair colour phase occurs when the vlogger uses whole body language to enact her reaction to how dark her hair is. She throws her head back and leans back as her arms rise up – literally overwhelmed with emotion (82).

(82)
language //1 *so*:: / ***dark*** I //
paralinguistic force
image

Alongside paralanguage of this kind converging with FORCE, Hood (2011) notes the potential for precise hand shapes and muscle tension to resonate with FOCUS. In the following example, introduced as (67) and repeated below as (67"), the vlogger tightens her grip on the tiny virtual needle she is holding and frowns slightly in concentration as she role-plays the precision involved in the dermatologist piercing her bumps:

(67")
language //3 *under* / *each* like / ***bump*** and in- //
paralinguistic focus slight frown, increased facial and hand tension
image

Hao and Hood (2019) draw attention to the use of what they call de-centring postures to soften focus, using the example of a shoulder shrug converging with *fairly non-contractile* in a biology lecture. The paralinguistic generalization here would appear to be loss of equilibrium, for example, asymmetrical facial expression, out-of-kilter posture or a rotating prone hand (interpretable as between prone and supine). Clear examples in our data are the faces the vlogger pulls as she struggles to name her skin condition in the second tone group, the second of which is accompanied by two shakes of her head.

(83) //4 **any**way, it was

(84) //3 *some* / *gran*u- / *loma*:: / ^ [out-breath] / **some**thing

(85) //1_ *I* don't know – it's / *called* – it's / *some* sort of / **skin** thing. //

(84')

language	//3 *some* / *gran*uloma:: / ^ [out-breath]	/ **some**thing //
paralinguistic focus	skewed left	skewed right
image		

Turning to ENGAGEMENT, Hao and Hood (2019) note the significance of hand position as far as supporting the expansion and contraction of heteroglossia is concerned – with supine hands opening up dialogism and prone hands closing it down. In the following example the vlogger's supine hands converge with the modalization *probably*, reinforcing acknowledgement of the viewer's voice:

(86)

language	//1 *probably* / *seeing* how / *dark* my / **hair** is well //
paralinguistic engagement	supine hands
image	

Two moves later the hands flip over to prone position in support of the negative move shutting down the expectation that the vlogger was in control of the new colour of her hair.

(87)
language   //4 *but* I could / *not* / *find* the / **hair** dye that I //
paralinguistic engagement prone hands
image

Voice quality was noted in Section 1.5.1 in relation to the sing/song pitch (high then low) movement the vlogger uses in her last four tone groups to close down her hair dye narrative. From the perspective of APPRAISAL the sound quality resonates with her feeling that she is resigned to her current hair colour, at least for now. Work on this interpersonal aural dimension of paralanguage, drawing on van Leeuwen (1999), will be further explored in Chapter 5.

As noted earlier, interpersonally semovergent paralanguage, as formulated in Chapter 5, does not involve resources for explicitly distinguishing moves in dialogue and so does not converge with NEGOTIATION in spoken language. Gestures treated as playing a speech functional role in dialogue in other models are treated as emblems in our framework (see Section 1.6 for discussion).

1.5.2.3 *Information flow (textual semovergent paralanguage)*

From a textual perspective[32] we need to take into account how spoken language introduces entities and keeps track of them once there (IDENTIFICATION) and how it composes waves of information in tone groups, clauses and beyond (PERIODICITY). Semovergent paralanguage potentially supports these resources with pointing gestures and whole body movement and position.

As far as pointing deixis is concerned we can return to the examples contrasting past and future in Sections 1.5.1 and 1.5.2.1. The vlogger's hand points to the past in (58'), and alongside motioning to the future both the vlogger's index fingers point there (14'''').

(58')
phonology //3 *loved* the / ***first*** time //
paralinguistic deixis whole hand pointing to past
images

(14''''')
language //3 *hope*fully next / ***time*** I will //
paralinguistic deixis hand/arm motion to right
image

As far as longer wavelengths of information flow are concerned,[33] our vlogger is seated, and so whole body movement from one location to another is not a factor (as it would be, e.g. for a lecturer roaming to and fro across a stage; cf. Hood, 2011; Hood and Maggora, 2016). As noted in Sections 1.5.1 and 1.5.2.3, however, the vlogger does end the phase with a contrasting high then lowered pitch. The higher pitch penultimate tone group begins rhythmically speaking with a handclap foot and then a foot comprising the 'filler' / *um* /.

(15''')
phonology // 3 / *um* / *but* for / ↑***now*** //
paralinguistic periodicity handclap high pitch
images

This is followed by the low pitch tone group; the vlogger is winding down. Following this there is a suspension of both language and paralanguage as her eyes shut and her head slumps forward (88).

(88)

phonology	//3 *this* will / ↓*do* //	[silence]
paralinguistic periodicity	lowered pitch	no gesture
somasis		eyes shut; head down
images		

The preceding phase to the one we are using to explore sonovergence here ends in a similar way (lowered pitch, with eyes shut, head down). So shutting down language and paralanguage and handing over to somasis is clearly a strategy for punctuating longer waves of discourse. It is at these points that the vlogger cuts from one filmic segment to the next (as she thinks of something more to say).

(89)

phonology	//13 *I'm* a picky / ↓*eat*er //	[silence]
paralinguistic periodicity	lowered pitch	no gesture
somasis		eyes shut; head down
image		

1.5.3 Multidimensionality (multiplying meaning)

The sonovergent and semovergent paralinguistic systems discussed thus far are outlined in Figure 1.9. Although presented as a simple taxonomy, all five

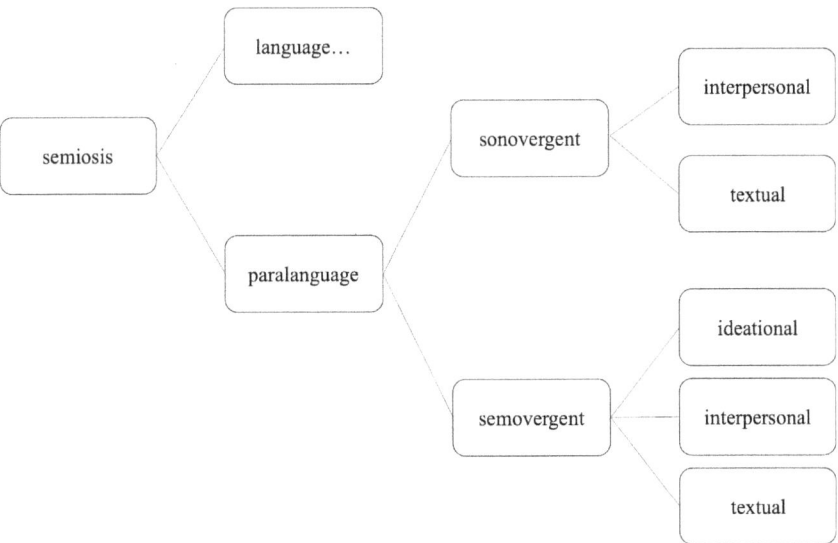

Figure 1.9 Sonovergent and semovergent paralanguage.

subtypes of paralanguage can combine with one another in support of a single tone group.

Several examples of multiple dimensions of paralanguage converging on the same tone group were in fact presented earlier (e.g. the combination of motion towards the future and pointing deixis in Example (69) of Section 1.5.2.1). As we will illustrate in the chapters which follow, it is probably safe to claim that whenever semovergent paralanguage is deployed, it will be coordinated with TONALITY, TONICITY and RHYTHM; this is equivalent to arguing that semovergence implies sonovergence. Sonovergent paralanguage on the other hand can be deployed without semovergence, through gestures in tune with or in sync with prosodic phonology (but no more).

1.6 Emblems

We conclude with a comment on what Kendon (2004) refers to as emblems, drawing on Ekman and Friesen (1969). Included here are gestures such as thumbs-up or thumbs-down (as praise or censure, respectively), index finger touching lips (for 'quiet please'), hand cupped over ear (for 'I can't hear'), middle finger vertical (for 'get fucked') and so on. Our vlogger uses one of these gestures to introduce the first of her explanations as to why her hair is darker than usual – raising her index finger as an emblem for the numeral '1'.

(90)

phonology   //1_ ↑*one* it's   / ↓*wet* //
'gesturology'   emblem '1'
image

These gestures differ from the semovergent ones illustrated thus far in critical ways (cf. McNeill, 2012: 7–10). For one thing they commit very specific meanings and can be readily recognized without accompanying co-text (linguistic or paralinguistic). As part of this specificity they can enact moves in exchange structure on their own, for example, statements and requests, alongside greetings and leave-takings (hand waving), calls (beckoning gestures), agreement (nodding head), disagreement (shaking head), challenges (upright palm facing forward for 'stop') and so on. For another they are the first thing that comes to mind when someone mentions gesture. And in this regard they are often commented on as culturally specific (e.g. the difference between an Anglo supine hand beckoning gesture and its Filipino prone hand equivalent). In both respects emblems contrast with common-sense dismissals of the paralanguage as idiosyncratic (although none of us has any trouble successfully interpreting another speaker's sonovergent and semovergent systems). From the perspective of the sign languages of the deaf, emblems most strongly resemble signs; they are expression form gestures explicitly encoding meaning. Similarly, from the perspective of character-based writing systems (such as those of Chinese), emblems most strongly resemble characters (but gestured rather than scribed).[34]

This indicates that from an SFL perspective emblems are better treated as part of language than as a dimension of paralanguage. The relationship we are emphasizing between emblems and alternative expression form systems is outlined in Figure 1.10, using the words *zero*, *one*, *two*, *three*, *four* and *five* as examples. These words can be alternatively expressed in English through

Embodied Meaning 43

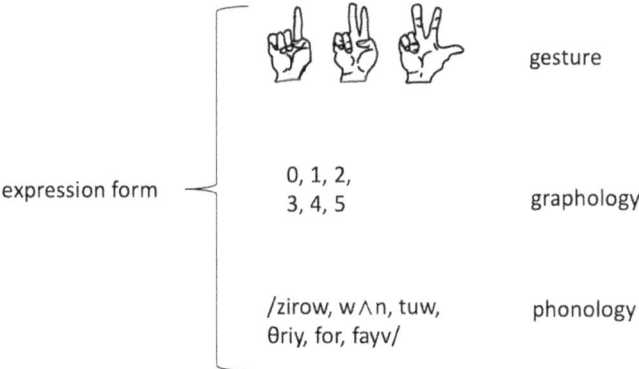

Figure 1.10 Alternative realizations of expression form in language (gesture, graphology, phonology).

segmental phonology (e.g. /tuw/), graphological characters (e.g. '2') or hand gestures (e.g. index and middle finger vertical).

An outline of the place of emblems in our overall system is presented in Figure 1.11. Rather than treating them as a dimension of paralanguage, we treat them as part of language proper – as an alternative manifestation of its own expression form.

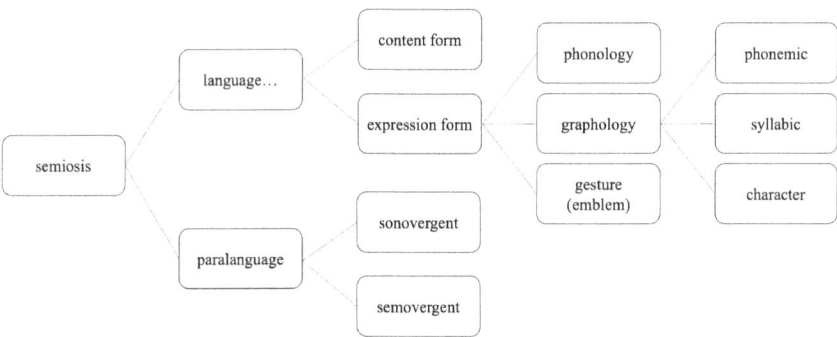

Figure 1.11 Emblems as gestural signs.

1.7 Overview of the chapters in this book

The remainder of this book proceeds as follows: In Chapter 2 we review the SFL ontogenesis research that inspired Zappavigna and Martin's (2018) model of paralanguage and consider its implications for the revision of terminology and some of that model's parameters here. In Chapter 3 we introduce the SFL description of English rhythm and intonation, which paralanguage converges with in spoken interaction. We then explore paralanguage from an ideational perspective in Chapter 4, from an interpersonal perspective in Chapter 5 and from a textual perspective in Chapter 6. Chapter 7 concludes the book with a discussion of intermodality, including consideration of mime, emblems and the place of paralanguage in a functional model of language and semiosis.

2

An ontogenetic perspective on paralanguage

2.1 Introduction

This chapter elaborates in greater detail the ontogenetic perspective underlying the accounts of paralanguage provided by Matthiessen (2009) and Cléirigh (2010) – the latter informing Martin et al. (2013b) and Zappavigna and Martin (2018) – which have influenced our model. Initially (in Section 2.2) we will consider the nature of pre-linguistic infant communication, which involves a range of expressive modalities, including face, voice and body, and eventually leads to the emergence of the first instances of semiosis – the first purposeful acts of meaning. These are described in Section 2.3 and discriminated from earlier and continuing forms of 'somasis'. The following two sections (2.4 and 2.5) describe the 'protolanguage' and 'transition' phases of linguistic development, respectively, using data from SFL case studies of three individual children (Halliday, 1975, 2004; Painter, [1984] 2015; and Torr, 1997). Here we will discuss the nature of the child's first semiotic system, the protolanguage, with its multimodal expression forms, and then the way the 'transition' into the mother tongue (with the appearance of true lexical words) heralds significant changes. These include the differentiation of various expressive resources, enabling them to function paralinguistically alongside verbal language, with both eventually organized along metafunctional lines. Following this account, Section 2.6 presents a case for our current adaptation of the model of adult paralanguage found in Martin et al. (2013b) and Zappavigna and Martin (2018) by expanding the semovergent category of adult communication to include aspects previously regarded as 'protolinguistic body language'. Section 2.7 briefly summarizes the key points of the ontogenetic perspective presented in the chapter.

2.2 Pre-linguistic communication

In recent years there has been renewed interest in the development of pre- and non-verbal forms of infant communication. There are several reasons for this, one being the belief that understanding the earliest development of communication in infancy can illuminate the origins of language in the human species (Matthiessen, 2004; Davis, 2011; Meguerditchian et al., 2011; McNeill, 2012). Since one leading proposal in theorizing the evolutionary origins of language is the 'gesture-first' hypothesis – the idea that gestural communication preceded oral-aural communication in our hominid ancestors (Corballis, 2003; Tomasello, 2008; Arbib, 2012) – pre-linguistic gesture, in particular, has come under new scrutiny (Tomasello et al., 2007; Colletta and Guidetti, 2012). Infant gesture has also been attended to in relation to the development of sign languages in deaf children and how their earliest attempts at gestural communication compare with those by hearing children (Volterra and Erting, 1990). Finally, the question of whether adult gesture and speech constitute components of an integrated communicative system in the mind, contrary to the Chomskyan notion of language as a distinct mental organ, has also provided a fresh impetus for the study of the ontogenetic origins of communication (McNeill, 1992; Bates and Dick, 2002; Capirci et al., 2005; Liszkowski, 2008, 2014).

Much of this recent work is focused on meaningful gestures, such as pointing, which do not emerge until towards the end of the first year of life; but it is worth putting this phase of development in the context of even earlier forms of communicative interaction involving the face and voice, as well as the body. Since the 1970s, there has been an accumulation of research demonstrating that human beings enter the world with innate capacities for emotional expression and for attending to other humans, which in turn facilitate the emergence of apparently communicative interactions from as early as two months of age – a development upon which all later semiosis is founded. (See Bullowa (1979) and Bråten (1998) for key collections of papers and Lee et al. (2009: chapter 4) for a useful summary of research.)

In early work Trevarthen (1979: 324) discriminates a baby's 'feeding, defensive or distress behaviour and signals of physiological state' on the one hand from 'expressions which lead to interpersonal communication' on the other. In relation to the latter, he observes that 'almost all adult facial expressions can be found in photographs and video records of new-borns and infants', including smiling, scowling, sneering and disgust faces, and he cites

Ekman and Friesen's (1971; [1975] 2003) research as evidence for 'an innate, pan-human facial "vocabulary" of emotional signs' (Trevarthen, 1979: 327). In addition to these facial expressions, Trevarthen notes early mouth shaping and tongue movements and head and body postures, together with hand, arm and finger gestures. All are evident in the early weeks of life and are likely to be 'based on innate templates as Darwin (1872) proposed' (see also Ekman (2009) for Darwin's contribution to the field). In sum, quite apart from self-regulatory behaviours such as feeding, crying, burping or hiccupping, babies enter the world with a repertoire of potentially communicative expressions involving both the face and the body.

This expressive repertoire is important in relation to a second characteristic of the newborn – the 'innate capacity for attuning to others' (Thibault, 2008: 288), which in turn leads the infant to participate in communicative interactions with caregivers from about two months of age. Attention to others involves various predispositions, including a preference for looking at and tracking human faces (Goren et al., 1975; Johnson et al., 1991), a preference for faces with direct rather than averted gaze (Farroni et al., 2002, 2004), an ability to discriminate voices from other sounds (Eisenberg, 1975) and a capacity to synchronize body movements to the rhythms of the mother's voice (Condon and Sander, 1974; Kato et al., 1983). By two or three months of age, these capacities, along with the baby's expressive repertoire, are brought into play in brief episodes with the caregiver that Bateson (1979: 65) refers to as 'protoconversations'. They are so named because the behaviours 'exhibit many of the dynamic and physiognomic characteristics of the paralinguistic part of adult conversation: they resemble "utterances" emitted in turn that integrate vocalizations, smiling, eye-contact and hand gestures' (Reddy et al., 1997: 250). In such episodes, which are 'swimming with emotion' (Reddy, 2008: 41), each party's expressive behaviour is contingent upon the other's (Brazelton and Tronick, 1980) to create what Trevarthen (1993: 66) has described as 'a precise interplay of address and reply of emotions in time'.

By two or three months of age, then, the infant's expressive but pre-symbolic behaviour can be modelled, as shown in Figure 2.1, as either 'biological behaviour' or 'social communion'. The former may have meaning for the adult but is unaddressed, while the latter involves shared address but no content. Both are regarded here as examples of 'somasis', that is, human vocal and bodily behaviour that is not being deployed for meaning-making.

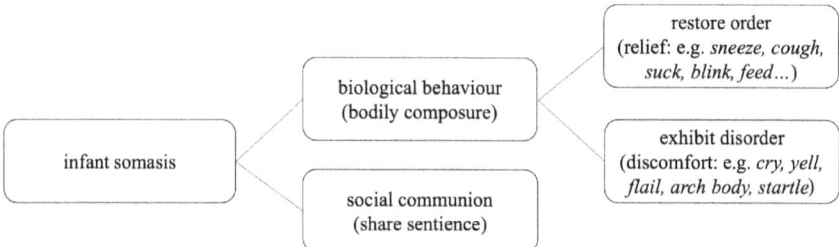

Figure 2.1 Early somasis (at approximately two months of age).

2.3 The emergence of 'signs'

Over the next six months or so, the protoconversational interactions involving 'mutual regulation of affect and attention' (Reddy et al., 1997: 247) become more playful, pleasurable and co-operative, enabling routines involving songs, rhymes, teasing, laughter and rhythmic games. At the same time, the developing infant explores the world beyond the conversational dyad, crawling and manipulating objects in activities which may compete with earlier forms of interpersonal play (Trevarthen, 1987). Halliday ([1992] 2002) suggests that reconciling the contradiction between inner and outer experience – that is, between the conscious world (already set up as a social one of 'you and me') and the material third-party world – may provide the impetus for the infant to participate in the first fully semiotic exchanges, where attention is shared about something through the use of baby symbols or 'signs'.[1] A number of studies, quite apart from the SFL sources, have confirmed this milestone as occurring from about nine months of age (Dore, 1975, 1978; Carter, 1978; Lock, 1978; Menn, 1978; Blake, 2000; Bates, [1979] 2014). To count as a sign, there must be a specific form of expression systematically and repeatedly paired with some recognizable 'content'.

An example from Painter's ([1984] 2015) case study of Hal can serve to illustrate. At ten months Hal would look at his parent while reaching to an object beyond his grasp and utter a particular vocalization, [amamamama], spoken quickly with a falling tone on the last syllable. He was satisfied when handed the object and frustrated when not.[2] The content of his sign clearly approximates to 'I want that' and the expression is an idiosyncratic multimodal complex of gesture, gaze, vocal articulation, tempo and pitch movement – all aspects of expressive behaviour long rehearsed in protoconversation. The multimodal utterance constitutes a sign because the content-expression pair is bi-unique; that is, for a period at least, the particular expression complex always carries the same

Table 2.1 Somasis contrasted with Nigel's gestural signs at nine months

Somasis (non-symbolic action)	Semiosis (symbolic action)	
	Expression	Content
Snatch object	Grasp and let go, leaving hand near	'I want that'
Knock away object	Touch object lightly and withdraw hand	'No, I don't want that'
Move adult's hand on object	Touch object firmly	'Do that (with it) again'

meaning and the particular meaning is always expressed in the same identifiable way. While initially, perhaps well before nine months of age, an isolated sign may emerge (Halliday, [1983] 2004: 215), once there is a set of contrasting signs in evidence, the baby can be said to have created a small 'protolanguage'.[3]

In explaining the distinction between a sign and an action that may have meaning for the observer but is not addressed as a form of symbolic communication, Halliday ([1978] 2004: 131) offers the example of his son Nigel's use of hand and arm movements at nine months of age, set out here in Table 2.1.

In the examples of somasis in Table 2.1 (column 1), the child acts on material reality directly in order to achieve his goal. By contrast, the examples of semiosis show Nigel acting on the world symbolically by deliberately addressing another person with a gesture of his own devising. In further clarifying the criteria for recognizing a vocal or bodily behaviour as symbolic in nature, Halliday defines a symbolic act as 'one of which the meaning and success criteria do not reside in its own performance' ([1978] 2004: 114). Ramenzoni and Liszkowski's (2016) experimental research on eight-month-olds similarly illustrates the difference between somasis and semiosis with respect to infant gesture, when they describe how their infant subjects reached out to grasp objects that were near enough for them to do so (somasis) but would only reach towards more distant, unobtainable objects in the presence of an adult who could act for them (semiosis).

Although there is a clear distinction between somasis and semiosis in principle, it needs to be recognized that there are fuzzy boundaries along the ontogenetic pathway. For example, when a baby routinely struggles to get out of its baby chair uttering grizzle-like sounds, or 'bicycles' legs at the tasting of favourite food, it may not be clear whether the vocalizations and body movements are signifiers addressed to the parent or simply involuntary manifestations of frustration or delight in the way an increased heartbeat might be. Similarly, when Halliday ([1992] 2002: 353) describes Nigel just before the age of six months as uttering a high-pitched squeak and looking about on hearing some commotion in the environment, it is hard to know if this is a symbolic act to share interest (as Halliday interprets it) or an involuntary biological response. Either way of course, just as with a screaming neonate expressing hunger or pain, the observer can interpret the behaviour as meaningful.

While we may not always know in the ontogenetic context whether an expressive behaviour is 'biological' somasis (unaddressed but displaying a feeling or state) or a symbolic signifier, this does not invalidate the principle of the difference between the two and the milestone achieved once there are clear contrasting symbols in use by the child. However, it does raise the issue for paralanguage theory of how to treat the realm of facial expression in particular, which is so much in evidence prior to the first symbols being created and continues uninterrupted throughout life. A relevant fact is that humans have limited voluntary control over what the face displays moment by moment, even though, past infancy, we can of course intentionally arrange our faces and perform specific emotional expressions when the occasion demands. Involuntary physiological actions, such as those involved in unintended facial expressions, do not in principle instantiate semiotic systems. However, given their capacity for being consciously controlled to a degree, or on occasion, or in performance, and given their ubiquity in the interpretation of meaning, there is an argument for following Martinec (2001) and modelling facial expressions in adult communication as if their manifestation were always semiotic in nature. This is the descriptive strategy we adopt in this book.

2.4 Protolanguage: The first semiotic system

This section will outline the nature of the protolanguage system from the descriptions in the case studies by Halliday (1975), Painter ([1984] 2015) and Torr (1997). This will provide a basis for a later discussion of the proposal put forward by Cléirigh (2010) and found in Martin et al. (2013b) and Zappavigna and Martin (2018) that some aspects of adult paralanguage remain protolinguistic in nature. It will also clarify the significance for paralanguage theory of the emergence of the mother tongue during what Halliday (1975) calls the 'transition' phase – a matter to be considered in the following section.

The data for the protolanguage case studies (cited earlier) comprised extensive pen and paper notes and/or audiotaped recordings of utterances and interactions involving children up to the age of eighteen months or two and a half years, by which time they were using the lexicogrammar of their mother tongue. Vocalizations were counted as protolanguage signs when there was 'an observable and constant relation between the content and the expression' (Halliday, [1975] 2004b: 35) and there were at least three distinct but comparable occasions of use within a six-week period.[4] As a rule, there were relatively few ambiguous cases: either there were fewer than three (so ignored in the analysis) or many more. Sign expressions were specified in the descriptions in terms of vocal articulation and tone, with facial expressions, gaze and gestural movements noted down in various cases where they seemed criterial to the recognition of a particular sign. The relative emphasis on the vocal in the aforementioned SFL case studies contrasts with some of the more recent work on infant gesture, where the presence of concurrent pre-lexical vocalizations may be ignored (Acredolo and Goodwyn, 1988), or else noted but not described (e.g. Caselli and Volterra, 1990; Meguerditchian et al., 2011), and where gesture accompanied by such vocalizing may be counted as 'gesture alone' (Goldin-Meadow and Morford, 1990; Capirci et al., 2005).

In the SFL case studies, the protolinguistic expressions seemed to have various origins. Some have been described as iconic[5] in nature (Halliday, [1978] 2004: 114) in that they related transparently to a somatic instance and were thus easy for the addressee to interpret. An example would be Nigel's grasp-and-let-go as his first symbolic expression of 'I want that' (see Table 2.1). As Kendon (2017: 164) observes, 'Perhaps the appearance of intelligible gesture prior to intelligible speech has been reported because adults can more readily interpret semantically a baby's kinesic expressions than its oral expressions.' Arguably less iconic but still derived in some way from the child's body are vocal examples such as the following:

- Both Nigel and Anna developed sighing kinds of sounds to express a response 'yes, do that' to adult offers (e.g. to a game), as if imitating the sound of a release of tension.
- Hal used a velar fricative to acknowledge a greeting, probably originating from hearing himself voicing a dribbly smile.
- All three children at some point used bilabial nasals in relation to food appreciation and grizzle-based sounds as demand expressions.

Other signs were imitations of adult words, although not functioning yet as lexical items: an example would be Nigel's [bø] as a demand for his toy bird or Hal's version of *oh dear* to express dismay. In the remaining cases the expressions were simply invented by the child.

In relation to the meaning potential of the protolanguage, one important issue is that meanings necessarily have to be interpreted in terms of the contexts of their use. In the case studies, this is done by describing the earliest meanings in terms of four such contexts, or 'microfunctions'. Two of the microfunctions are oriented to acting on the world – the instrumental ('I want') and the regulatory ('you do (that)'); and two are oriented to reflection on the world – the interactional ('you and me together', 'let's attend together') and the 'personal' ('I like', 'I wonder'). These are outlined in Table 2.2, adapted from Halliday ([1995] 2003: 401). In later months, a few additional functions, such as the imaginative and heuristic, are included in the description until the point where the system transitions into a more adult-like semiotic.

Despite the strongly emotional nature of earlier protoconversation, in this interpretation, symbolic expressions of feeling are seen as restricted to the personal microfunction, where the child uses symbols to construe a sense of self in contradistinction to the environment. However, it could be argued that

Table 2.2 Microfunctions of protolanguage: Active and reflective (after Halliday [1995] 2003: 401)

Form of consciousness Domain of experience	Action (what should be)	Reflection (what is)
1st/2nd person (you & me)	Regulatory 'do for me!'	Interactional 'you and me together'
3rd person (all else)	Instrumental 'give me!'	Personal 'I like/wonder'

Table 2.3 Emotions underlying early microfunctions

Microfunction	Meaning gloss	Emotion
Regulatory	'I like/don't like that – do/don't do it (again)'	Enjoyment or lack of
Instrumental	'I want that – give me' 'Help!'	Desire, frustration
Interactional	'I love being/doing this together'	Happiness, trust, security
Personal	'That's nice/interesting'	Pleasure (later, excitement, surprise, pride); curiosity

emotional states underlie each of the four initial microfunctions as shown in Table 2.3.

This makes room for an alternative interpretation of the early protolanguage as a system of semioticized affect, as argued in Painter (2003). Figure 2.2 presents a representation of Hal's protolanguage at ten-and-a-half months in these terms. The system is a small one compared with the entirety of a child's somatic emotional expression because only systematically vocalized (and therefore clearly semiotic) expressions of affect have been included. It is relevant that Malatesta, who tracks the development of emotion expression more broadly, comments as follows:

> In the course of the first year of life, infant emotional expressive behaviour proceeds from spontaneously emitted complex reflexive behaviours through a period of susceptibility to instrumental conditioning, to the eventual capacity to use these behaviours voluntarily and instrumentally. (1985: 212)

She regards this capacity as having been attained by about seven months of age, which is before the emergence of a protolanguage system.

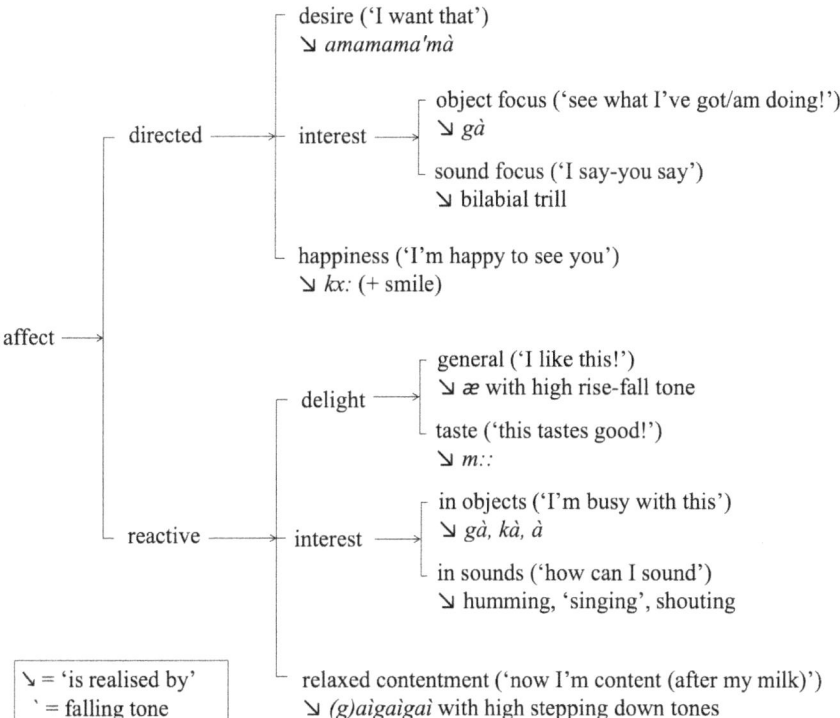

Figure 2.2 Hal's protolanguage at ten-and-a-half months shown as a system of affect.

While modelling protolanguage from the perspective of affect does not lend itself as readily to tracking the development of the system as proto-dialogue (involving calls, greetings, offers, refusals, acknowledgements, playful exchanges) and imaginative play, it has the advantage of emphasizing the continuity with the earlier, emotion-charged forms of social communion and of allowing for a clearer focus on the origins of the verbal ATTITUDE system in the adult semantics of APPRAISAL (Martin and White, 2005). Different possible framings of protolanguage are possible because there are no lexicogrammatical oppositions to ground the description as there are with mature adult language.

In whatever way the protolanguage is interpreted, there are defining features of the semiotic that can be specified. In relation to the expressions, a key point is that the signs are multimodal. They involve any combinations of pitch, tone, articulation, loudness, voice quality, gaze, movement of finger/hand/limb/head/face or repetition of a syllable as invariant and non-separable features of the expression. A few examples from the case studies are given here to illustrate. Most content/expression pairs did not persist for the entire protolanguage so the relevant period is indicated in each case:

Hal:
- a smile and direct gaze always accompanies [kx:], his vocal acknowledgement of being greeted (interactional function, nine–twelve months)
- a rise-fall intonation is invariant with [ou], meaning 'ooh, that's surprising!' (personal function, twelve–fifteen months)
- a pointing gesture always accompanies variants of [ga], the vocal articulation for 'that's interesting' (personal function, ten-and-a-half to thirteen-and-a-half months)
- miming of drinking goes together with a satisfied *aaah!* sound in pretend-play drinking (imaginative function, twelve-and-a-half to fifteen months)

Nigel:
- high-level tone is invariant with [na] or [an:a] for greeting of Anna or with [da] or [dada] his greeting for Daddy (interactional function, twelve–fifteen months)
- curling up on the floor accompanies a specific repeated low-pitched vocalization to signify 'I'm sleepy' in pretend play (imaginative function, thirteen-and-a-half to fifteen months)

Anna:
- a reaching gesture and alternating gaze (object/caregiver) accompanies the vocal expression of 'I want that' (instrumental function, nine to ten-and-a-half months)
- level then falling tone, together with loud volume, is inherent to [mami] the vocal expression of 'Mum get me!' (regulatory function, ten to thirteen-and-a-half months)

In sum, with few exceptions, multimodal fusion is the basic form of instantiation for protolanguage expressions.[6]

The other distinctive and corresponding characteristic of the protolinguistic sign is that the 'referential' (or proto-'ideational') aspect of the meaning is inseparable from the expression of affect or function (or proto-'interpersonal' meaning). For example, Nigel's instrumental [bø], spoken on a mid-tone, expressed not just 'bird' but the entirety of the meaning 'I want my toy bird.' It could not be used to refer to the bird in any way other than to demand it, and conversely the meaning of 'I want' signified by [bø] could not be separated out from the meaning of 'my toy bird'. A demand for another object would require an entirely new sign. Similarly, Hal's appreciative [m::], within the personal microfunction, encompassed the whole complex of 'this tastes good', while Anna's instrumental utterance [bɛ] on a randomly varying level or falling tone meant all and only 'take off my bib'; it was not a lexical item *bib* that could be used in non-instrumental contexts.[7] In short, the fusion of expressive modalities (articulation, tone, volume, gesture etc.) in the signifier and the fusion of (proto) ideational and (proto) interpersonal aspects of meaning in the signified are essential aspects of the protolanguage sign.

2.5 The transition to language

The SFL longitudinal case studies show that as the child's meaning system expands in the latter part of the second year of life and incorporates mother tongue lexical items from the adult language, the nature of the semiotic transforms. There are three aspects to this, the most striking being the emergence of two overarching functions for speech that are more general than the individual microfunctions. These are the 'pragmatic' function for 'language as action' and the 'mathetic' for 'language as reflection', each vocally signalled (rather than simply contextually inferred). In effect, during a phase of 'transition' into the mother tongue, ideational and interpersonal aspects of meaning become separable: the articulatory aspect of the lexical word is used to express the ideational content, such as 'ball', while tone (or, in Anna's case, voice quality) carries the more interpersonal aspect, such as the active meaning of 'I want' or the reflective one of 'I see'. Thus, for Nigel, *ball* on a rising tone signified a demand 'I want the ball', while *ball* on a falling tone expressed observations such as 'I see the ball' or 'I played with the ball'. This systematic distinction between active demands and reflective comments is achieved by separating the expressive modality of tone (or voice quality) from that of lexical articulation, so that they can be combined and recombined in a systematic and meaningful way.[8] While at first most of the lexis or simple structures are restricted to use within either the pragmatic or mathetic function with only a minority of items available on either tone, this restriction gradually disappears over the course of the transition phase.

A second way in which the semiotic system transforms in the move to the mother tongue is that meanings in general begin to be graduated by varying volume, voice quality or vowel length or by repetition of an expression (rather than by the invention of a new sign). For example, whereas Nigel had neutral and intensified meanings at ten-and-a-half months created through the use of quite different expressions, Hal at eighteen months used creaky voice quality on words as a general means to intensify any demand and an elongated vowel and crescendo-diminuendo volume to add force to the pragmatic use of any food name. Even before the transition, there are a few instances of variable force within the protolanguage itself, especially by Anna. For example, at twelve months, she sometimes whispered her 'interest' sign, perhaps upscaling its force to that of 'wonder', while her refusal sign was optionally accompanied by head shaking from ten-and-a-half months, perhaps to indicate greater force. Hal at sixteen and a half months, very close to the transition phase, could intensify one variant of 'I want' through syllable repetition and foot shuffling. But at this stage these protolinguistic forms of proto-graduation related to individual signs and were not extended throughout the system as began to happen during the transition.

Finally, there are examples from Hal where accompanying gestures and even facial expressions become clearly separable from articulatory or tonal aspects of the sign. For example, the pointing gesture, arising as an invariant part of his 'interest' sign within the personal microfunction, becomes generalized and available for deictic identification in any context, as for adult speakers. Thus during the transition, a point might sometimes accompany Hal's (pragmatic) verbal response to an adult offer *Which one do you want?* or his (mathetic) answer to a question like *Where's the cat?* In addition, his playful use of language during the transition phase shows a new ability to separate and recombine strands of expression. By eighteen months he had a vocal expression approximating *oh dear* which was used initially at such times as when his tower of bricks fell down or he failed to dislodge a toy when it had become stuck under an armchair. On such occasions his facial expression naturally expressed the consternation he felt. However, during the transition he began to use *oh dear* teasingly; for example, deliberately knocking over his tower of bricks and uttering *oh dear* with a delighted grin. He would also use *bad boy*, not only as an expression of remorse accompanied by a solemn face, but in a cheeky manner while deliberately doing or threatening a forbidden act, with an appropriately gleeful glance at the addressee.

In summary, the protolanguage gradually undergoes three transformations:

- the meaningful and systematic use of tone or voice quality to signify proto-grammatical mood (demand vs comment) with respect to a lexically coded representation;
- the graduation of lexical meanings through such means as creaky voice, loud volume and vowel elongation; and
- the separation of gestural, facial or tonal expression from segmental vocalization with both the generalization of pointing as a deictic gesture and the playful use of 'inappropriate' facial affect and intonation.

All these changes involve the teasing apart of different aspects of meaning (the interpersonal or textual aspects from the ideational, or the lexical attitude from facial affect) together with the corresponding separation of different aspects of hitherto invariant multimodal expressions. The case study data therefore clearly support Matthiessen's (2007) assertion that in the transition to language a range of expressive effects can be separated out, becoming available to be combined and recombined with any content. In his words, 'The multimodality of protolanguage is distributed across language, body language (face, gesture) and paralanguage (timbre, tempo, loudness … etc.)' (Matthiessen, 2007: 6–7). In later work, Matthiessen (2009) includes both bodily and vocal resources as 'paralanguage', the overarching term also adopted in this volume.

Towards the end of the second year of life, the transition strategy of a two-way mathetic/pragmatic distinction, realized by a systematic distinction in tone (falling vs rising) or voice quality (relaxed vs tense), itself gives way as the language develops further. Pragmatic demands (initially for material action) come to include demands for information, while mathetic comments (initially resharing shared experience) develop into statements genuinely giving information. To enable this, a system of SPEECH FUNCTION emerges realized by grammatical choices in MOOD (imperative/polar and Wh-interrogative/declarative). Once interpersonal meaning has in this way become more complex than the mathetic/pragmatic binary allows, intonation and voice quality are freed up for further grammatical or paralinguistic effects, as in adult usage. The system of tones is mapped onto MOOD choices as in adult language and as

Torr (1997: 147) notes with respect to Anna's use of voice tension (originally indicating pragmatic meaning):

> By 24 months voice tension could no longer be considered criterial in determining to which function any utterance should be assigned. Early adult Mood forms such as WH- and polar interrogatives were now being used in ... [all] contexts to indicate the interpersonal status of the utterance. Voice tension continued to mark certain utterances, but now its use may be regarded as paralinguistic as is the case in the adult language.

By this time too, interpersonal grammatical and paralinguistic choices combine with ideational meanings that are now expressed as activity sequences and TRANSITIVITY structures as well as lexically (and perhaps occasionally, paralinguistically through gesture; Mayberry and Nicoladis, 2000; Pizzuto and Capobianco, 2005).[9] By the end of the transition period, then – at about two years of age for these particular children – there are simultaneous strands of interpersonal and ideational meaning expressed in every utterance, both linguistically and paralinguistically. And alongside these developments, experience with both dialogue and monologue propels a corresponding development with respect to textual meaning. This involves, for example, appropriate placement of the tonic syllable in dialogue, something that seems to emerge as soon as there is a grammatical structure to sustain it, as in the following exchanges (1), when Hal is twenty-two months old:

(1)

    M: //1 *where's* / **Daddy**
    H: //1 ***there's*** Daddy

    M: //1 *that's* / *Daddy's* little / ***brush***
    H: //1 *that's* / ***Hal*** / *brush*

Similarly, resources for IDENTIFICATION (such as pronouns, determiners, locative adverbs) emerge early but in exophoric usage (e.g. *that's mine*; *put it there*). However, the dialogic context soon allows some examples to function anaphorically as well, as in *What colour's Mummy's pen? – That's blue* (Painter, [1984] 2015: 245). In Nigel's case especially, longer turns in dialogue provide greater opportunity for anaphora as well as for chunking information via clause and tone group structure. This can be seen in the following dialogue (2) where he uses his imagination in the final clauses (intonation analysis for Nigel interpreted from Halliday's ([1975] 2004a: 191) formatting):

(2)

N: //1 *chuff*a walk on **rail**way line

//1 *chuff*a walk on **rail**way line

//1 *fast* **chuff**a

//1 *one* day might **go** on fast chuffa

//1 *one* day might **go** on fast chuffa //

F: yes, we might

N: //1 *one* day go on blue **chuff**a

//1 *next* chuffa **com**ing

//1 go on **that** one //

Once there are three relatively distinct sets of options for interpersonal, ideational and textual meaning, and corresponding co-present strands of meaning in the utterance, the language can be regarded as metafunctionally organized along the adult model. Thus at the same time as paralinguistic resources involving the voice, face and body become available to make meaning in their own right, the resources of verbal language have become organized into three metafunctional strands.

Both the linguistic and paralinguistic systems continue to develop further once the mother tongue is established. For example, some textual systems such as those of THEME, TONICITY and TONALITY within language and the kind of gesturing McNeill (1992) refers to as 'beats' depend for contrasts on longer conversational or more 'narrative' turns than those of the single word, phrase or clause moves that are typical of the immediate post-transition period. Mayberry and Nicoladis's (2000) research on gesturing in bilingual children is interesting here in showing that the variety and distribution of gestures increase with increasing mean length of utterance, which argues against interpreting them as a temporary prop filling in for inadequate language resources.[10] In sum, both linguistic and paralinguistic resources within all three metafunctions are in place by the end of the transition phase but continue to develop further with greater meaning-making experience.

2.6 Modelling adult paralanguage

Although the term 'protolanguage' in SFL theory referred in origin to a phase in linguistic ontogenesis, Martin et al. (2013b) and Zappavigna and Martin (2018) have suggested that for the adult communicative system, one of three proposed

Table 2.4 Categories of 'body language' (drawn from Martin et al., 2013b)

Microfunction	'Protolinguistic' examples
Regulatory	Glower with raised fist
Instrumental	Extended palm; forearm raised in rejection
Personal	Smiling and other facial expressions; fidgeting, posture shifts etc.
Interactional	Gaze, facial and body orientation, body uprightness
Metafunction	**Sonovergent examples**
Textual	Hand, head gesture in sync with speech rhythm
Textual	Hand, head gesture in sync with tonic placement
Textual	Hand, head gesture coextensive with tone group
Interpersonal	Face, hand gesture in tune with tone choice
Metafunction	**Semovergent examples**
Textual	Pointing with hand, head, eyes to phenomena or to metaphenomenon (as regions of gesture space)
Interpersonal	Oscillating gestures of hand, head to illustrate modality, polarity
Ideational	Drawing, mime, to illustrate phenomena

categories of paralanguage can be interpreted as 'protolinguistic' in nature. This is on the grounds that, like the infant meaning system, but unlike the other two categories they propose, it is organized in terms of microfunctions rather than metafunctions. See Table 2.4, based on Martin et al. (2013b), where the terms 'sonovergent' and 'semovergent' replace the terms 'linguistic and 'epilinguistic' used in the original.

This model usefully distinguishes paralinguistic behaviour that can only accompany speech (being closely tied to the interpersonal and textual systems of spoken language) from all the rest. This is our category of sonovergent paralanguage, where paralinguistic expression moves with speech prosodies. The remaining paralinguistic behaviour is divided in Table 2.4 between protolinguistic and semovergent categories, both of which may (but need not) accompany speech. The question, then, is whether it is helpful to separate out some of this expressive behaviour as protolinguistic – which would be to suggest that the adult semiotic communicative system simultaneously deploys language and (paralinguistic) protolanguage.

The first point to be made is that some of the phenomena counted as protolinguistic in Zappavigna and Martin (2018) may in fact be somatic rather than semiotic. For example, forms of fidgeting, scratching a cheek or crossing feet may simply be a matter of relieving some bodily discomfort, rather than having symbolic import. It is necessary to have criteria for discriminating somatic and semiotic expression in such cases (see Chapter 1, Sections 1.4–1.5), but their ambiguity is not grounds for classing them as protolinguistic. Secondly, it is clear that not all forms of adult facial or bodily gesture that first arise in the protolanguage are assigned to the 'protolinguistic body language' category by Zappavigna and Martin (2018). The pointing gesture, for example, has already been discussed as arising in early protolanguage but becomes generalized during the transition to function in concert with a variety of ideational and interpersonal forms of linguistic (or paralinguistic) expression. This gesture is accordingly accepted by Zappavigna and Martin as semovergent and part of the textual metafunction. In addition, forms of mime that first arise within the imaginative microfunction of protolanguage (e.g. raising an imaginary cup to the lips) are recognized in Table 2.4 as ideational and so also within the semovergent paralanguage category. It is not therefore the case that having a clear origin in protolanguage is regarded by Zappavigna and Martin as sufficient grounds for classing an adult gesture as a protolinguistic 'leftover'.

Nor is it possible to argue that certain forms of adult paralanguage are organized in terms of microfunctions simply because it is possible to interpret them this way. As explained earlier, there is no formal way to determine the microfunction of an infant expression – it is an interpretation from context. Therefore, given that any adult communication could be assigned to a microfunction on contextual grounds, since adult language has limitless uses, this does not in itself count as evidence for microfunctional organization. It would therefore be more appropriate for the term 'protolanguage' to be used only if it can be shown that the defining characteristics of protolinguistic communication are apparent, that is, if the expression form is an irreducible multimodal complex and if the meaning is similarly an inseparable bundle of ideational and interpersonal meaning.

To explore this, some examples of adult paralinguistic behaviour classified by Zappavigna and Martin (2018) as protolinguistic will be briefly discussed. One group comprises various facial expressions such as smiling, raising, lowering or widening the eyes, opening the mouth and the presence or absence of eye contact with the addressee, all features of 'social communion' that predate even protolanguage (see Figure 2.1). As has been discussed, during the transition phase there is evidence that facial affect can be separated from other strands of interpersonal expression (e.g. looking happy while saying *oh dear*) and in the adult semiotic system affective facial expressions can clearly combine freely with any ideational meaning. In these respects, such expression forms are unlike protolinguistic signs, and the issue to be resolved in a particular case is whether that instance is somatic or semiotic.

Another group of behaviours from Zappavigna and Martin's (2018) 'body protolanguage' category involves relative uprightness of body posture, frontal or oblique facial and body orientation and the leaning forward or backwards of the torso in relation to the addressee. These expressive movements of the body are similarly independent from any ideational meanings with which they may combine and, similarly to facial movements, may also combine with other interpersonal strands of meaning, whether linguistic (e.g. a variety of spoken MOOD forms) or paralinguistic (e.g. smiling or widening the eyes). There is thus neither fusion of ideational/interpersonal meaning in relation to 'content' nor multimodal fusion in the form of expression. The characteristics of protolanguage as a developmental semiotic are not therefore in evidence.

If we turn now to other SFL theorists, particularly those who have considered the visual depiction of human communicative interaction, we can see some common threads. There is a general agreement about the meanings of the way the body is oriented in relation to an addressee. For example, Kress and van Leeuwen's (2006) system of INVOLVEMENT within their 'visual grammar' explains the meaning as relative detachment or involvement of the viewer with the content of the image. The meaning is realized by horizontal angle, with an oblique angle signifying greater detachment than a front-on angle. Painter et al. (2013) extend this to analysis of the depicted interacting characters in picture books to propose a system of ORIENTATION with different orientations between characters (face to face, side by side, back to back) comparably realizing different degrees of engagement, solidarity or detachment. Martinec (2001) similarly has a comparable system of ANGLE (operating alongside one of SOCIAL DISTANCE) again with similar realizations. In all of this work the meaning systems are placed within the interpersonal metafunction and are thus seen as available alongside textual and/or ideational paralanguage systems and all three metafunctions of language.

What is common to most of the meanings assigned by Zappavigna and Martin (2018) to 'protolinguistic' microfunctions is that, if not simply somatic, they are interpersonal in nature – but not accommodated by a linguistic model that includes only SPEECH FUNCTION, MOOD and MODALITY in that metafunction. As we have seen, much of what is assigned to body protolanguage involves the expression of emotions. Here we meet again the challenge of discriminating somasis and semiosis. Nonetheless, in the analysis of visual depiction, Painter et al. (2013) propose VISUAL AFFECT as an interpersonal meaning system complementing that of verbal AFFECT within the linguistic domain of APPRAISAL. The details of the system remain unspecified by them, but Martinec (2001) provides networks of meaning options for basic emotions with realizations specified in terms of facial movements. These systems are again treated by him as belonging within the interpersonal metafunction and thus able to be put into play alongside meanings originating from within the other metafunctions. For our own work in this domain, see Chapter 5.

In sum, given that there is no formal way to discriminate the proposed adult 'protolinguistic' body language from the semovergent category, no evidence that the proposed instances operate as protolinguistic signs and a common recognition that the meanings in question belong within the interpersonal domain, they are subsumed in this book within the semovergent category. Our position will be that paralanguage, like verbal language, is organized metafunctionally and that different metafunctional strands of both language and paralanguage can be instantiated simultaneously.

2.7 Summary

In recent years, the growing awareness that adult face-to-face communication involves the face and body as well as the voice has impacted on studies of its ontogenesis, resulting in a new interest in gestural forms of infant communication and their relation to early mother tongue speech. This has generally meant observing or eliciting different forms of gestures from infants and attempting to establish the extent to which they predate, accompany, substitute for or are overtaken by early language forms. A limitation of this work is that there is little consistency in the classification systems used in different studies, and the mother tongue rather than the protolanguage is seen as the starting point of meaningful vocal communication. Nonetheless there appears to be a consensus that meaningful communication predates the mother tongue and evidence that different kinds of gestures may be deployed in the early years.

Taking an ontogenetic perspective to the theorization of paralanguage inevitably reminds us how thoroughly both the face and body are implicated in the expression of meaning from the very beginnings of communication. Newborns are innately equipped to express emotion facially and demonstrate an impressive gestural repertoire involving arm, hand and finger even before harnessing these movements communicatively at two or three months of age. At that point babies engage in emotion-charged, rhythmic interactions with caregivers involving gaze, voice, facial expressions and movements of limbs, hands, head and body, where the only meaning exchanged is that joyful mutual address is taking place.[11] It is on this foundation of 'protoconversation' that older infants, by now engaged in exploring the world beyond the communicative dyad, begin to create their first semiotic system – the protolanguage. This semiotic system makes use of expressive resources that are both vocal and gestural as documented in three SFL longitudinal case studies.

Exploring this developmental pathway raises the issue of discriminating the semiotic status of different classes of behaviour. There is behaviour which carries meaning for others, such as screaming, arm flailing, lip smacking and burping (the baby is in pain, startled, hungry, 'windy'), but being instinctive or biological in nature it can be excluded from the realm of paralanguage. More problematic are the protoconversational behaviours of gaze and facial expression which are clearly addressed and where both parties are 'reading' each other's behaviour. Ontogenetically this is a temporary phase, where moving and meaning are not yet distinct (Halliday, 2004: 7), and these behaviours become incorporated into the expression complexes of protolanguage once the infant has begun to create signs and come under voluntary control in due course.

Given its basis in protoconversation, it is not surprising that the initial protolanguage, serving various functions relevant to a one-year-old, constitutes a meaning potential that strongly expresses the child's affect. And while the original SFL protolanguage descriptions focus mainly on vocal expression, the role of gaze and facial expression, as well as gesture in some cases, forms an integral part of the multimodal realizations of protolanguage meanings. These meanings in turn are a fusion of affective or microfunctional status in relation to some representational content (e.g. desire in relation to visible food or surprise in relation to an observed commotion). Later, with the transition into the mother tongue, the interpersonal and ideational strands of meaning become distinct, the former initially expressed through tone or voice quality and the latter through lexis. Once this happens, interpersonal and ideational meanings can be freely combined and recombined. At the same time, the various strands of protolinguistic multimodal expressions, such as articulation, tone, voice quality, gesture and facial expression, become separable (from each other and from specific verbal expressions), each capable of realizing systemic choice and thus warranting description as semiotic systems in their own right.

By the time a child's language has passed through the transition phase, it can be shown to be organized into three simultaneously available metafunctions (ideational, interpersonal and textual) allowing for systemic options at different strata. There is also evidence that by this time there are various paralinguistic expressive domains in play in a way that is different from the protolanguage phase. Where some of these expressive resources have been described by SFL scholars concerned with the semiotic potential of action or the visual depiction of human interaction, they too have been assigned to one of the three metafunctions. It remains to build on such work by providing more detailed descriptions of a wider range of paralinguistic systems. This will be done in Chapters 4, 5 and 6 of the book.

3

The semiotic voice: Intonation, rhythm and other vocal features

3.1 Introduction

In this chapter we explore the voice as semiotic instrument. In particular, we explore the contributions made to meaning by the phonology of intonation and rhythm. We will also briefly consider other semiotic aspects of the vocal signal such as pitch height and vocal quality, with further discussion to follow in Chapter 5. Our main aim in this chapter is to provide a description of those phonological systems of language that interact with the sonovergent systems of paralanguage presented elsewhere in this book.

Building on the discussion in the previous chapter on the transition from infant protolanguage to adult language, this chapter provides a brief introduction to the phonetics and phonology of rhythm and intonation in English. The field of English intonation presents a diverse range of views, both on the same and on different phenomena. One fundamental contrast involves approaching the study of pitch segmentally, as pitch levels (e.g. Pike, 1945; Silverman et al., 1992) or prosodically, as contours (Halliday, [1963] 2005b, [1963] 2005a; Brazil, 1975; see Bolinger (1951) for an early discussion on the 'levels vs contours' debate). The approach to the form as well as the functions of intonational phonology in discourse varies depending on theoretical background and purposes of the scholars (for a discussion, see Kohler, 2006; Halliday and Greaves, 2008).

In the present book we take a systemic functional, social semiotic approach (Halliday, [1978] 2003). This allows us to relate the choices in intonation and other semiotic systems of the voice to other aspects of language and paralanguage within a coherent, holistic theory and description and address the challenges therein (Martin, 2011b). The discussion draws primarily on Halliday's systemic functional theory and description of intonation (for an introduction,[1] see Halliday and Greaves, 2008; Smith and Greaves, 2015) and on work by van Leeuwen (1992, 1999) and Martinec (2000a, 2002) on rhythm and other semiotic resources of the voice. Our approach to the functions of vocal semiotic systems, in their interactions with bodily semiotic systems, is developed from the perspective of the discourse semantics described in Martin and Rose ([2003] 2007) and briefly introduced in Chapter 1 (see also Tann, 2017; Martin, 2019). This chapter uses illustrative excerpts from the Chatty Vlog text introduced in Chapter 1 and presents texts that will be featured in later chapters – in order to introduce rhythm and intonation systems and illustrate the nature and functions of these systems in their contributions to meaning in discourse.

3.2 An introduction to phonetics and phonology

The human vocal tract is capable of making an immense variety of sound distinctions. Firstly, using air pushed up from the lungs, the vocal cords vibrate with variable frequency, heard as distinctive variations in pitch (fundamental frequency, F_0, measured in Hz) – including pitch contours (rising, falling etc.), jumps up and down in pitch height and variations in duration of pitch events. Other features such as breathy or creaky voice are created through variation in the vocal fold aperture; and the amplitude of vocal fold vibration, referred to as intensity, is heard as loudness of the voice. Then, at various places within the vocal tract above the larynx, movements and positions of articulators (e.g. uvula, tongue, roof of the mouth, teeth, lips) shape the airstream to create the various features that, in combination, form the vowels and consonants of languages (for an accessible introduction to phonetics and phonology, see Clark et al., [1990] 2007; for descriptions of how these sound distinctions are taken up in particular languages across the world, see Ladefoged and Maddieson, 1996). In Chapter 2 we showed that meaningful distinctions are already present in early infant sounds, ranging across features such as pitch variation, creaky voice, loudness and nasality – including the protolinguistic formation of what will, in the adult language, be vowels and consonants and intonation contours. Many of the sounds featuring in the production of adult semiosis are already being used by infants and drawn into the creation of meaningful signs.

While the infants' utterances described in the previous chapter are clearly meaningful, it is debatable whether the infant child's protolanguage can be said to have a developed phonological system. At this point in the protolanguage, there is a unitary fusion of expression (sound) and content (meaning) as bundles of features which do not enter into independently variable systemic oppositions of either content or expression. For example, as described in Chapter 2, in the protolanguage of the infant Nigel in Halliday ([1975] 2004b) [bø] with mid-tone expresses the composite meaning of bird plus demand ('I want my toy bird'). It is only when these features become independently variable that a bona fide phonological system becomes available to encode systemic choices in meaning. In Nigel's early speech, for example, the rising/falling pitch contour distinction became a phonological choice encoding, respectively, a distinction between pragmatic and mathetic meanings. This distinction could be independently mapped onto other sounds, such as [bø], 'bird', with a rising or a falling pitch contour thus meaning, respectively, 'I want/look at my toy bird'. Similarly, at eighteen months, during the transition phase, the infant Hal described in Chapter 2 used creaky voice quality on various words as a general means to intensify any demand. Such a combination of independently variable features creates a significantly increased semiotic potential. The child can now 'mean more than one thing at once' (Halliday, [1974] 2009).

The study of phonetics refers to the description of such sounds as sound – phenomena of the concrete, physical realm; phonology, on the other hand, describes the way sounds pattern and relate to one another to make meaning-bearing distinctions – phenomena of the abstract, semiotic realm. The influential principles espoused by Trubetskoy ([1939] 1969: 10) for the study of linguistic phonology have applications in the study of all sounds that make meaning (and indeed all meaning-creating phenomena): 'It is the task of phonology to study which differences in sound are related to differences in meaning in a given language.' That is, while phonetics must consider 'the acoustic and articulatory properties' of speech sounds, a phonological description 'needs to consider only *that aspect of sound which fulfills a specific function in the language*' ([1939] 1969: 11, italics in original). This principle can be extended to mean that if any feature of the vocal sound signal is found to make or help to make a distinction in meaning, it should be included in a phonological description of a language or of a text (for an application of this principle to speech, music and sound, see, e.g. van Leeuwen, 1999). This point is echoed in comments by Halliday and Greaves (2008: 16).

> When we talk about the sound system of English, the significance of any category we refer to (whether a prosodic category, such as pitch movement, or an articulatory one, such as the shape and position of the tongue) will be its semogenic value – its function in the total meaning potential of the English language. This is a phonological consideration.

In this book we consider intonation and rhythm as part of language, while other features such as voice quality and loudness are treated as paralanguage. When an infant moves into the adult language, protolanguage distinctions such as 'nasal/non-nasal' in English form phonemic combinations that serve to realize morphemes, words and wordings within clauses. Other features that may be prominent as signifiers of meaning in protolanguage, such as creaky voice, whisper, loudness and the many variations of pitch and pitch movement, also remain in adult speech. However, in English, as in many language cultures, such meanings tend to be sidelined in our consciousness; it is the phonemic distinctions and the meanings they realize that are privileged in the writing system and in education systems.[2]

As meaning-makers, we know how to interpret and produce with great accuracy and semiotic power the pitch movements and other semiotic systems of the voice, together with those of the body – which we use continually in our daily lives to make meaning from an early age. Our aim in this chapter is to provide an accessible introduction to the basics of intonation and rhythm, as well as other semiotic systems of the voice, within a social semiotic approach. Our work takes a discourse semantic view on the semiotic functions of speech. It can be placed broadly within the Firthian prosodic tradition of phonology (e.g. Firth, 1948; for a discussion, see Sampson, 1980) and is multi-metafunctional, multimodal and meaning-focused in scope. The various sound distinctions produced in the vocal tract can be broadly classified into those that realize phonemic distinctions (the vowels and consonants of a language) and those realizing non-phonemic distinctions – the latter often referred to under the heading prosodic phonology (e.g. Firth, 1948; Crystal, 1969; Hirschberg, 2002; Jun, 2005). It is the latter resources that we focus on in this chapter.

3.3 Rhythm and SALIENCE

In this book we follow the tradition of description which treats English as a stress-timed language (Pike, 1945; Abercrombie, 1965).[3] In this tradition syllables are organized rhythmically in terms of their relative prominence as speech unfolds, that is, some syllables are made to sound prominent relative to others. In Halliday's terminology the relative prominence of such a syllable is referred to as 'salience'. A salient syllable is termed Ictus, while non-salient syllables are termed Remiss. The pattern of salient (Ictus) and non-salient (Remiss) syllables is referred to as rhythm. Choices from the systems of SALIENCE and RHYTHM are presented in

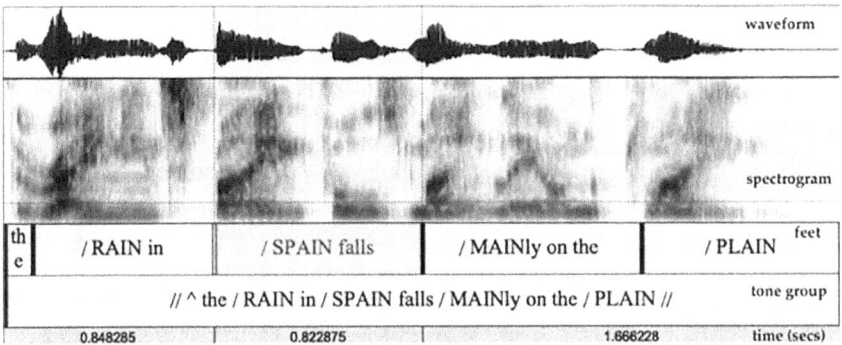

Figure 3.1 Praat visualization (with annotated Praat functions) showing RHYTHM and SALIENCE.

example (1) (satirized in George Bernard Shaw's (1913) play *Pygmalion*) and visualized in the Praat (Boersma and Weenink, 2019) visualization in Figure 3.1 (which we have annotated at the right of the image to show the main functions of Praat).[4]

(1) // ^ the / *rain* in / *Spain* stays / *mainly* in the / *plain* //

The purpose of the phonological transcription is simply to indicate those aspects of the sound signal that enter into meaning-making distinctions – in this case, which syllables are salient. In the transcription system here, taken from Halliday and Greaves (2008), each salient syllable begins a foot[5] – so a salient syllable is the one preceded in the transcription by a single or double forward slash, '/' or '//' (the double forward slash also indicates TONALITY; see Section 3.5).[6] For ease of reading our transcription, in this book we also italicize the syllables which carry salience.[7] Thus, in the excerpt given earlier, the salient syllables are '*rain*', '*Spain*', '*main-*' and '*plain*'. These syllables compose a regular rhythm across these feet. To indicate cases where the first tone group in an utterance begins with a non-salient syllable, the caret symbol, '^', is used; and this is generalized to cases where there is a silent Ictus within an utterance – that is, silence where a salient syllable would be expected in an established rhythm.

Salience is achieved in various ways: through the lengthening of a syllable relative to preceding syllables, a distinct jump up or down in pitch or by a syllable falling in beat position within an established rhythm – or some combination of these features. Rhythm is established as the regular (isochronous) occurrence of salient syllables at equivalent time intervals. In English, there is a tendency towards isochrony:[8] successive feet tend to be of roughly the same length for a certain period of spoken discourse, producing the perception of a consistent rhythm. Thus, as in music, we hear a 'beat' in speech and can clap our hands or tap our feet to it. The 'beat' of language need not be precisely consistent in terms of the temporal duration of feet for it to be perceived as rhythmic. As in music, once a regular rhythm in speech is established, it can be to some extent assumed, and those syllables in 'beat' position will then be 'heard' as salient, in phonological terms.[9] The spoken equivalent of a bar in music is the foot. Seen in these terms, spoken English is a succession of feet, each foot having one salient syllable, an Ictus, and (optionally) one or more non-salient (Remiss) syllables. The structure of a foot is, therefore, Ictus ^ (optional) Remiss – with the possibility of a silent Ictus.[10]

Although rhythmic and often perceptually isochronous, due to variations in the demands of discourse, everyday speech is not always metronomically regular (for a discussion of rhythm and culture, see van Leeuwen, 1999). A perceived change in rhythm, where a regular isochronous beat is broken, is thus significant (for a discussion of variation from isochronous rhythm and its significance, see Couper-Kuhlen, 1993). Such a shift is considered here a choice in the system of RHYTHM. To return to the Chatty Vlog text introduced in Chapter 1 (https://youtu.be/YRx-zDoPbVw),[11] we can see choices in both SALIENCE and RHYTHM, displayed example (2) and Figure 3.2.

(2)

// [*oh* and *you're*][12]

// *probably* / *seeing* how / *dark* my / *hair* is well

// *one* it's / *wet*

// *but* I could / *not* / *find* the / *hair* dye that I //

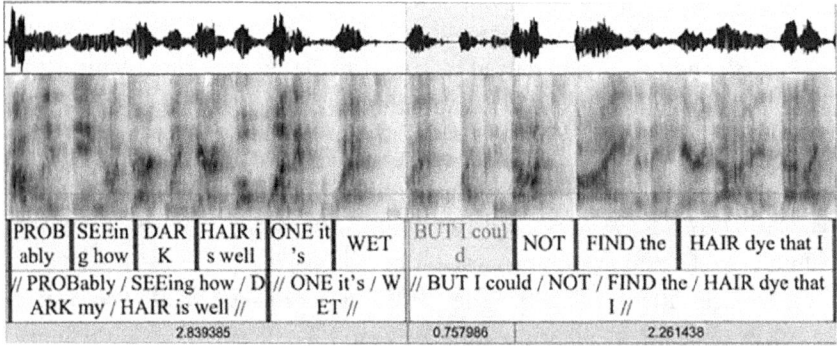

Figure 3.2 Praat visualization showing RHYTHM and SALIENCE.

In this excerpt, the following lexical items involve salient syllables: *probably, seeing, dark, hair, one, wet, but, not, find* and *hair* (dye).[13] A clearly isochronous rhythm is set up in the earlier part of this excerpt (*[you're] probably seeing how dark my hair is, well one it's wet*); in this part the salient syllables appear at roughly equivalent time intervals of about half a second (between 0.45 and 0.5 seconds) for each foot. But this isochrony is broken after *but*; its foot is about three-quarters of a second long (0.76 seconds). There follow three salient syllables, *not, find* and *hair*, in feet of varying length relative to each other and to the feet before. Although the second part ('but I could not find the hair dye') is considerably shorter, lexicogrammatically speaking, than the first part ('oh and you're probably seeing how dark my hair is, well, one, it's wet'), the first and second parts of this excerpt take roughly the same time period (about 2.8 and 3 seconds, respectively).[14] This shift in the temporal patterning of the feet has the effect of creating a disjunction between the first and second parts of this excerpt – there is a shift in rhythm. Furthermore, the salience on both *not* and *find*, as successive syllables, gives additional prominence to this verbal group.

As mentioned earlier, a silent beat (a silent Ictus) in an established rhythm is indicated by a caret symbol, '^'. We refer to this silent Ictus as a pause – a deliberate semiotic choice. Another excerpt from the Chatty Vlog text is presented in example (3) and Figure 3.3.

(3)
// […when I]
// *dyed* my / *hair* which I
// *loved* – I
// *loved* the / *first* time
// ^ so I / *end*ed up having to / *do* like a / *diff*erent / ^ / *shade* … //

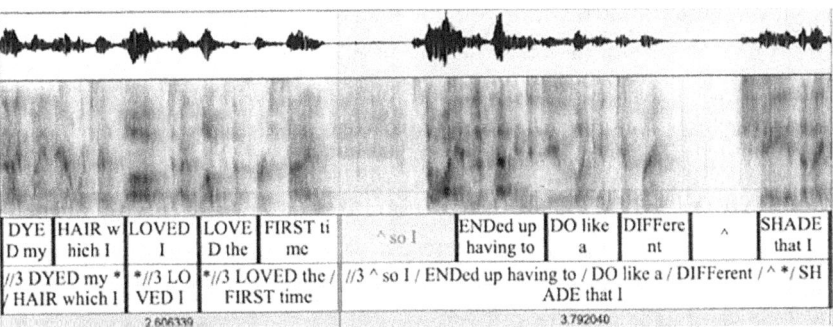

Figure 3.3 Praat visualization showing rhythmic pauses.

After *time*, a silence occurs where the expected 'beat' falls. And there is another silent beat after *different*. Both silences are visible in the waveform and spectrogram of the Praat visualization. As we can also see, the feet are not precisely even in duration, so the salient syllables do not occur at precisely regular intervals. For example, for *loved the first time*, the foot containing the syllable *loved* is shorter than the preceding foot and the one following. But through a succession of feet of roughly equivalent duration, the perception of a regular rhythm through these first few feet sets up an expectation that a salient syllable will be heard where the silent Ictus occurs. We will discuss further the analysis of these choices and their discourse functions in Section 3.7.

3.4 Tone

As mentioned earlier, our vocal cords vibrate and produce what is heard as pitch (F_0). Through increases or decreases in the rate of vocal fold vibration, the pitch of the voice moves higher or lower, either in jumps up or down in pitch or through distinctive contour shapes – rising or falling pitch contours. We can analogize this, phonetically, with a stringed instrument such as a guitar or violin. Steps up or down in pitch are like playing different fret positions on a guitar to make higher or lower musical notes, as the guitar string is thus made shorter or longer – these are discrete jumps up or down in pitch. A pitch contour, on the other hand, is like moving one's finger up or down a violin's fingerboard while bowing, or playing slide guitar, producing smoother pitch transitions.

As we discussed in Section 3.3, distinct jumps up or down in pitch along with other features help to signal rhythm and salience. Pitch contours, on the other hand, serve three systemic functions in English. The location of pitch contours on specific items in the flow of discourse determines choices in the system of TONICITY, better known within SFL for their functions in realizing choices of Given and New information structure. In addition, the occurrence of these contours also serves to divide the flow of speech into tone groups, in the system of TONALITY, and thus the flow of discourse into chunks of information. We will return to a discussion of the functions of these phonological systems in Section 3.5. Finally, the type of contour, whether falling or rising pitch (or combinations of these contours), realizes the system of TONE. In a typical reading (without any context) of the earlier excerpt from *Pygmalion*, the reader's pitch (whether reading aloud or internally) will fall across the articulation of the syllable for the final lexical item, *plain*, creating a falling pitch contour. The syllable which

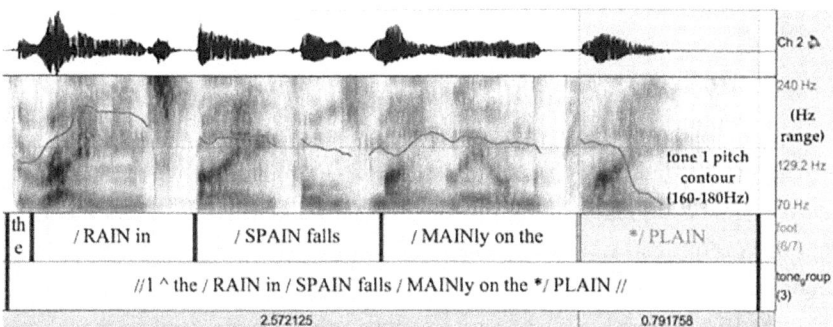

Figure 3.4 Praat visualization showing tone 1.

begins the pitch contour is called the Tonic syllable, indicated in this book using bold and shown in example (1').

(1')   // ^ the / rain in / Spain falls / mainly in the / **plain** //

In the annotated Praat visualization in Figure 3.4 (1"), this falling pitch contour, on 'PLAIN', is shown as a line (representing Hertz values) across the spectrogram.[15] The pitch falls from about 160 Hz to about 80 Hz on this single syllable.[16] This falling pitch contour is labelled tone '1', with the numeral placed at the beginning of the tone group.

(1")   //1 ^ The / rain in / Spain falls / mainly in the / **plain** //

While the domain of a salient syllable is the foot, the domain of a Tonic syllable, and the pitch contour that it carries, is the tone group. Tone group divisions are indicated in the transcription by a double forward slash at either end, '//.... //'. A tone group is composed of one or more feet. The syllables prior to the Tonic syllable are called pre-Tonic syllables.[17] Thus, a tone group has a phonological structure of (optional) pre-Tonic and (obligatory) Tonic feet. Any post-Tonic syllables form part of the Tonic pitch contour, with the tone choice continuing its contour up until the end of the tone group if there are any post-Tonic salient syllables – that is, a rising tone will continue at the highest point till the end of the tone group, and a fall will similarly remain at the low point.[18]

The TONE system can be seen as a system of five primary tones: falling (tone 1), rising (tone 2), level-rise (tone 3), falling-rising (tone 4) and rising-falling (tone 5) contours. In example (5), we can hear a tone 5 rise-fall contour followed by a tone 1 in the first two tone groups.

(5)
//5 **oh** and you're
//1 *prob*ably / *see*ing how / *dark* my / **hair** is well //

The Tonic syllable *Oh* carries a distinct, rise-fall pitch contour – the rising-falling pitch contour, tone 5, begins at about 280 Hz, rising to 385 Hz, then falling to about 250 Hz for the following two syllables ('and you're'). The tone 1 contour that begins on 'hair' falls from 330 to 210 Hz. A little further in this text (6), we see a fall-rise pitch contour, tone 4, followed by rising pitch contour, tone 2.

(6)
//4 *but* I could / *not* / *find* the / **hair** dye that I
//2 *bought* / *prev*iously when I //

We find two instances of tone 3 in succession a little later (7) in the Chatty Vlog.

(7)
// … which I
//3 **loved** – I
//3 loved the / **first** time //

It can take some time to learn to distinguish the different tones. Tone 4 typically has a slight rise at the beginning of the contour, which makes it like a tone 5 rise-fall, except that the fall is not 'to the basement' (William S. Greaves, personal communication, July 2005) as with the tone 5. Instead, there is a rise at the end – sometimes quite slight, as in this instance, but enough to identify it as a tone 4 not tone 5. Here, as elsewhere, the principle of systemic opposition should be kept in mind during analysis: the tone is either one or the other of these two possible tone choices, and the speaker need only articulate clearly enough so that the systemic distinction can be heard.[19]

One issue in analysing tone 3 is deciding on the boundary between a tone 3 level-rise and the full rising contour of the tone 2. In example (7) earlier, the two tone 3s in succession illustrate this difficulty. The second instance, beginning on 'first', is clearly a tone 3, since the rise is quite moderate (190–245 Hz) and sounds more like a level-rise than the full rise of the tone 2. However, the first instance is not so clear, as there does seem to be a significant rise in pitch on 'loved' (190–265 Hz). As mentioned earlier, when analysing from a social semiotic perspective one should always keep meaning in mind – or 'listen for meaning'. As we will discuss in Section 3.7, the discourse semantic functions of a tone 2 and tone 3 are distinct, and this distinction needs to be kept in mind during phonological analysis. Thus, in deciding whether an instance is a tone 2 or tone 3, one should listen for whether it is similar to a prototypical 'listing' tone 3 or similar to the interrogative 'elicitation' of a yes/no question. A useful technique in phonological analysis is to model the different possible choices oneself – speak out loud the text in question, using the different possible tone choices. Doing this, and then listening back to the source audio, is an effective way to determine the analysis.

Halliday's PRIMARY TONE system also includes two compound tones, tones 13 and 53, which as their names suggest are a fusion of either tone 1 or tone 5 with a tone 3 which is tacked onto the end. Example (8) of a tone 13 is from the film *Coraline* (dir. Selick, 2009), which will appear again in Chapter 5. Note that there are two Tonics, for the tone 1 and the tone 3. The first tone is considered the major Tonic and the second tone a minor Tonic (the first Tonic is always the major Tonic, in this case tone 1, and the second is always the minor Tonic, tone 3).

(8)   Coraline: //13 *don't* even / *think* about / *going* / **out** / *Coraline* / **Jones** //

These are not considered separate tones because there is no potential for pitch variation between the major Tonic and minor Tonic: the pitch will remain low after the fall of the tone 1 or the tone 5 until the level-rise of the tone 3, usually at the end of the tone group (for two successive tone groups with separate major Tonics, there is the possibility of pre-Tonic variation before the second Tonic).

Halliday's TONE system also includes what he calls secondary tones, which are variants on the primary tone system of five tones – either variations of the Tonic syllable or pre-Tonic pitch variations. We will briefly discuss and illustrate SECONDARY TONE choices in Section 3.7. Choices in TONE resonate with voice quality, and facial expressions and other bodily features of paralanguage, to make interpersonal meanings (see Chapter 5). We will discuss further the analysis of choices in the TONE system and their discourse functions in Section 3.7.

3.5 TONALITY and TONICITY

As discussed in Section 3.4, in a typical reading (without any context) of the sentence (1") from *Pygmalion*, the speaker's pitch will fall across the articulation of the syllable for the final lexical item, *plain* (see Figure 3.4 earlier). Such a pitch contour is a distinctive, significant event for the human ear. In the so-called tone languages, tones are used to distinguish one lexical item from another. In these and other languages, including English, a pitch contour is also used to give special, added prominence to one salient syllable above others. Following Halliday, we call this the Tonic syllable. As mentioned earlier, the location of a pitch contour on a particular syllable (and thus lexical item) signals a choice in TONICITY – these Tonic syllables pick out particular discourse items as having an additional prominence over and above that given by SALIENCE. The division into tone groups created through occurrences of pitch contours, in the system of TONALITY, distributes the flow of speech into manageable 'chunks' – or waves of information.

Our *Pygmalion* excerpt earlier (1″) had one clause, which was realized on one tone group. This is considered the default choice in tonality: one tone group per clause. Alternatively it could have had its information distributed into two tone groups, as shown in example (1‴), each with its own pitch contour – with Tonic syllables located on *Spain* and *plain* (tone group boundaries are indicated by the double forward slash, '//').

(1‴)
// ^ the / *rain* in / **Spain** stays
// *main*ly in the / ***plain*** //

TONALITY not only determines how many tone groups a clause is broken up into but also where that division lies. In the *Pygmalion* example (1″″), the division could be as follows: still two tone groups but with a different division of the clause.

(1″″)
// ^ the / *rain* in / *Spain* stays / ***main**ly* in the
// ***plain*** //

So, in one sense the TONALITY choice is the same here (i.e. one clause, two tone groups), but the second version distributes the clausal information differently.

Independent of these choices in TONALITY (although related to them), the choice in location of the Tonic realizes the TONICITY choices – *Spain* and *plain* in the first version, *main*(*ly*) and *plain* in the second. We can also vary choices in TONICITY with precisely the same choice in TONALITY; in example (1‴)', we could have the following choices in TONICITY:

(1'''')
// ^ the / ***rain*** in Spain stays
// ***main***ly in the / plain //

This is the same TONALITY choice as example (1'''), but the locations of both Tonics are different: rather than *Spain* and *plain*, they are *rain* and *main(ly)*. The default is for the final lexical (content) item in a tone group to be Tonic (with some exceptions, discussed in Halliday and Greaves, 2008: 101–8). Variations from this default pattern are considered marked, as in (1''''), where both *rain* and *main*(ly) are marked choices in TONICITY. In the Chatty Vlog excerpt (9), the items *oh, hair, wet, hair* (dye), *prev*(iously), *hair, loved* and *first* are all Tonic syllables, with eight tone groups realizing seven clauses.

(9)
//5 ***oh*** and you're
//1 probably / *see*ing how / *dark* my / ***hair*** is well
//1_ one it's / ***wet***
//4 but I could / *not* / find the / ***hair*** dye that I
//2 bought / ***prev***iously when I
//3 *dyed* my / ***hair*** which I
//3 ***loved*** – I
//3 loved the / ***first*** time //

This text shows mostly unmarked choices in TONALITY and TONICITY (the exclamation, *oh*, is assigned a separate tone group from the clause following). In excerpt (10), from a biology lecture (which will be discussed again in Chapter 6), we can see marked choices in both TONALITY and TONICITY.

(10)
// 3 ^ the / *last* one is the / *distal* /*con*voluted / ***tub***ule
//1 ^ / ^ / ***now*** by the
//4 *time* the / *filt*rate has / *reached* the distal convoluted / ***tub***ule
//1 *most* of the / *good* stuff has / ***gone***
//3 ^ / ^ / *most* of the / ***gluc***ose is
//3 *back* in the / ***blood***stream
//3 *most* of the / ***vit***amins are / *back* in the / ***blood***stream //

The first clause in this excerpt is a single clause mapped onto one tone group. The next clause is distributed into three tone groups. It has a single tone group for one constituent of the clause, the conjunction *now*, signifying a shift in phase. This clause also contains an embedded clause within a marked Theme circumstance, *by the time…*, which is assigned a separate tone group from the remainder of the clause. Such marked Themes, particularly when they include an embedded clause, are often assigned their own tone group. This plays a role in a text's 'method of development' (Fries, [1981] 1983; Martin, 1992; Martin and Rose, [2003] 2007). The next clause also is mapped into two tone groups, but this time it is an unmarked Theme, *most of the glucose*, that is given its own tone group. In the final clause, we see a canonical instance of marked TONICITY, with the previously mentioned phrase *back in the bloodstream* being post Tonic.[20]

As with TONE, it takes practice to determine whether one is dealing with an Ictus (salient syllable) or a Tonic, and modelling the different possibilities out loud can help in working out the actual choice in the source text. Choices in TONALITY and TONICITY work together with those in RHYTHM and SALIENCE and synchronize with gesture and other bodily features of paralanguage to make textual meanings. We will discuss some of the typical discourse functions of these choices in Section 3.7. From this and the previous two sections it is already evident that there are potentially many choices afforded by intonation and rhythm systems, however short is the text. There are also many more systems at work in relation to the semiotic voice (e.g. van Leeuwen, 1999). In the next section we briefly discuss some other examples of these which we have found to be relevant to our discussion of paralanguage in this book.

3.6 Other features of the semiotic voice

We mentioned earlier that jumps up or down in pitch help to identify salience. Scholars (e.g. Brazil, 1997; O'Grady, 2013; Tench, [1965] 2015) have also pointed to the potential of changes in pitch height to organize speech into the spoken equivalent of written paragraphs. However, there are two types of pitch height change that do not appear to be involved in the creation of either salience or phonological paragraphs. The first is where there is a significant jump in pitch, usually upwards, which does not involve a choice of tone, but which seems to be more than is required to merely indicate salience.[21] We term this phenomenon 'super-salience', indicated in the transcription via a vertical arrow, ↑, before the super-salient syllable. In example (11) from the Chatty Vlog text shown in Figure 3.5 and transcribed here, the pitch moves from 265 to 450 Hz on the syllable 'not' (then to 110 Hz on 'find').

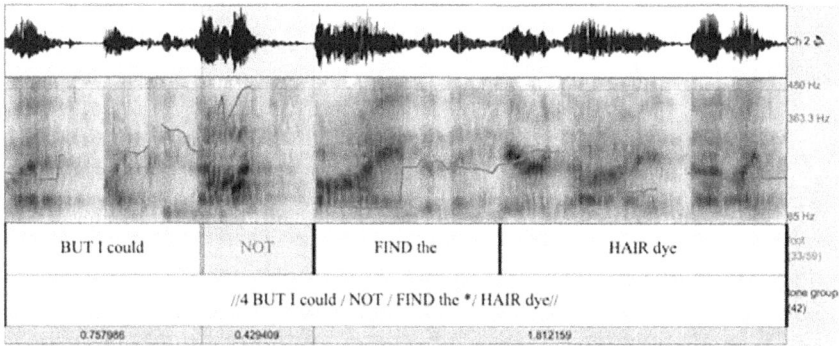

Figure 3.5 Praat visualization showing super-salience.

(11)   // *but* I could / ↑*not* / *find* the / **hair** dye that I... //

Although there is thus a distinct change in pitch upwards on *not*, there is no tone choice made. If a tone choice had been made, it would have been a tone 2 (rising pitch contour); but in such a case, there would have been either a silent Ictus following the Tonic syllable, or the rising pitch contour would have continued through 'find' thus clearly indicating *not* as a Tonic.[22] This additional level of textual prominence is distinct from the prominence afforded by a Tonic pitch contour – that is, it is one that lacks the interpersonal function afforded by a tone choice (see Section 3.7 on functions of TONE choices; see van Leeuwen (1992) for an alternative approach to analysing intonation and rhythm).[23] Through such choices of super-salience, a speaker can add additional waves of textual meaning (cf. Martinec, 2000a) which are not restricted in their function to phonological paragraphing, although these functions may coincide.

Another aspect of pitch change is what van Leeuwen (1999: 172) refers to as 'pitch range'. This refers to the capacity speakers have to make significant shifts in the bandwidth of their pitch in a particular passage of discourse. This is clearly visible in the Praat visualization shown in Figure 3.6.

The transcription of example (12) shows pitch height (in Hz) in brackets for each salient syllable (Figure 3.6 shows pitch movements within each syllable).

(12)
//3 (188) *thought* that'd be / (172) *really* good for the / (164–167) **kids**
//3 (245) *and* my- / **self** since
//13 (235–162) *I'm* a *picky* / (154–172) *eat*er
//5 (278-385-250) **oh** and you're
//1 (350) *probably* / *see*ing how / (310) *dark* my / (329–209) **hair** is well

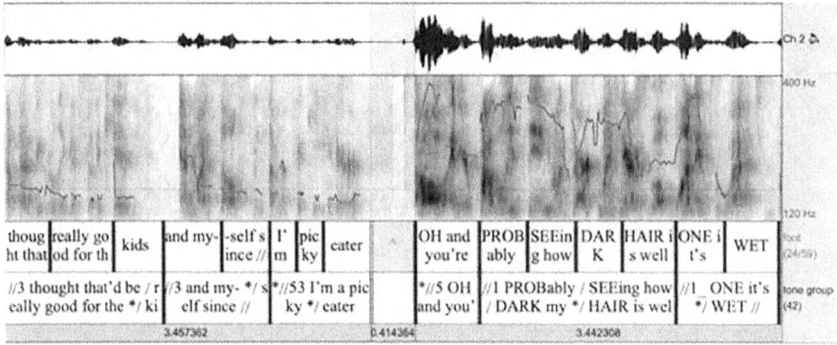

Figure 3.6 Praat visualization showing pitch range.

//1 (360) *one* it's / (170–150) **wet** //

There is a both a marked shift up in pitch and an increase in pitch range, at roughly midway in this image, between 'since I'm a picky eater' and 'Oh! And you're probably seeing'. (Note also the quantum shift in loudness (intensity) evident in the change in bandwidth of the Praat waveform at the top of the image.) Thus, there are two distinct phenomena mapped onto this disjuncture: the reset of the pitch from low to high; and the expansion of the pitch range. It is important to distinguish between pitch height and pitch range, as they have different discourse semantic functions. Shifts in pitch height are a textual phenomenon, assigning an additional level of prominence to particular items in the discourse, as in super-salience on 'not' in the excerpt earlier. However, the expansion in pitch range appears to be an interpersonal phenomenon, signalling vocal affect – a prosody of excitement for the new phase. Such a change in pitch range could potentially appear within a phase without necessarily adding additional textual prominence or signalling a new phase – although one often finds these interpersonal and textual choices together, as is common at change-points in discourse. As we discuss further in Chapter 5, other semiotic resources of vocal quality express interpersonal meanings (for an extended discussion on the social semiotics of the voice, see van Leeuwen, 1999).

3.7 Analysing the semiotic voice: Prosodic and periodic systems in discourse

The systems of intonation and rhythm we discussed earlier serve to make meaning across three metafunctions: interpersonal, textual and logical. RHYTHM, SALIENCE, TONALITY and TONICITY all make textual meaning. TONE makes interpersonal meaning. But two tones, tones 3 and 4, are also called into service, within specific local contexts, to create logical relations of subordination and coordination between tone groups. Whereas textual choices are periodic, or wave-like, interpersonal choices are prosodic in nature – they spread across the unit in which they are made, both in terms of their expression and the meanings they express (see Pike, [1959] 1972; Halliday, [1979] 2002).

To see the TONE system working at its full potential, interpersonally speaking, we need to examine dialogue. In the following excerpt (13) from *Coraline*, the rising pitch contour of tone 2 combines with the polar interrogative to enact a yes/no question:

(13)
Coraline: //2 ^ do / *you* know where the / **gard**en tools / are //
Dad: //1 ^ / *it's* ah – it's / **pour**ing out there
//1 **is**n't it //[24]

The father's response combines a falling tone 1 with a declarative for a simple statement, but with a polar tag combining polar interrogative and tone 1. The latter is thus not used as a question on polarity but to demand a response. Likewise, when a tone 2 occurs with a declarative (14), the resulting meaning is that of a statement and a polar question combined (or statement proffered as a yes/no question).

(14)   Coraline: //2 ^ you're / *talk*ing about your / **gard**en catalogue //

We also hear examples of what has been termed a 'high rising terminal' (HRT; see Warren, 2016), as in the following excerpt (15) from a lecture (which appears again in Chapter 6), where the rising pitch contours on the statement present an appeal or challenge to the audience – opening up the potential, even if rhetorically, for dialogic interaction (an important technique in lecturing).

(15)   Lecturer: //2 ^ she's / *passed* / **out** after a
        //2 *bit* too much hash- / **ish** //

Tone 5 is commonly associated with exclamations of surprise or amazement such as 'Wow!' – as exemplified by the tone 5 '*oh*' in the Chatty Vlog example (12). This rising/falling tone is commonly associated with statements where the certainty about the polarity is emphasized as though in response to a question about polarity (i.e. 'with regard to some uncertainty (rise), I am certain (fall)') or where interpersonal commitment to a proposition is expressed, as in the following example (16) from *Coraline*:

(16)   //5 Dad I / missed you / so / **much** //

Tone 3 can have both interpersonal and logical functions in discourse. Interpersonally, in the following excerpt (17) from the Chatty Vlog text, the speaker wraps up one phase of her discourse with a tone 3 that expresses a certain interpersonal nonchalance in ending this phase (in terms of interpersonal energy, this tone 3 is at the opposite end of the scale to the interpersonal commitment of a tone 5 or challenge of a tone 2):

(17)   //3 [handclap] / um / but for / **now** //3 this will / **do** //

In terms of the logical metafunction, tones 3 and 4 are also used to make meanings of coordination (listing) and subordination (linking tone groups together in dependent relations), and as such are common in lectures and monologues in general – where tone 3 serves to chunk up complex information (e.g. into lists) and tone 4 creates logical dependencies between units of information. Here are two examples (18, 19), from the biology lecture used earlier and a law lecture also discussed in Chapter 6.

(18)

//3 ^ / most of the / **gluc**ose is

//3 back in the / **blood**stream

//3 most of the / **vit**amins are / back in the / bloodstream

//3 most of the / ah – a- / **min**o / **ac**ids are / back in the / bl – / back in the / bloodstream

//1+ lots of / **wat**er is

//1 back in the / **blood**stream //

(19)

//4 ^ / ^ it / **turns** out that the / policy of / British / **Air**ways along with

//4 many of its com- / **pet**itors

//1 ^ / was to / over- / **book** //

In (18), the listing function of tone 3 allows the lecturer to present a long list of items which 'are back in the bloodstream'. The tone 4s in the law lecture and the other hand create a logical dependency between the first two tone groups on the final one on tone 1. This 'subordination' function of the tone 4 may take on an interpersonal meaning of reservation in certain local contexts (e.g. Halliday and Greaves, 2008: 112; Smith, 2008: 1–2, 116–17).

As mentioned in Section 3.4, Halliday's TONE system also includes what he calls 'secondary tones', which are variants on the primary tones that have distinct functions in discourse meaning. For example, in the biology lecture excerpt earlier, we saw a tone 1+, '//1+ *lots* of / *wat*er is //', which is a high falling variant of the tone 1 falling contour. This tone adds interpersonal emphasis, not to the whole tone group but to one specific lexicogrammatical item. It is often employed for counter-expectant or contrastive effect; as in the example (20) from *Coraline*, where she emphasizes the correct pronunciation of her name (i.e. it is *not* 'Caroline').

(20)   //1+ ^ it's / ***Cor***aline //

Another tone 1 variant, the low falling contour tone 1_, has the reverse meaning – a sense that something is expected, as shown in example 21.[25]

(21)
//3 ^ like / *two* days / *lat*er and there was a
//1_ whole / ***stack*** of them so I ... //

An important variant of tone 2 is the sharp fall-rise of a tone 2_; rather than a fall, the pitch jumps down from the initial pitch level ('rain-', in example (22) from *Coraline*) then sharply rises, as represented in the following graphic showing the initial pitch level then the jump down in pitch for the rise:¯/. This tone is phonologically quite distinct from that of the more rounded fall-rise of the tone 4 and has the sense of challenge of the declarative tone 2, but usually with a sharper sense of indignation or incredulity.

(22)
Dad: //1 ^ / *it's* ah – it's / ***pour***ing out there
//1 ***is***n't it //
Coraline: //1 ***hmm*** it's
//2_ just / ***rain***ing //

Compound tones are often used, as in the instance of example (8"), for second-person address tacked onto the end of clauses, as we saw in example (8) from *Coraline* earlier (imitating her mother's voice).

(8")   Coraline: //13 *don't* even / *think* about / *going* / ***out*** Coraline / ***Jones*** //

Textual choices form waves of prominence, assigning varying textual statuses to different elements of a discourse. In choices in RHYTHM and SALIENCE, there tends to be a correlation between lexical items and salient syllables, and between grammatical items and non-salient syllables – although this can be varied to background certain lexical meanings or give prominence to particular grammatical ones. In example (23), from the law lecture, salience is assigned to the conjunction *if* which refers to a condition of the commercial contract at issue.

(23)
//5 ^ cheap / ***air*** fare
//3 ^ was on / ***off*** er
//1 *if* you were the / ***ear*** ly bird //

Like RHYTHM and SALIENCE, TONALITY and TONICITY work together to assign special textual status to particular lexicogrammatical items or stretches of discourse. As mentioned in Section 3.4, the default, without taking relevant contextual or co-textual information into account, is for each clause to have one tone group – with variations on this default pattern considered marked or in some way motivated (in Halliday's terms, the default pattern is chosen unless there is a 'good reason' not to; cf. Halliday and Greaves, 2008: 108). To return to our law text, in example (23) we can see how choices in textual systems synchronize to instantiate waves of textual meaning.

(24)
//1 ***so***
//1 ^ / *Brit*ish airways and / ***Tay***lor
//1 ^ / *Tay*lor was a / *guy* who ah / *worked* for a con- / *sum*er / ^ / ***ag***ency – a
// government / ***ag***ency
//1 ^ / *he* was representing a / *guy* called / ***Ed***monds
//3 ^ / *Ed*monds / *had* / *lived* on the / *isl*and of Ber- / ***mud***a for a
//3 long / ***time*** //

Firstly, the internal conjunction 'so' is given its own tone group at this point in the lecture – to signal a shift in the lecture from one phase to another. There are also pauses after both 'so' and 'British Airways and Taylor', to highlight what is functioning as a hyper-Theme predicting the following discourse. Choices of this kind work together to organize longer wavelengths of information flow and as such are often used in lectures to signal higher-level organization of discourse and in general to chunk up the flow of information into manageable chunks (as further discussed in Chapter 6). We can see, in example (25) from another lecture, the way in which TONALITY is used to vary the pace and flow of information in the lecture, with tone groups of varying lengths.

(25)
//1 ^ now Sa- / *id's* a- / *na*lysis / *made* it / *pos*sible for / *scho*lars to cri- / *tique* / *lite*rary and his- / *to*rical / **texts** a-
//3 *bout* / *um* the / *Mid*dle / **East** and to
//1 *un*der- / *stand* / *how* they re- / **flect**ed and
//1 *rein-* / **forced** the um Im-
//1 *pe*rialist / **pro**ject … //

The first tone group is quite long, with the following tone groups considerably shorter but of varying lengths – the verbal group complex, *reflected and reinforced*, is, for example, assigned two tone groups. In example (26) from another lecture, TONALITY works together with TONICITY to assign textual prominence to the Finite *is*, thus textualizing (drawing attention to) the interpersonal aspect of this part of the lecture.

(26)
//1 **now**
//1 *where* – it's / *just* th – that's fan- / *tas*tic that you / **said** that be-
//1+ *cause* that / **is**
//1 *one* ex- / *treme* of a – of a / *West*ern / *know*ledge of a / **har**em and
//1 *how* it was de- / **pict**ed //

Thus, although there are default mappings in TONICITY and TONALITY (see discussion in Section 3.5), marked choices are taken up for various reasons (see Matthiessen (1992) for a discussion of the textual metafunction and Smith (2007) for an extended illustration of textual choices at work in televised political debate).[26] In another excerpt from the same lecture (27), we can see how the speaker, through successive restarts, eventually assigns the desired textual status to the Finite *is*.

(27)
// *what* – what / *is* – what / **is** that is
// *that* a – an ex- / *am*ple of just / *how* relaxed she can / *be* – / ^ in / *what* sort of / **space** is she
//1 **oc**cupying //

Given the way this utterance begins, the Finite *is* would have been Remiss (// what is…//). The first restart assigns *is* the status of Ictus (//… what / is … //). Finally, after another restart, the Finite *is* is made Tonic (//… what / ***is*** that… //). Once established as a focal point at this phase in the lecture, *is* is then returned to Remiss status in the following clause, and the textual attention shifts from the interpersonal back to the experiential (eventually, to *space* and *occupying* as Tonic foci). In fact, many restarts in speech are the result of such shifts in textual strategy, indicating the importance speakers assign to intonation and rhythm systems for managing information flow in unfolding discourse. At times, speakers will restart what they are saying for no other reason than to make a different choice from these textual intonation systems.

As van Leeuwen (1992: 253) shows, such choices 'receive their precise colour from the context', while also construing a specific social context, as they map textual status onto particular aspects of the discourse. Shifts in patterns of such choices, for example, from a focus on ideational meaning to one on interpersonal meaning, can have significant consequences for the discourse itself and the context in which the language is taking place (see Smith, 2007; for a discussion of how such choices impact on discourse and context, see Smith, 2008: 218–51; see also Bowcher (2004), who tracks choices in these systems in sports commentary).

In analysing these systems, as mentioned, it is important to keep in mind that there is a distinct choice being made at each point which has a contribution to meaning. Getting to know the discourse semantic functions of various choices in intonation, rhythm and other systems of the semiotic voice can also help in the phonological analysis. As mentioned, one should always 'listen for the meanings' of intonation choices in distinguishing which choice is being made: in each instance it is either this or that choice, and the SFL analyst's job is to determine which choice is being made through consideration of system *and* function.

3.8 Conclusion

In this chapter we began with the child's transition from protolanguage to adult language reviewed in Chapter 2 and what this means in terms of the development of phonological systems – introducing basic concepts from mainstream phonetics and phonology. We then introduced examples from the texts used in this book to illustrate some of the various semiotic systems of the voice, with a focus on the periodic systems of RHYTHM and SALIENCE, TONALITY and TONICITY and the prosodic system of TONE. Choices in the periodic systems of the phonology of intonation and rhythm synchronize with choices in visual paralanguage systems such as gesture and body movement, while prosodic phonological choices resonate with paralanguage systems such as facial affect. As we will show in later chapters, these systems work together to create meaning in discourse across the interpersonal (Chapter 5) and textual (Chapter 6) metafunctions.

4

Ideational semovergence: Approaching paralanguage from the perspective of field

4.1 Representing experience

This chapter explores how ideational meaning is realized in paralanguage. Ideational meaning is concerned with how experience is represented: 'what kinds of activities are undertaken, and how participants undertaking these activities are described and classified' (Martin and Rose, [2003] 2007: 17). The linguistic systems of IDEATION and CONNEXION, described in Martin (1992) and developed by Hao (2015), model ideational meaning at the level of discourse semantics as sequences of figures made up of elements of different kinds: entities (objects), occurrences (happenings/motion) and qualities (attributes/manner) (Table 4.1). As discussed in Chapter 1, we set aside CONNEXION, since, as in filmic discourse, there is no way of making it explicit in paralanguage alone and linking relations among gestures have to be abduced (Bateman, 2007, 2014).

Chapter 1 provided a brief overview of the ways in which paralanguage can converge semovergently with spoken language in terms of ideational meaning. The reader is reminded that we are not envisaging a one-to-one mapping of these discourse semantic systems to paralinguistic systems but are instead interested in degrees of concurrence between these systems (see Table 1.3). Chapter 1 described how, in terms of articulation, ideational paralanguage is mimetic – meaning that it resembles a material thing or action (i.e. 'draws' a material reality). This chapter provides further details on the ways in which Figures and Elements are supported by paralanguage, and presents system networks modelling this meaning potential.

Previous work on IDEATION has focused on the production of technical knowledge in science (Martin, 1993, 2017b; Martin and Veel, 1998; Hood and Hao, in press; Doran and Martin, 2021), geography (Wignell et al., 1989) and history (Eggins et al., 1993; Martin and Wodak, 2003; Martin et al., 2013a),

Table 4.1 Terminology for describing ideation at each stratum of language (based on Hao, 2015: 192)

Stratum	Field	Discourse semantics	Lexicogrammar
Terminology	activity, item, property	sequence	clause complex
		figure	clause
		element (entity, occurrence, quality)	participant, process, circumstance

where technical entities, and their qualities, are involved in uncommon sense activities. The discourse considered in this chapter is the lived experience of a YouTube vlogger who discusses dimensions of her everyday life such as shopping, beauty routines, care of children and use of social media platforms. The text used to illustrate the model of ideational paralanguage under discussion is the seven-minute YouTube video titled 'Let's Talk. | Random Chatty Vlog,'[1] hereafter 'Chatty Vlog', introduced in Chapter 1. The description accompanying the video gives us a sense of the fields of experience covered in the vlog, ranging from the minutia of domestic life to the vlogger's aspirations for her YouTube channel. The entities introduced include thing entities (*coffee*, *a snack*, *kids*, *food*, *hair* and *feet* etc.) and her *video*, a semiotic entity (see Section 4.2 for an explanation of entity types).

This chapter will explore gestures occurring across the nine phases within this vlog:

1. Intro
2. 'National Night Out' phase – about a neighbourhood 'potluck' gathering
3. 'Hair Dye' phase – about the vlogger dying her hair
4. 'Caring for Children (A)' phase – about the vlogger's children asking her for food
5. 'Visit to the Dermatologist' phase – about a visit to the dermatologist for treatment for granuloma on the vlogger's feet
6. 'Parking Lot' phase – about an incident in which the vlogger was hurried from her parking spot
7. 'Social Media' phase – about the vlogger's social media posting schedule and goals
8. 'Caring for Children (B)' phase – when the vlogger's child interrupts the vlog
9. Outro

Each phase involves figures and entities that have different degrees of concurrence between language and paralanguage: some are realized only in language, some co-realized in language and paralanguage and some are realized only in paralanguage (see the discussion of mime in Chapter 7). We begin by exploring how entities are multimodally realized in the vlog and then move on to consider figures.

4.2 Entities

Entities are the ideational discourse semantic units construing items in a field of experience. The primary types of entity are thing entities (a person, place, or object), activity entities (an activity or sequence of activities) and semiotic entities (verbiage or ideas). In the Chatty Vlog, the 'National Night Out', 'Hair Dye', 'Caring for Children (A)', 'Dermatology' and 'Parking Lot' episodes tend to realize concrete thing entities from the fields of domestic/daily life and medicine (e.g. *people, neighbours, kids, feet, syringe*). By way of contrast, the 'Social Media' phase at the end of the vlog, where the vlogger reflects on her own social media posting practices and goals, tends to realize fewer thing entities and more semiotic entities relating to her social media text production (e.g. *vlog, text message, clips, videos, comments*). Activity entities are not common (one example being *vacation* in the Intro) in the vlog. Examples from other studies include entities that realize activity sequences such as *method, pipette calibration, study* and *experiment* (in scientific discourse; Hao, 2015, 2020b; Hao and Hood, 2019).

All of these linguistic entity types can be realized concurrently in paralanguage as gestures. Paralinguistic entities are often realized through a flat hand suggesting the boundaries of an object (e.g. parallel hands implying the sides of a box) or through a curved hand suggesting something being held or moulded (e.g. a cupped hand implying the weight or shape of an object). We introduced three entities from the 'Visit to the Dermatologist' phase in Chapter 1. In this phase the paralanguage concurred with two entities in the language (*needle* and *bump*) (Table 4.2).

Research within gesture studies into how gesture construes experience has tended to emphasize representational meaning, focusing on how gestures visually represent the things in the world referred to by language (McNeill, 1992; Kendon, 2004). This work has drawn heavily on the concept of iconicity and contrasted representational with indexical or emblematic gesture. According to McNeill (1985) 'iconic gestures' are 'imagistic' because they look like the phenomena, activities or scenes expressed in speech, whereas non-imagistic

Table 4.2 Concurrent construals of entities

Phonology	//3... *took* like this / *need*le and		//3 *under* / *each* like / *bump* ... //
Paralanguage	Holding needle	Holding syringe	Cupped hands
Images			

gestures are either deictic or rhythmic. In other words, iconic gestures manifest 'a certain degree of isomorphism between the shape of the gesture and the entity that is expressed by the gesture' (Kita, 2000: 162). Imagistic gestures may also be metaphoric, standing for abstract concepts such as semiotic entities (see later, e.g. the Instagram stories gesture in example (11)).

Some studies have also acknowledged that it may be problematic to assert that gestures function uniformly in terms of iconicity (Streeck, 2008) and that 'because the driving principle of iconicity is generally assumed to be based on similarity (and not conventionality), the role that social and individual practices play in the creation and use of these semiotic forms can be easily misunderstood' (Mittelberg and Evola, 2014: 1733). In addition, the validity of distinguishing iconic gestures from other types of gesture has been disputed. For instance, Goodwin (2003: 229) questions the validity of distinguishing iconic from deictic gestures and of separating gestures into types more generally:

> Pointing gestures can trace the shape of what is being pointed at, and thus superimpose an iconic display on a deictic point within the performance of a single gesture. Instead of using this distinction to separate gestures into distinct classes, it seems more fruitful to focus analysis on an indexical component or an iconic component of a gesture, either or both of which may contribute to the organization of a particular gesture.

In our social semiotic model, rather than classifying gestures into types, we are concerned with degrees of convergence between gestures and discourse semantic entities, occurrences, qualities – that is, degrees of ideational concurrence. Here we draw on the concept of commitment 'which refers to the amount of meaning instantiated as a text unfolds' (Martin, 2011b: 255) as developed in Martinec

(2008) and Martin (2010). Language and paralanguage can vary in terms of the amount of meaning that is specified by each semiotic mode. For instance, returning again to the example from the 'Visit to the Dermatologist' phase, and as noted in Chapter 1, some entities were committed in the language alone (e.g. the occurrence *film* in *I didn't film it*) and not in the paralanguage. There can also be differences in how delicately meaning is committed in language and paralanguage. For example, the needle and the foot bump were more delicately committed in the paralanguage than in language, as far as qualities such as size and shape are concerned. So rather than separating gestures into a catalogue of types based on their purported resemblance to things in the world, the approach adopted in this chapter considers how gestures function as a resource which supports ideational meaning-making – focusing on how they concur with ideational discourse semantic selections.

4.2.1 A system network for paralinguistic entities

In terms of how they are construed in paralanguage, entities vary across two main dimensions – SPECIFICITY and DEPICTION, as represented in the system network in Figure 4.1. SPECIFICITY deals with how much meaning is committed

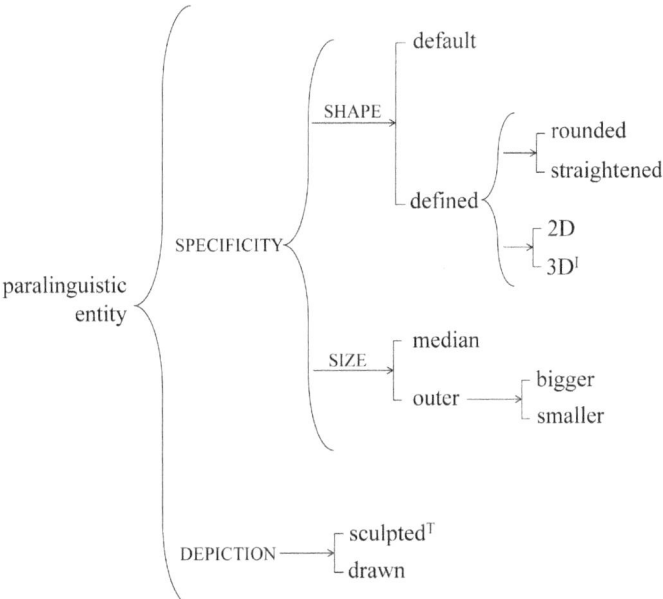

Figure 4.1 Paralinguistic entity network.

in terms of shape and size, while DEPICTION addresses how the entity is visually formed.

The SHAPE of a paralinguistic entity may be default, which means that it is rendered simply as a thing held in one or two hands in front of the body – with hand and fingers in a relaxed naturally cupped configuration. At the end of the 'Hair Dye' phase, for example, the vlogger is interrupted by her hungry children, and when filming resumes she explains that she has already given them a heaping bowl of 'Chex Mix' with applesauce squeeze – and she uses a default entity gesture for the applesauce.

(1)

phonology	//4 *applesauce* / ***squeeze***... //
paralinguistic entity	[specificity: default]
image	

Alternatively, the paralinguistic entity may be shaped as either two- or three-dimensional, with rounded or straightened hands and fingers. For example, the vlogger gestures defined entities when referring to the *bump* formation of the granuloma on her foot (2).

(2)

phonology	//3 *under* / *each* like / ***bump*** and in- //
paralinguistic entity	[specificity: defined: rounded/3D] + [specificity: outer: smaller]
image	

Paralinguistic entities may also vary in terms of SIZE relative to the amount of gestural space taken up by the prosodic unfolding of gestures in a stretch of discourse. In other words they may be, for instance, bigger or smaller than other entities that have occurred up to a given point in the speaker's discourse. For example, the 'heaping bowl of Chex Mix' gesture in (3) is large relative to the 'applesauce squeeze' gesture in (1) that it precedes.

(3)
phonology   //4+ ... like a / ↑*heaping* / **bowl**
                 //3 *full* of / **Chex** Mix ... //

paralinguistic entity   [specificity: defined: rounded/3D] +
                             [specificity: outer: bigger]

image

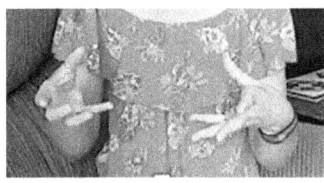

DEPICTION considers whether the paralinguistic entity has a defined contour that is visually 'drawn' in space (by, e.g. drawing the outline of an entity with a pointed finger in the air) or 'sculpted' (by, e.g. cupping a hand as in the example in (3)). The features sculpted and drawn correspond to two of Müller's (1998) four modes of expression used in representational gestures: *drawing* (tracing the silhouette of an object in the air with a finger or hand) and *moulding* (sculpting or shaping the form of an object with the hands). Müller's (1998) two other modes, *imitating/acting* ('acting out' an action) and *representing/portraying* (where the hands represent an object, e.g. a 'V' shape made with middle fingers to represent scissors) are dealt with in Chapter 1 in terms of somasis and emblems, respectively.

The first phase in the Chatty Vlog, the 'National Night Out' phase, features thing entities relating to food that are realized with sculpted gestures specified in size and shape that mark out the boundaries or sides of an object. During this phase the vlogger describes the food that she plans to bring to this event ((4)–(8)).

(4)   // [...I'm] //3 *bring*ing / *two* big / *ma*caroni and / **chees**es just like the
(5)   //2 **Stouff**er's brand I / *think*
(6)   //1 *Andy* went and / *got* it um / **yest**erday at the
(7)   //4 **store**
(8)   //3 *yeah* I got / *two* / **big** ones... //

In this sequence paralanguage converges with the thing entities *two big macaroni and cheeses* – which are qualified verbally in terms of size and number (8). The vlogger makes a gesture 'sculpting' the size of the entity, with flat vertical hands indicating the sides of a food container (perhaps a tray or dish) as she completes the first two tone groups in the sequence ((4)–(5)). The gesture incorporates movement to indicate that there are two entities, with the second entity placed slightly to the left of the first in the gestural space (9).

(9)

phonology [...I'm]
//3 *bring*ing / *two* big / *ma*caroni and / *chees*es just like the //2 **Stouff**er's brand I / *think* //

paralinguistic [specificity: defined: rounded/3D] +
entity [specificity: outer: bigger] +
[depiction: sculpted]

images

The vlogger then maps out the boundaries of the paralinguistic entity in terms of quality (*two big ones*) with a series of hand gestures indicating the edges of the object in width and length (10). In both cases the entity is sculpted with her hands. The alternative choice (see Figure 4.1) would be to draw the object in the air, for instance, tracing a square shape in the air with a pointed finger to indicate the shape of a tray of macaroni. The sculpting option is restricted to 3D entities, as formalized by the 'if/then' I and T superscript notation in the network in Figure 4.1 (read as if [3D], then [sculpted]). In other words, an object that is represented by a cupped hands gesture to make a shape that has more than two dimensions (i.e. a shape with depth) always selects the option 'sculpted'. These are distinctions in the rendering of the gesture rather than distinctions in the physical properties of the object represented (since an object can be represented by drawing or sculpting regardless of its materiality).

(10)

phonology //3 *yeah* I got / *two* / ***big*** ones… //

paralinguistic entity [specificity: defined: rounded/3D] +
[specificity: outer: bigger] +
[depiction: sculpted]

images

In addition to gestures that concur with 'tangible' thing entities in the discourse, semiotic entities are also construed paralinguistically in the vlog. The ideational meaning in the social media observation phase tends to involve more semiotic entities than the other phases, largely entities related to the use of social media platforms (e.g. Instagram stories). These semiotic entities are also realized with sculpting gestures suggesting a bounded object. For instance, when the vlogger refers to Instagram stories (Ephemeral videos streamed to viewers on Instagram) in her speech, she uses a flat hand gesture positioning the entity as an object to her left (11).

(11)

phonology //3 … *In*stagram / ***stor***ies … //

paralinguistic entity [specificity: defined: rounded/3D] +
[specificity: outer: bigger] +
[depiction: sculpted]

image

Similarly, video clips are construed as a wide entity with very slightly curved fingers in front of the speaker (12).

(12)

phonology //1 … / ↓*four* little / *clips* of / ***vid***eos so //

paralinguistic entity [specificity: defined: rounded/3D] +
[specificity: outer: bigger] +
[depiction: sculpted]

image

While these paralinguistic entities are sculpted, *comments* (gesturing the responses that appear beneath a YouTube video) are instead represented with a flat hand moving vertically downwards, 'drawing' the direction of the unfolding comment feed in space (13).

(13)

phonology //2 … / *you* have / *all* the / ***comm***ents and / *stuff* but //

paralinguistic entity [specificity: defined: rounded/ 3D] +
[specificity: outer: bigger] +
[depiction: drawn]

images

In order to explore paralinguistic entities in more detail it is necessary to consider how they enter into paralinguistic figures in discourse. This will enable us to account for how paralinguistic entities are variously manifested, or presented as relating to other paralinguistic entities, and/or involved in actions or happenings in the discourse.

4.3 Figures

Figures comprise change or states, involving one or more entities. For example, the figure *and injected this like steroid* in the Dermatology anecdote construes an activity experienced during a visit to the dermatologist. This figure is a moment in an activity sequence: *And so, the dermatologist um took like this needle and under each like bump and injected this like steroid and it would like all bubble up.* In terms of lexicogrammar, this figure is realized congruently as a clause with a material Process (*injected*). Hao (2015: 198) distinguishes between occurrence figures which involve an occurrence realized congruently through relevant clause types (e.g. material and behavioural clauses) and state figures realized through relational clauses. The following instances from the 'Visit to the Dermatologist' phase illustrate occurrence (14) and state (15) figures:

(14)　and injected this like steroid
(15)　and it was all like bumpy and stuff

The system network in Figure 4.2 outlines the paralinguistic figures which can concur with these kinds of meanings. It distinguishes between paralinguistic occurrence figures, in which a paralinguistic entity is involved in an activity, and paralinguistic state figures, where a paralinguistic entity is manifested. Each type

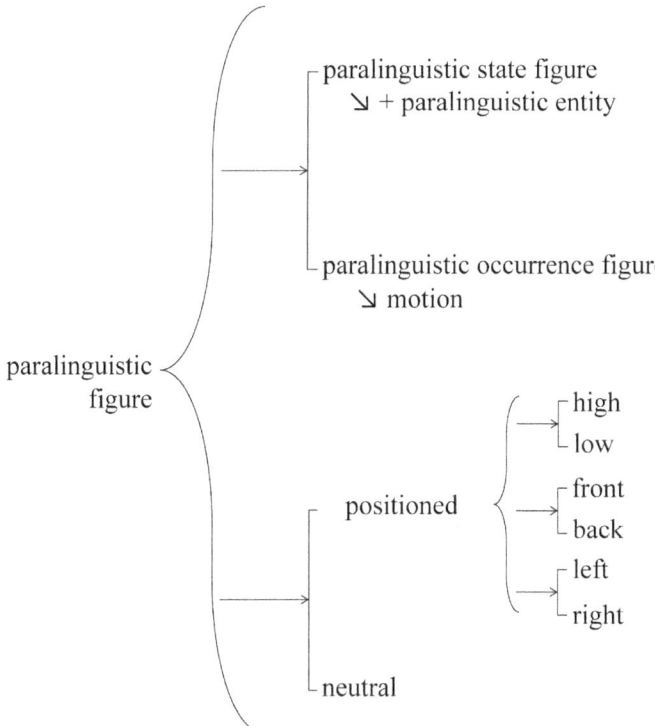

Figure 4.2 Paralinguistic figure network (general systems).

of paralinguistic figure can be positioned in space, relative to the neutral position adopted by a speaker where most of their gestures occur (in front of the speaker's solar plexus with elbows slightly bent). Paralinguistic state figures necessarily involve an entity; paralinguistic occurrence figures necessarily involve motion (as specified by the realization statements following the downward slanting arrows in the network).

For example, near the end of the 'Visit to the Dermatologist' phase the vlogger offers an explanation of why she did not film a video about the details of her foot problems. Concurrent with her verbiage explaining the existence of *feet people* (people with foot fetishes in the YouTube audience that such a video might attract) is a paralinguistic state figure manifesting the imagined group of people through a wide slightly curved entity gesture (16). Aside from slightly oscillating fingers (perhaps to soften the focus and suggest the group is an imagined/intangible threat rather than a known audience) the entity in this gesture does not move in the gestural space.

(16)

phonology   //2 ... there's like / ***feet*** people / *out* there ... //

paralinguistic [paralinguistic state figure] +
figure   [non-positioned]

image

By way of contrast, earlier in the phase the vlogger described a steroid injection forming part of an activity. In that example she employed a paralinguistic occurrence figure with a hand shape suggestive of holding an entity (the syringe) and thumb movement suggestive of the act of pressing down on a syringe to release its contents as the drug is injected into the foot (17).

(17)

phonology   [in-] //3 *ject*ed this like / ***ster***oid ... //

paralinguistic [paralinguistic occurrence figure] +
figure   [non-positioned]

image

4.3.1 Paralinguistic state figures

State figures involve either single paralinguistic entities that are simply manifested or more than one entity that enters into an association with another one (the [presentational] vs [relational] options in Figure 4.3). These paralinguistic entities are not involved in a paralinguistic occurrence. For relational state figures, the association may be represented via variations in either the relative size or relative position of the entities, or both, within the gestural space.[2]

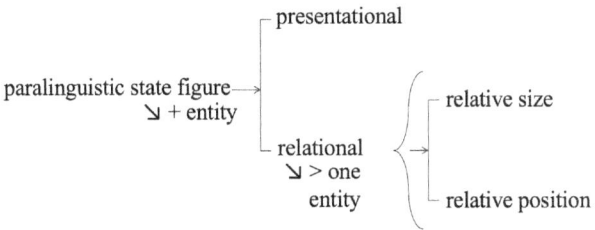

Figure 4.3 Paralinguistic state figures.

An example of a presentational state figure is shown in (18), where the vlogger refers to neighbours she only sees once a year at her local neighbourhood 'National Night Out'. In this figure the neighbours are presented as an entity realized by a shaping of slightly cupped hands stretching from the chest outwards away from the body.[3]

(18)

phonology   //3 there are / **neigh**bours that I
                   //3 see ... //

**paralinguistic   [paralinguistic state
figure**   figure: presentational]

image

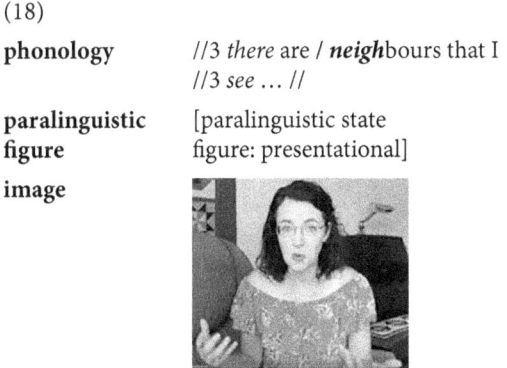

An example of a relational state figure occurs in one of the phases of the video where the vlogger complains about how frequently her children ask for snacks (19). When she talks about giving them 'Chex Mix' and applesauce she makes a rounded gesture with her hands sculpting the side of a bowl. She then combines this with a downward movement of her right hand to indicate the shape of the applesauce squeeze packet as if it is sitting next to the bowl – which she continues to gesture with her left hand (signalling relative position). This example can also be interpreted as realizing relative size, since the heaping bowl of 'Chex Mix' is gestured as larger than the applesauce squeeze. The act of giving, which is the activity construed in the verbiage, is not concurrently realized in the paralanguage.

(19)

phonology [I] //4+ *gave* them / *each* a / *bowl* – like a / ↑*heap*ing / ***bowl*** //3 *full* of / ***Chex*** Mix and an //4 *ap*plesauce / ***squeeze*** //

paralinguistic figure [paralinguistic state figure: relational: relative size/relative position]

images

 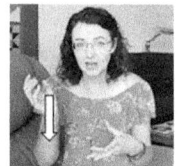

4.3.2 Paralinguistic occurrence figures

Paralinguistic occurrence figures incorporate motion to construe a happening or activity. Unlike paralinguistic state figures which always visually incorporate a paralinguistic entity, a paralinguistic occurrence figure can occur both with or without committing a definable entity. There are three other dimensions along which such figures vary: whether or not the motion repeats (iterated/isolated), the speed of the motion (constant/adjusted) and the direction of the motion (omni/linear) – as shown in the system network in Figure 4.4. The features at greater levels of delicacy for all of these dimensions are detailed in the sections which follow.

4.3.2.1 Paralinguistic occurrence figures with or without paralinguistic entities

Where an entity is present in the paralinguistic realization of an occurrence figure this entity may change, [transformative] versus [non-transformative] in either size, [increase] versus [decrease] or [shape]. These options are outlined in Figure 4.5. If it remains a constant size or shape, it may impact another entity in the gestural space, [impacting] versus [non-impacting].

There are multiple examples of paralinguistic entitied occurrence figures used by the vlogger to describe her skin condition and treatment in the 'Visit

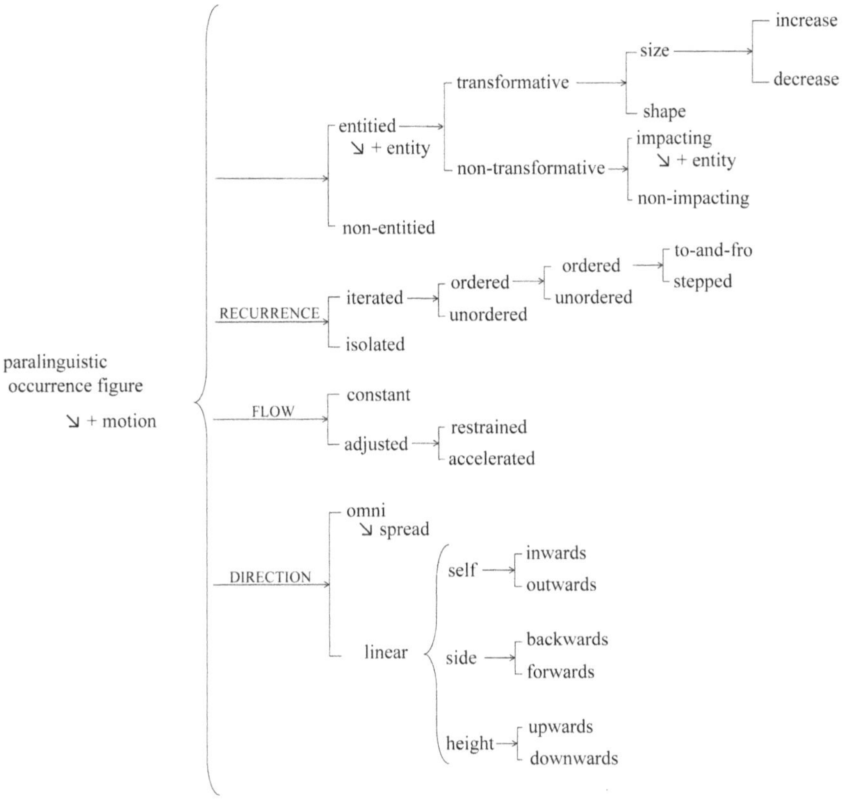

Ideational Semovergence

Figure 4.4 Paralinguistic occurrence figures.

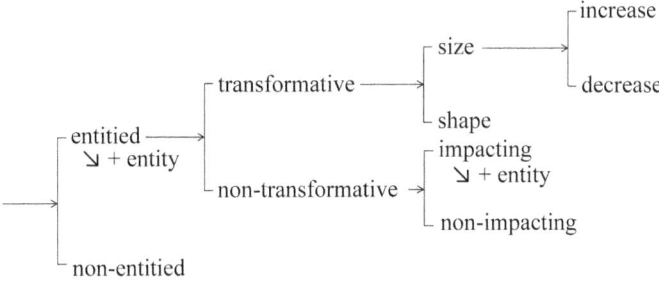

Figure 4.5 Paralinguistic entitied occurrence figures.

to the Dermatologist' phase. For example, she refers to the spreading of the condition with a gesture representing a dispersal movement as she says *and it was spreading*. In this gesture an entity is represented at first by pincer-clasped thumbs and index fingers and then increases in size, transforming as it does so into splayed fingers (20).

(20)

phonology   //3 *And* it was / ***spread***ing ... //

paralinguistic   [entitied: transformative: size: increase]
figure

images

The vlogger also uses an entitied gesture when she talks about how the condition *tripled – quadrupled in size in a year* (21). This gesture incorporates an entity by beginning with a round, curved shape that she makes with the index finger and thumb on her right hand (to suggest a part of the perimeter of a circular region of her foot). She then closes this shape into a full circle with her left index finger. Two 'waves' of this circular gesture are repeated (on *tripled* and *quadrupled*) with fingers transforming from circular to splayed to circular again.

(21)

phonology   // ... and it had like
//3 *trip*led – quad- / *rup*led in / *size* in a / ***year*** ... //

paralinguistic   [entitied: transformative: size: increase]
figure

images

Rather than transforming a single entity, occurrence figures that contain multiple entities can incorporate gestures that represent the impact of one entity on another, for example, an entity knocking into another. This might include clapping gestures where the two entities coming together is realized through the sound of the hands hitting each other. In relation to example (17) earlier and (24) that follows, had the vlogger's left hand been deployed to construe the bumps the steroid was injected into, then the occurrence figure would have been an impacting one.

Non-entitied occurrence figures, on the other hand, do not realize a visible entity in the paralanguage. For example, during the 'National Night Out' phase the vlogger indicates that she wants to look more presentable by appearing in different clothing to the usual outfit that she wears walking with her children. Concurrently there is a non-entitied circular gesture in which she makes three horizontal circles in the air with her index finger (22),[4] suggesting both her regular activity of walking around the neighbourhood and its location.

(22)

phonology //3 *diff*erent than they / *norm*ally / *prob*ably / *see* me / *every* / *sing*le day / *walk*ing with the / **kids** ... //

paralinguistic figure [occurrence Figure: non-entitied]

image

A vertical circular gesture appears in the 'Hair Dye' phase. In this case the index fingers of each hand are moving in opposite directions (away from/towards the body) and so are construing a non-entitied paralinguistic occurrence figure (*washing*) but not a location (23).

(23)

phonology [so I've] //1 *tried* washing it / ***out*** ... //

paralinguistic figure [occurrence Figure: non-entitied]

image

4.3.2.2 *Iterating paralinguistic occurrence figures*

Another dimension of occurrence figures has to do with whether or not they incorporate gestures that repeat – [iterated] versus [isolated], and if so, in what manner – [ordered] versus [unordered], and if [ordered], then [to-and-fro] or [stepped]. These options are outlined in Figure 4.6.

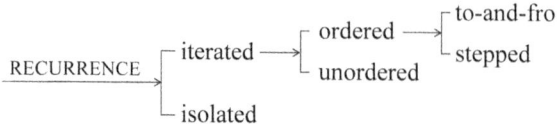

Figure 4.6 Iterating occurrence figures.

An example of an iterating occurrence figure is seen in the dermatology anecdote where piercing gestures are used to construe the steroid injections (17 and 24). In each case the entity indicated by the hand shape is in motion, as the dermatologist picks the needle up and pierces the bumps. This figure is also an example of an [accelerated] occurrence figure (as opposed to [restrained]), as the piercing gesture involves half a dozen rapid movements. The example shown in (22) earlier is another example of an iterating figure, as the vlogger makes the circular gesture three times to suggest repeated trips around the neighbourhood.

(24)

phonology   //3 *under* / *each* like / **bump** … //

paralinguistic figure   [paralinguistic occurrence Figure: iterated: ordered: stepped]

images

Another example of an iterating occurrence figure is found in the social media observation when the vlogger is discussing the 'Q and A' session that she plans to run *with the family – with Andy or whoever has questions* – once she achieves twenty thousand YouTube subscribers. The entities (*the family*, *Andy* and *whoever has questions*) are realized as a series of gestures with a flat hand and splayed figures; each entity in turn involves 'to-and-fro' gestures that iterate the entities on different sides of the body. The 'family' entity is construed with a forward movement gesture of the vlogger's right hand, positioning the entity in front of her. The 'Andy' entity is positioned with the vlogger's left hand moving to the left of her body. And the 'whoever' entity is positioned with her right hand moving to her right – the third image in (25).

(25)

phonology   //3 *with* the / *fam*ily – with
                           //4 *Andy* or / *who*ever
                           //3 *has* / *quest*ions … //

paralinguistic figure   [paralinguistic occurrence Figure: iterated: ordered: to-and-fro]

image

The alternative choice to this to-and-fro positioning would be to order the entities sequentially in the gestural space, for instance, when listing items or events (the feature [stepped] in Figure 4.6). For example, the vlogger uses a stepped occurrence figure when recounting the amount of food her children have already eaten that day as justification for why she will deny them more when they come and ask for it. This figure begins with the vlogger pushing her pinkie finger downwards with her index finger (as if she is about to use her fingers to list items) as she says *They had a big lunch*. Then keeping her index and pinkie fingers extended she moves her left hand to the right and repeats the downward motion of her pinkie finger (but this time without touching it with the index finger).

(26)

phonology   //3 … they / *had* a big / ***lunch***
                           //1 ^ then they / *had* a / ***snack*** … //

paralinguistic figure   [paralinguistic occurrence Figure: iterated: ordered: stepped]

images

4.3.2.3 The systems of FLOW and DIRECTION

The final two dimensions to consider when analysing an occurrence figure are FLOW and DIRECTION – as outlined in Figure 4.7.

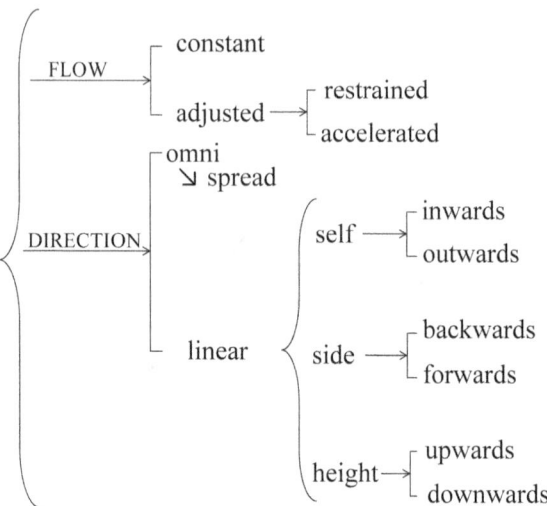

Figure 4.7 The system of FLOW and DIRECTION in occurrence figures.

The FLOW system allows for the speed at which gestures are made to be either constant or adjusted, and if adjusted, either accelerated or restrained. Returning to the figure where the vlogger discusses her plans for a question-and-answer session (specifically *I am going to do a big Q and A*), the concurring paralinguistic occurrence figure involves an [accelerated] gesture where the hands increase in speed as the gesture spreads outwards (27). The alternative [restrained] choice would be a gesture that slows down.

(27)

phonology [I am] //3 going to do a / *big* / ↑Q and / *A* //

paralinguistic figure [occurrence Figure: accelerated]

images

As far as DIRECTION is concerned, this gesture moved outwards from the vlogger's body. The system in general allows for [omni] gestures such as that illustrated in (20) earlier – where the splaying fingers construe something spreading in all directions. Alternatively gestures can move in various [linear] directions. Examples were provided in Chapter 1. Example (81) in Chapter 1 also involved an [outwards] gesture, registering the amount of hair dye now in stock. Example (82) involved an [inwards] gesture, construing a wave of emotion overwhelming the vlogger. Examples of gestures to one side or the other were also provided in Chapter 1. In example (14'''''') in Chapter 1 the gesture moved to the right, construing future possibility – generalized as [forwards] in the network; and in example (58') it moved to the left, construing past experience – generalized as [backwards] in the network.[5] The piercing gestures in (24) were [downwards] ones. And the [inwards] gesture in (82) in Chapter 1 was also an [upwards] one. This shows the potential for choices from the DIRECTION systems [inwards] versus [outwards], [backwards] versus [forwards] and [upwards] versus [downwards] to combine.

A system network bringing together the various choices we have covered in the previous sections is provided in Figure 4.8.

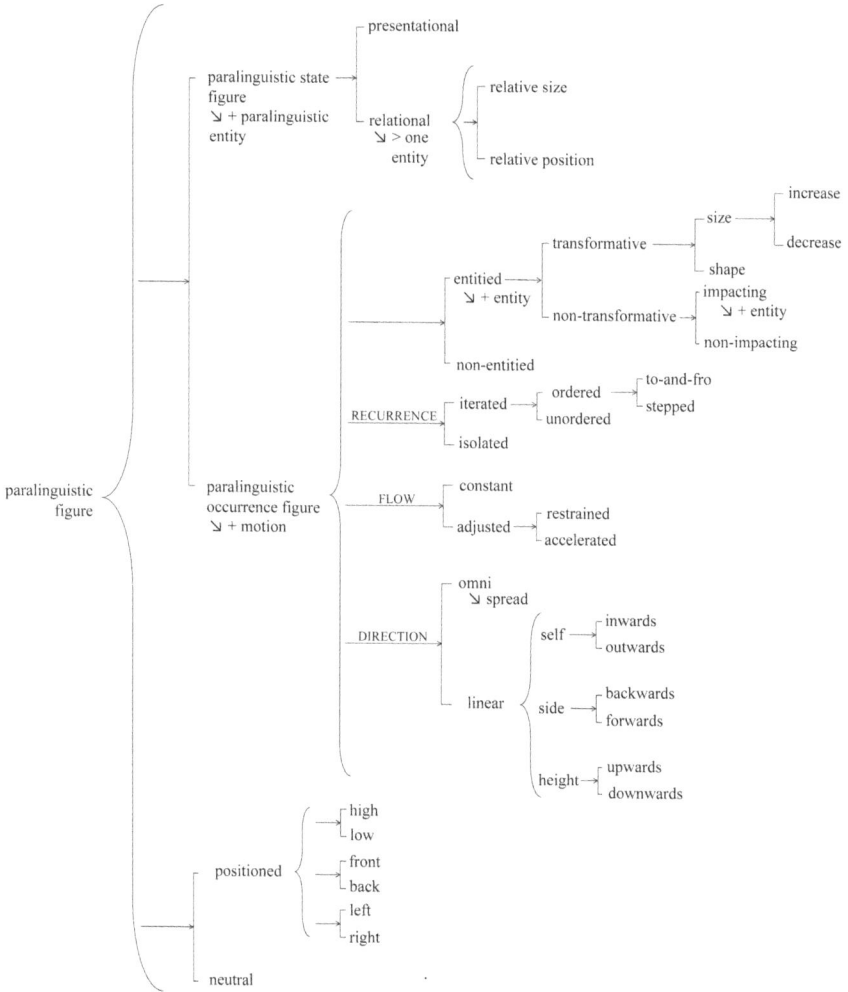

Figure 4.8 A system network for paralinguistic figures.

4.4 Co-construing experience

This chapter has described how semovergent systems construe ideational meaning and has explored entities and figures as resources for embodied ideational meaning across language and paralanguage. These systems have been formalized in system networks that can be used by an analyst as they consider how gestures interact through a relationship of concurrence or divergence with the ideational meanings made in spoken discourse.

Different semiotic modes have different affordances in terms of the degree of ideational meaning that can be committed, with language appearing to have more resources for more delicately or specifically construing figures and entities. For example, a gesture can be used to represent macaroni and cheese but is unlikely to be able to represent the particular brand in the way language can (e.g. the Stouffer's brand macaroni and cheese mentioned in the 'National Night Out' phase). In addition, as noted in Chapter 1, language also has the capacity to realize the discourse semantic system of CONNEXION, while paralanguage does not. Paralanguage also appears to be unpredictable in terms of whether or not it concurrently realizes ideational meanings realized as linguistic figures and entities. For example, in terms of the data considered in this chapter, at times both language and paralanguage construe an entity (e.g. the syringe in the 'Dermatologist Visit' phase), and at times only one mode commits the ideational meaning (e.g. the figure in the 'National Night Out' phase where the macaroni and cheese is realized in both the paralanguage and language but the act of bringing it is only realized in the language).

A robust analytical framework for investigating ideational meaning offers a key resource for understanding human experience in social life. The ideational paralinguistic systems presented in this chapter have important potential in applied linguistics where adopting a multimodal approach to studying communication involving multiple modalities is becoming increasingly important. Ideational paralanguage also has particular importance in fields such as science education where investigating and classifying entities, activities and their relationships are central to knowledge-building (Danielsson, 2016). There has been some work investigating inter-semiotic relations between spoken language and body language in science lectures (Hood and Hao, 2021). While technical fields tend to foreground classification practices, all areas of social life construct fields of experience that may be construed in paralanguage. We look forward to seeing how the systems explored in this chapter are taken up in disciplines such as the humanities and in studies of different semiotic modes (including face-to-face communication and communication in digital environments).

5

Interpersonal paralanguage: Approaching paralanguage from the perspective of social relations

5.1 Introduction

This chapter focuses on interpersonal meaning in paralanguage – on the ways in which the paralanguage of facial expression, voice quality, body gestures and positioning express feelings and enact social relations in cooperation with spoken language. The data are drawn from an award-winning stop-motion puppet animation film *Coraline*, directed by Henry Selick (2009) and based on a novella of the same name written by Neil Gaiman (2002).

Analyses explore the paralinguistic systems of interpersonal sonovergence in which movements of parts of the body or face rise and fall in tune with the intonation contours of the prosodic phonology (see Section 5.2) and interpersonal semovergence in which paralinguistic expressions converge with interpersonal meanings in spoken discourse (see Section 5.3). In the latter the relevant interpersonal discourse semantic system is APPRAISAL with its three subsystems of ATTITUDE (as AFFECT only in this case), ENGAGEMENT and GRADUATION (Martin and White, 2005; Martin and Rose, [2003] 2007; Martin, 2017a). Reviews of these discourse semantic systems precede introductions to related paralinguistic systems – PARALINGUISTIC AFFECT, PARALINGUISTIC ENGAGEMENT and PARALINGUISTIC GRADUATION. Systems of body ORIENTATION, PROXIMITY and POWER are also briefly discussed. System choices are illustrated in instances from *Coraline* and discussion focuses on intermodal convergences in expressions of emotion and the enactment of inter-character relations.

The story depicts the return adventure of the central character, Coraline, a pre-teenage girl who moves from the real world into a mirror (other) world through a tiny passageway behind a locked door in an empty room in the house her family has just moved into. Having been ignored by her busy parents and bored in the real world, Coraline finds herself the centre of attention from an 'Other Mother' and an 'Other Father' in the alternate world. However, she soon comes to realize that she has in fact been trapped by a sinister villain, Beldam, appearing in the disguise of Other Mother with the intention of capturing the souls of children. The clever and brave Coraline is eventually able to save herself as well as her real parents and the souls of three other trapped children. She returns to her real world with a greater appreciation of her real parents.

In stop-motion animations such as *Coraline* story characters are portrayed by puppets. Their movements, body language and facial expressions are designed by animators to match the pre-recorded speech of voice actors. The animations are developed frame-by-frame as animators make very small changes to the puppet's face or body. Each change is captured as a 'stop-motion' or static frame before being collated and camera recorded to create movements in film (Laika Studios, 2017). In films, the characterization of the main characters conveys the thematic message; accordingly, every facial or body movement of the main puppet characters (including the way they walk) is designed to express meaning – and so everything they do can be interpreted as semiotic rather than somatic behaviour (see Chapter 1; Mohamed and Nor, 2015; van Leeuwen, 2005). That said, the body movements of secondary characters arguably include both semiotic and somatic behaviour in order to progress the storyline. In this chapter we concentrate on the meaningful behaviour of the main characters.

5.2 Interpersonal sonovergence

Sonovergent paralanguage is only meaningful in its relation to the prosodic phonology of co-expressed speech (Halliday, 1967, 1970a; Halliday and Greaves, 2008; Smith and Greaves, 2015) (see Chapters 1 and 3). The five primary tones in prosodic phonology of English are a falling tone 1 signalling 'certain', a rising tone 2 signalling 'uncertain', a level-rise tone 3 signalling 'unfinished', a falling-rising tone 4 signalling 'reservation' and a rising-falling tone 5 signalling 'surprise' (see Chapter 3). The major pitch movement that realizes the tone choice occurs on the stressed *tonic* of the tone group and is transcribed in bold italics in examples (see Chapter 3). Where interpersonal sonovergent paralanguage resonates with tone choices it is frequently expressed in up or down movements of the head, eyebrows or arms in tune with pitch movements in co-articulated speech.

Interpersonal Paralanguage

The example in (1) shows paralinguistic expressions sonovergent with each major tone choice (other than the level-rise tone 3 which offers minimal phonological scope for convergent body-part movement). A phonological transcription records the tone (as, e.g. //1), and the intonation contour describes and interprets it (as, e.g. falling – 'certain'). The paralanguage which is sonovergent with each intonation contour – which visualizes it – is then described. The resonance of the visual and phonological contours adds further salience to the tonic and hence the given tone choice.

(1)

language	I want to go home	Don't believe me?	I didn't break it.	It was so amazing.
phonology	//1 ^ I / *wann*a go / *home* //	//2 *don't* be- / **lieve** me //	//4 *I* didn't / *break* it	…it was //5 *so* / *so* a- / *maz*ing //
intonation contour	tone 1 (falling) signalling 'certain'	tone 2 (rising) signalling 'uncertain'	tone 4 (falling-rising) signalling 'reserved'	tone 5 (rising-falling) signalling 'surprise'
para-language	eyebrows dropping and arms falling	rising left eyebrow	fall-rising eyebrows and arms	rise-falling eyebrows and arms
images				

5.3 Interpersonal semovergence

Before introducing interpersonal paralinguistic systems we briefly review the interpersonal system of APPRAISAL in language. A skeletal overview of the dimensions of APPRAISAL as ATTITUDE, ENGAGEMENT and GRADUATION is provided in Figure 5.1. (For detailed accounts, see Martin and White, 2005; Martin and Rose, [2003] 2007.)

The discourse system of ATTITUDE (Figure 5.1) differentiates AFFECT as the expression of feelings or emotions from JUDGEMENT as the evaluation of

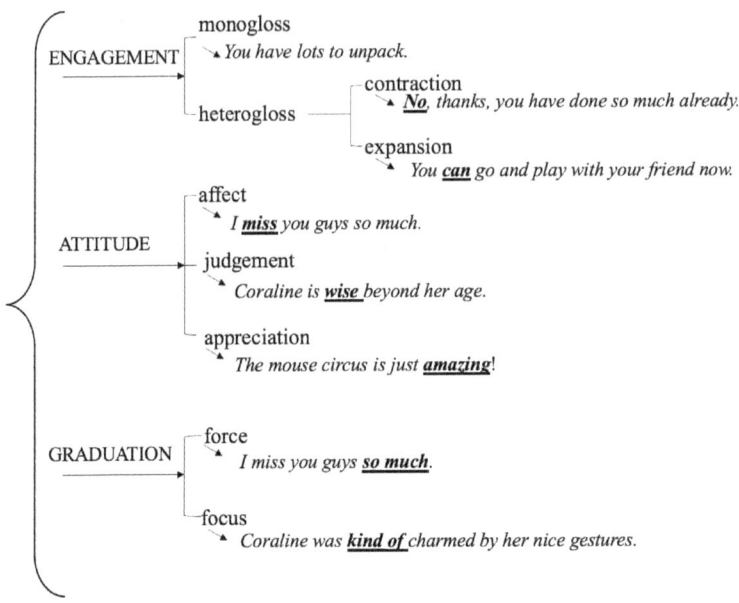

Figure **5.1** The system of APPRAISAL in English.

people and behaviour and APPRECIATION as the assessment of phenomena (Martin and Rose, [2003] 2007; Martin, 2020). Of these three kinds of ATTITUDE only AFFECT is relevant to a discussion of interpersonal semovergence as paralinguistic expressions of attitude are restricted to those of emotion (e.g. Tian, 2011; Welch, 2005; Painter et al., 2013: 31–2). Basic oppositions that hold for AFFECT in language are presented in Figure 5.2 before introducing the system of PARALINGUISTIC AFFECT.

The opposing features in Figure 5.2 are reconfigured as a paradigmatic diagram in Table 5.1.

In Table 5.1 the left column presents a basic opposition between [irrealis] AFFECT and [realis] AFFECT. [Irrealis] AFFECT refers to an emotion response to what might happen. It selects only for the feature [positive]/[negative]. If [positive], the [irrealis] feeling is glossed as 'desire', and if [negative], it is glossed as 'fear'.

[Realis] affect has three opposing features – [happiness], [security] and [satisfaction], each of which also selects for either [mood] or [directed] and for either [positive] or [negative]. An instance of AFFECT might, for example, select [realis:happiness], [mood] and [negative], with an alternate presentation as [realis:happiness; mood;negative]. Lexical instantiations might include, for example, *sad/unhappy/down*. The terms listed under the opposing features of

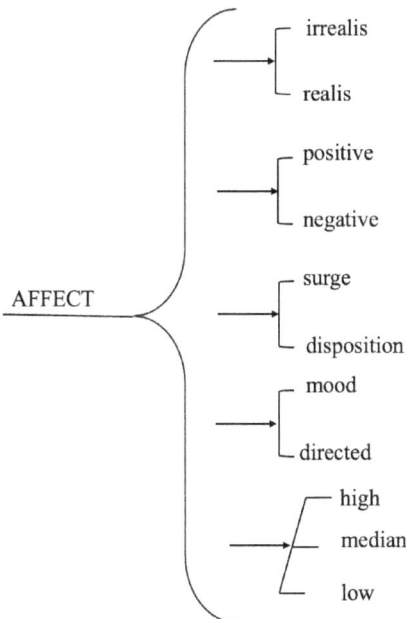

Figure 5.2 Oppositions in the system of AFFECT in language (from Martin, 2020).

Table 5.1 The linguistic system of AFFECT and opposing features (Martin, 2020)

AFFECT			[positive]	[negative]
[irrealis]			'desire'	'fear'
[realis]	[happiness]	[mood]	'cheer'	'misery'
		[directed]	'affection'	'antipathy'
	[security]	[mood]	'confidence'	'disquiet'
		[directed]	'trust'	'surprise'
	[satisfaction]	[mood]	'interest'	'ennui'
		[directed]	'pleasure'	'displeasure'

[positive] and [negative], as 'desire', 'fear', 'cheer' and so on, are neither features nor instances but simply glosses for a potential array of indicative instances. However, as discussed in following sections, in PARALINGUISTIC AFFECT, [fear] constitutes a feature. This is indicated in the use of square bracketing.

The linguistic system of AFFECT does not constitute a blueprint for the development of a system of PARALINGUISTIC AFFECT, its features or oppositions; the systems in the two modalities are named differently to reflect this (as in PARALINGUISTIC ENGAGEMENT and PARALINGUISTIC GRADUATION). PARALINGUISTIC AFFECT models expressions of emotion in FACIAL AFFECT with features realized through muscle movement of the face, and in VOICE AFFECT with features realized through qualities of the voice.

5.3.1 The system of FACIAL AFFECT

FACIAL AFFECT references the theorization of AFFECT in language (e.g. Martin, 2000, 2017a, 2020; Martin and White, 2005) and also engages with significant contributions from a broader literature. An early interpretive framework for facial expression of emotion comes from Darwin (1872) who proposed the principle of antithesis – meaning that opposing movements in facial expression are related to opposing emotions. Of more recent influence has been the work of Ekman and colleagues (Ekman, 2004; Ekman and Friesen, [1975] 2003). Ekman proposed six basic universal facial expressions of emotion, namely, those of happiness, anger, sadness, disgust, surprise and fear. These six emotions underpin the development of a Facial Action Coding System (FACS) (Ekman and Friesen, [1975] 2003) which has been applied in the creation of facial expressions in characters in the computer face-animation industry. The areas of the face considered most significant are eyebrows, eyes and mouth (Faigin, 1990: 256; see also Martinec, 2001).

The systemic functional semiotic system of FACIAL AFFECT presented in Figure 5.3 takes into account these important contributions in a number of areas, including descriptive terminology. For example, the naming of features in the model of FACIAL AFFECT avoids the use of Ekman's terms of 'happiness' and 'sadness' as [happiness] is already a feature in linguistic ATTITUDE. Instead emotion terminology is sourced to Darwin's (1872) opposition in facial movements of 'high spirit' and 'low spirit'. Darwin's influence is seen in Figure 5.3 in the naming of the feature [spirit] and its opposing features as [up] and [down].

An additional opposition proposed by Darwin (1872) is between facial movements interpreted as 'fear' and 'anger'. For Darwin, 'fear' is a feeling caused by the anticipation that one could be harmed (which we interpret as a response to what might happen, i.e. an irrealis trigger) and 'anger' is a feeling that might result in one harming others (which we interpret as a response to something real happening, i.e. a realis trigger). In the network of FACIAL AFFECT in Figure 5.3 [fear] and [anger] are opposing features of [threat]. Each feature is realized through a different set of facial expressions shown in italics. In the intersemiosis of facial expression and the unfolding storyline in language and action, the facial feature [fear] is interpretable as negative and irrealis, that is, it is a negative

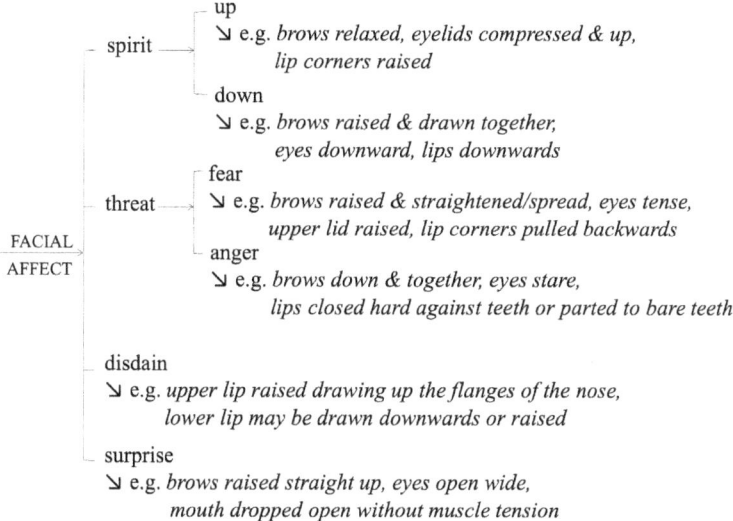

Figure 5.3 The system of FACIAL AFFECT.

emotional response to what might happen. In contrast the feature [anger] is interpretable as negative and realis, an emotional response to what is happening or has happened.[1] Neither [disdain] (akin to Ekman's 'disgust') nor [surprise] has further discriminating features. In summary, the network in Figure 5.3 models FACIAL AFFECT with six features of emotion: [spirit:up], [spirit:down], [fear], [anger], [disdain] and [surprise]. Each of these six features is illustrated and described in (2). Facial resources for expression are in bold.

5.3.1.1 Issues in analysing FACIAL AFFECT

As noted earlier, ATTITUDE in language can be expressed through systems of AFFECT, APPRECIATION or JUDGEMENT while paralinguistic expressions of attitude are restricted to FACIAL AFFECT (see, e.g. Tian, 2011). This means that the paralinguistic meaning potential for expressing emotion is relatively limited with respect to language. For example, an array of finely distinguished lexical instantiations of the feature [realis:happiness;mood;positive] (Table 5.1) are possible, as, for instance, in *happy/joyful/delighted/thrilled* and so on, such fine distinctions are not available in FACIAL AFFECT. In analyses of intermodal resonance in *Coraline*, fine distinctions in verbal instances (e.g. happy vs joyful) may be inferred for resonant facial expressions but cannot be attributed to specific variations in the facial expression. In other words a given expression of FACIAL AFFECT might couple with a diverse array of lexical realizations of [realis:happiness;mood;positive].

(2)

PARALINGUISTIC AFFECT			[threat]		[disdain]	[surprise]
subtype	[spirit]					
	[up]	[down]	[fear]	[anger]		
paralanguage	**eyebrows**: relaxed (no frown) **eyes**: eyelids slightly compressed by raised cheeks **mouth**: corners rising	**eyebrows**: inner portions of brows drawn together and raised **eyes**: usually cast downwards; lower eyelids slightly raised **mouth**: corners of mouth pulled downwards	**eyebrows**: raised and straightened **eyes**: upper lid raised and lower lid tense **mouth**: corners drawn backwards; tightening lips against teeth; teeth may be exposed	**eyebrows**: drawn down and together. **eyes**: staring (penetrating) **mouth**: lips closed hard against teeth or parted to bare them	**eyebrows**: lowered **mouth**: upper lip raised drawing up flanges of the nose; lower lip may be drawn down or raised	**eyebrows**: raised high; straight up **eyes**: open wide **mouth**: dropped open; no muscle tension
images						

Facial expressions can also function as emblems of culturally specific meanings (Ekman and Friesen, [1975] 2003). In many cultures a quick smile accompanying a slight nod without any co-occurring language constitutes an emblem read as a greeting by passers-by. A particular facial expression of emotion might also be read differently in different cultural contexts. Particular social norms might govern how people manage expressions of emotion appropriate to certain social settings (e.g. Ekman, 2004: 45). In example (3), a Vietnamese farmer is talking to a television news reporter about the devastation of his crops by a herd of monkeys. He smiles consistently throughout the interview, not as an expression of [spirit:up] but in response to a cultural expectation (for what Eckman (2004) calls 'display rules') whereby the farmer is not expected to display negative personal feelings in public. Cultural differences in interpretations of facial expressions are also discussed in Birdwhistell ([1970] 1990).

(3)

A further consideration in analysing and interpreting facial expressions is the potential for one feature of FACIAL AFFECT to transition very quickly into another in an animated expression. An instance in example (4) expresses both [surprise] and [spirit:up].

(4)

FACIAL AFFECT   [surprise] + [spirit:up]

image

From a systemic functional perspective, rather than describing this as a blending or merging of emotions it is considered as the co-instantiation of two different emotions with each realized through particular parts of the face (e.g. eyes, eyebrows, mouth) and often in very quick succession. In (4) the raised curved eyebrows realize [surprise] and the upturned lips realize [spirit:up]. A facial expression of [surprise], interpreted as a perturbance (Martin,

2017a) typically has the briefest duration and often transitions quickly to the expression of another emotion, one which responds to the specific trigger of the perturbance.

Our focus is on the semiosis of facial expression realizing emotion in human interaction, but it is important to note that the face can also manifest non-emotional (somatic) states. A frown, for example, might manifest concentrated thinking (Fasel and Luettin, 2003: 260) or physiological states of pain or fatigue (see Chapter 1). Instances of somatic facial expression can of course index purposeful feelings, which remains a challenge for analysts as discussed in Chapter 1. The approach taken in this book is that behaviours can be treated as paralinguistic (i.e. semiotic) depending on whether or not they are negotiated as meaningful in interaction.

5.3.1.2 *The systems of* PARALINGUISTIC GRADUATION *and* FACIAL AFFECT

Linguistic GRADUATION comprises two principal subsystems – FORCE and FOCUS. FORCE can function to adjust the relative intensity or quantity of inscribed attitude or to invoke an attitudinal meaning by grading ideational phenomena. FOCUS has to do with adjusting the categorical boundaries of phenomena as more or less sharply or softly defined (Hood, 2010, 2021; Hood and Zhang, 2020). However, unlike its linguistic counterpart and unlike the PARALINGUISTIC GRADUATION of body gestures (Hao and Hood, 2019; Hood and Zhang, 2020), FACIAL AFFECT can only be graded in FORCE. Features of [strong] to [weak] are shown as positions on a cline in Figure 5.4, realized through variations in muscle tension and/or the duration for which an expression is held.

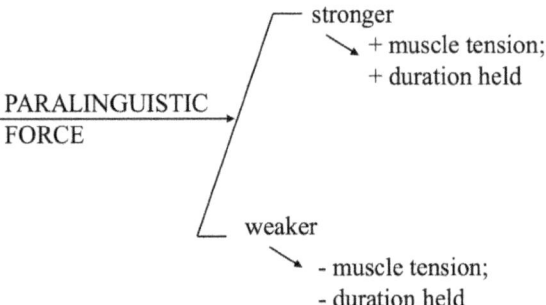

Figure 5.4 The system of FACIAL AFFECT and PARALINGUISTIC FORCE.

Illustrated in (5) are two instances of FACIAL AFFECT as [spirit:up]. Image 2 is graded up in PARALINGUISTIC FORCE through increased muscle tension in the face as evident in the curled up corners of the mouth.

(5)

FACIAL AFFECT   [spirit:up]   stronger [spirit:up]

images   1   2

Expressions of relative FORCE in FACIAL AFFECT are additionally realized through the relative duration over which an expression is held. While some studies measure duration in seconds or milliseconds, a systemic functional perspective considers duration in terms of the relative number of phonological feet or tone groups over which an expression is sustained (see Chapter 3).

In example (6), Coraline, having sensed danger, tells her Other Parents that she wants to go to bed. Her intention is to escape from the Other world in her sleep. However, the Other Parents follow closely behind her, the Other Mother even offering to tuck her into bed. Coraline's anxiety is not revealed in the spoken exchange with the Other Mother but rather in her expression of FACIAL AFFECT as [spirit:down] realized through eyebrows raised and drawn together and downcast eyes. The expression is extended in duration, sustained over the three tone groups of the exchange (marked as //…//…//…).[2]

(6)

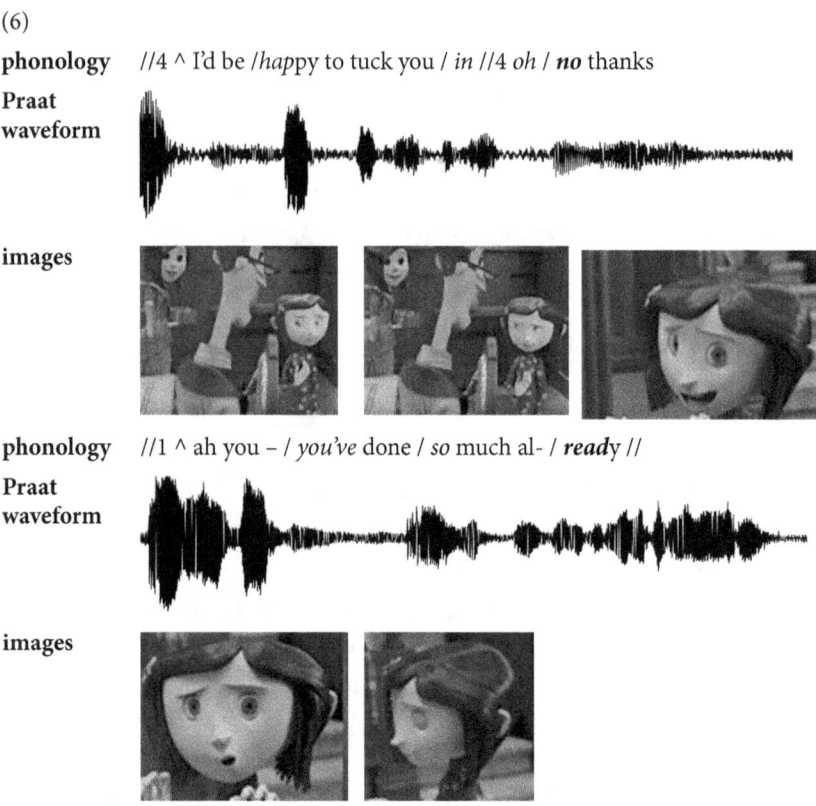

5.3.1.3 Triggering FACIAL AFFECT

AFFECT in verbal and visual texts is always triggered by ideational phenomena. These can be entities or occurrences of any kind. Ideational triggers for expressions of FACIAL AFFECT in *Coraline* may be sourced via a diversity of perceptual channels that are interpreted as available to the character in particular instances. A taxonomy of types of perceptual channel is presented in Figure 5.5.

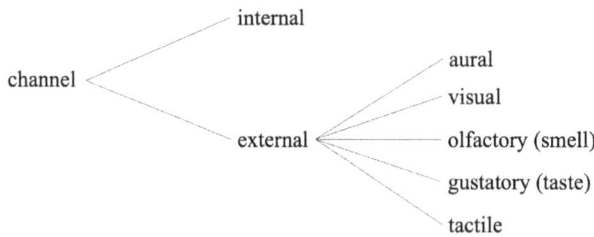

Figure 5.5 Perceptual channels for identifying ideational triggers.

The triggering information may be sourced externally through an auditory perceptual channel (as sound or silence) or a visual, olfactory, gustatory or tactile one (Feng and O'Halloran, 2013). Alternatively, it can be sourced internally through reflection, memory or imagination. In interpreting the trigger for a particular facial expression of emotion in multimodal discourse such as that in *Coraline* more than one perceptual channel is likely to play a part.

In (7), the trigger for facial expressions of emotion is apparently sourced internally. In the resolution stage of the narrative storyline in the film, Coraline meets the Cat, a good friend whom she has not seen since she threw him at the Other Mother in attempting her escape from the Other World. In image 1 in (7) Coraline expresses both mild [surprise] and [spirit:up]. There is no immediately convergent speech, and the trigger is not interpretable at this point by the viewer. However, in image 2 more visual information is made available. The Cat is now revealed as standing outside Coraline's bedroom window, and his presence retrospectively explains the trigger for her facial [surprise] and [spirit:up] in image 1. In image 2, convergent with her spoken language, Coraline's expression of FACIAL AFFECT changes from [spirit:up] to [spirit:down]. Again there is no apparent trigger in the visually available information. The resonant spoken language *I'm really sorry I threw you out at the Other Mother* suggests that the trigger at this point is sourced internally through her reflection on past events. The broader co-text of the story supports this interpretation.

(7)

phonology	[Ø speech]	//1 ^I'm /*really* /sorry I //3 *threw* you out /*at* /^/ //1 ^ the /**Oth**er /Mother //
PARALINGUISTIC AFFECT	[surprise] + [spirit:up]	[spirit:down]
images		

A further example in (8) shows how information acquired from past events can trigger a response in FACIAL AFFECT. The instance involves Coraline's first encounter with the Cat in the orientation stage of the film's narrative. The episode begins with Coraline exploring the neighbourhood along a steep hillside path. A rock falls onto her path from on high. She calls out but gets no response, then throws the rock in the direction from which it fell. A pained cry is heard. Extremely alarmed by this, she runs as fast as possible, sensing something is pursuing her. Startled by a loud 'meow' from behind, she turns to look. Seeing that it is only a cat, her facial expression of [fear] swiftly changes to [surprise], but then to [anger], as in the three images in (8).

(8)

| **phonology** | [Ø speech] | [Ø speech] | [Ø speech] |
| FACIAL AFFECT | [fear] | [surprise] | [anger] |

images

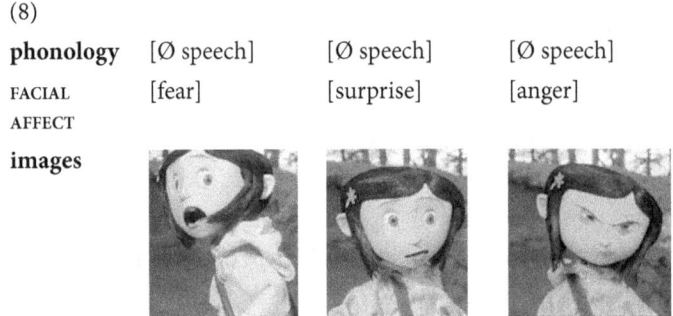

Just as an expression of FACIAL AFFECT supports the identification of the trigger, so available ideational information supports the interpretation of FACIAL AFFECT. A sequence of triggers is interpreted as prompting the sequence of emotions in (8). We interpret Coraline's expression of [fear] in image 1 of example (8) as triggered by the potential consequences of accumulated information sourced visually in the falling rock and auditorily in the cry of pain and the loud, angry 'meow'. We interpret the expression of [surprise] in image 2 as triggered visually by Coraline's first sight of the cat. The trigger for [anger] in image 3 is interpreted not as a response to seeing the cat but to an internal realization that it was the cat who had instigated her fear.

In (8) the facial expressions in the first two images are similar in a number of ways. The brows and eyes in both are raised and the eyes are wide open. However, there is a difference in the movement of mouth muscles in each. Ekman (2003) notes that for strong [fear] the lips are usually parted giving the mouth an open shape, while the lower jaw is drawn back. The mouth is also opened for [surprise] and the jaws are parted but not drawn back.

5.3.2 The system of VOICE AFFECT

A further semiotic resource for the expression of emotion is the voice. In this section we explore how the additional analysis of voice qualities can afford more delicate distinctions in PARALINGUISTIC AFFECT than can the facial expression alone. The proposed systems of VOICE AFFECT draw from both psychological studies of the emotional voice (Johnstone and Scherer, 2000) and the social semiotic perspective discussed in van Leeuwen (1999). Analyses of the vocalizations of the central character of *Coraline* also take into account acoustic and perception-based methods.

Descriptions of emotional vocalization in psychological studies propose four dimensions of acoustic signal: 'time-related measures', 'measures relating to fundamental frequency', 'intensity-related measures' and the combination of these known as 'time-frequency-energy measures' (Frick, 1985; Scherer, 1986; Banse and Scherer, 1996, cited in Johnstone and Scherer, 2000: 225–7). Intensity (or energy) related to loudness of the voice and is measured in decibels (dB); however, the accuracy of this measure may be affected by background noise in speech perception or by the distance of the speaker from the microphone in voice production. Fundamental frequency refers to the 'rate at which the vocal folds open and close across the glottis' (Johnstone and Scherer, 2000: 225) and closely relates to pitch since frequency refers to the physical transmission of sound in air while pitch refers to the way it is perceived by the human ear (Halliday and Greaves, 2008). The precise measurement of pitch level and pitch range relies on the measurement of fundamental frequency in Hertz (Hz) value.

The system network of VOICE QUALITY in Figure 5.6 is built upon van Leeuwen's (1999: 151) 'sound quality' system, which maps the potential for a set of simultaneous features each of which is graded. As van Leeuwen notes, 'Sounds are not either tense or lax, either high or low and so on' (1999: 130) but are relatively so. Discussed in van Leeuwen (1999), though not included in his diagrammatic representation are the subsystems of 'tension, roughness, breathiness, loudness, pitch register, vibrato and nasality'. (For explanations of sound (voice) production, see, e.g. van Leeuwen 1999: 131–6; Gordon and Ladefoged, 2001: 385.) Each voice quality system generates opposing features, as in, for example, TENSION [tense/lax] and ROUGHNESS [rough/smooth]. In Figure 5.6 we rename the system as VOICE QUALITY and conventionalize its formatting with the insertion of subsystems in small caps. To the van Leeuwen's systems are added those of DURATION with time-related features of [long/short] and TEMPO with features of [fast/slow]. As simultaneous systems, instances of voiced expression select from each system. As van Leeuwen (1999: 129) notes, 'Every sound quality is a mixture of different features. The voice is never only high or low, or only soft or loud, or only tense or lax.' It is the particular 'mixture' of options which realize one feature or another in the system of VOICE AFFECT (see Figure 5.7).

Features of voice quality can be perceived by ear and measured acoustically for segments of recorded speech and then visualized in waveform and spectrogram

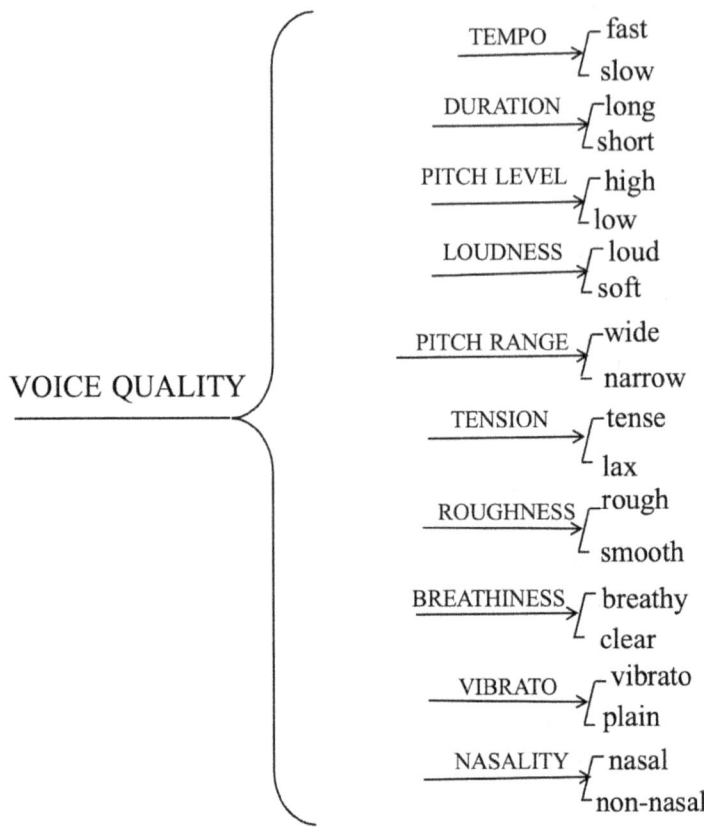

Figure 5.6 The system of VOICE QUALITY (extended from van Leeuwen, 1999).

images using Praat software. (Appendix C explains in greater detail how features of voice quality are measured and displayed in such visualizations.) Voice quality analyses of speech segments underpin the identification of options in the VOICE AFFECT system in Figure 5.7.

In this chapter analyses are restricted to variations in the voice quality of the main character, Coraline. We begin the process with sampled instances of her 'neutral' (non-emotional) speech. Since the character Coraline is never in an absolutely neutral state in the film, 'neutral' speech is taken from scenes in which she expresses the mildest of feelings. This provides a baseline of qualities against which the relative variations of features in Figure 5.6 can be compared. This is first undertaken as a perceptual examination of voice qualities by a single researcher and then blind-coded by other researchers in voice quality research by the research team to check for reliability. The perceptual examination results were triangulated with Praat spectrograms.

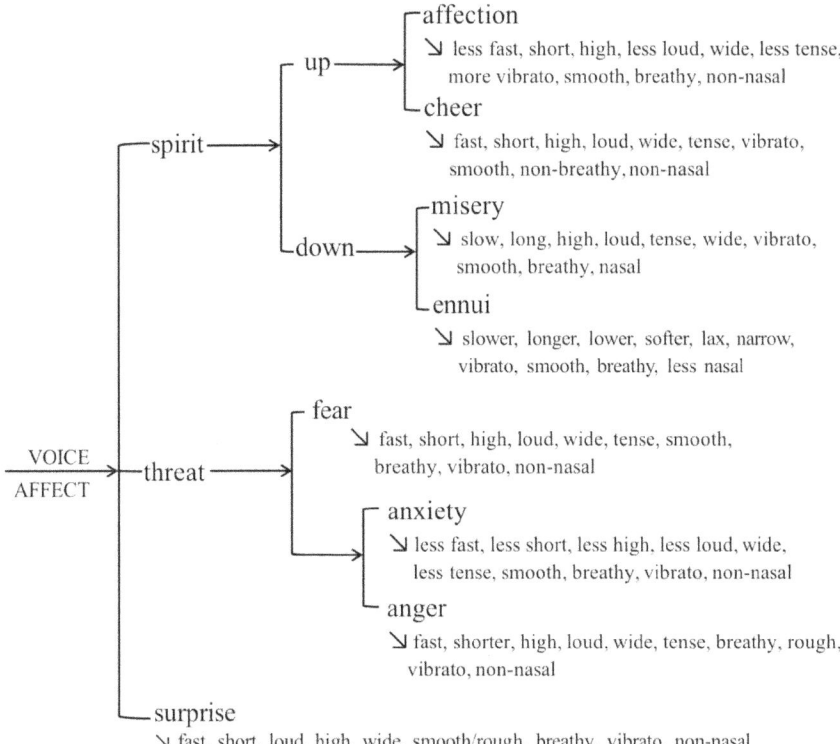

Figure 5.7 The system of VOICE AFFECT.

However, it is important to note that the computation of acoustic measures of voice in Praat cannot be assumed to be entirely accurate as the voice is sometimes recorded with background music or noise. In such cases the spectrogram may calculate and present values of all sounds in one measurement. For this reason, the perceptual examination is considered the more reliable method of voice quality analysis in this study.

Both the VOICE AFFECT system (Figure 5.7) and the FACIAL AFFECT system (Figure 5.3) share the names of features at the less delicate end of their networks (with the exception of [disdain] which is only afforded by facial expression). This is an indication of the same emotion manifesting in different physiological responses, that is, with different realizations. At further levels of delicacy the VOICE AFFECT system includes additional opposing features; for example, [spirit:up] opposes options of [affection] and [cheer] and [spirit:down] opposes [misery] and [ennui]. As shown in Figure 5.7 options within systems are realized through particular voice quality contours. Each contour is distinguished from another on the basis of degrees of similarity/difference in one or more qualities. Contours of voice quality are identified initially on the basis of perceptual analysis. If results are inconclusive, comparative measurements are made against Coraline's 'neutral' speech to support the identification of subtle degrees of difference in given qualities. The VOICE AFFECT system is discussed feature by feature with exemplifying instances from *Coraline* and accompanying spectrogram and waveform visualizations. For guidance on reading the visualizations, see Appendix C.

5.3.2.1 *The system of* VOICE AFFECT *as [spirit:up]*

In VOICE AFFECT as [spirit:up] opposing features are [cheer] and [affection].[3] As opposing features they are realized through different voice quality contours. Certain qualities are shared, as, for example, those of [short] and [high], while others differ by degree, for example, [affection] as considerably less [fast] relative to [cheer], as well as less [loud], more [vibrato] and more [breathy].

Voice qualities that oppose [affection] and [cheer] are illustrated in Praat visualizations for two examples in (9).

(9)

phonology	//5 ^ I / *missed* you / *so* much //	//5 *that* was / **great** //
VOICE AFFECT	[affection]	[cheer]
voice quality	less fast, less loud, more vibrato, breathy	faster, louder, less vibrato, more clear
Praat visualizations		

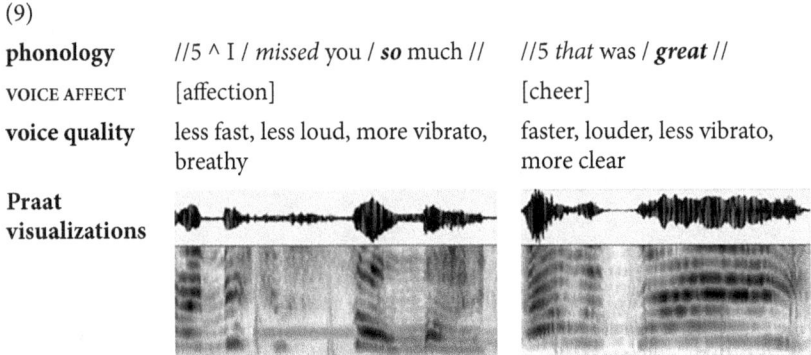

The first example in (9) captures a moment in the story where Coraline sees her parents again after a long time. In *I missed you so much* the voice quality realizes [affection]: a [breathy] voice quality resonates with *miss you* and *much* as shown in grey areas on the spectrogram. In the second example in (9) Coraline exclaims about her appreciation of a performance of a mouse circus. In *that was great* the voice quality realizes [cheer]: the relatively [clear] quality is evident in an absence of the kind of grey areas noted on the first spectrogram. The relatively [loud] quality in the expression of [cheer] is evident in the darker and sharper grey on the second spectrogram.

Example (10) revisits the speech segment in (9) with a focus on the voice feature of [vibrato] and variations with respect to [affection] and [cheer]. The Praat visualization for [affection] on *much* shows relatively greater pitch variability in the frequency waves realizing more [vibrato] than is evident for [cheer] on *great*.

(10)
phonology	//5… much //	//5 … / ***great*** //
VOICE AFFECT	[affection]	[cheer]
voice quality	more vibrato	less vibrato
Praat visualizations		

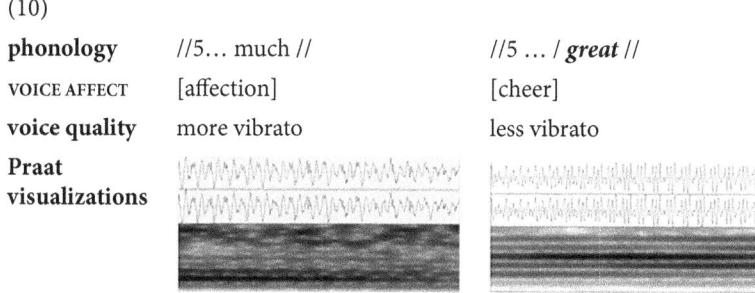

5.3.2.2 *The system of* VOICE AFFECT *as [spirit:down]*

VOICE AFFECT as [spirit:down] has opposing features of [misery] and [ennui]. The voice quality contours which realize these features are shown in Figure 5.8.

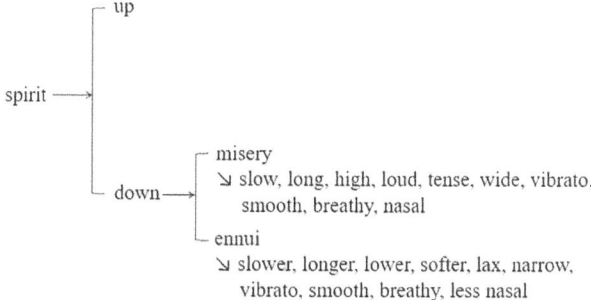

Figure 5.8 VOICE AFFECT as [spirit:down] with opposing features of [misery] from [ennui].

A number of voice quality features realizing [misery] are illustrated in example (11). The segment of speech occurs at a point in the story when Coraline sees her mum and dad trapped in the mirror world, trembling and signalling to her for help. She calls to her parents in *Mum Dad*. The Praat visualization displays a number of the voice quality features that contribute to the realization of [misery]. Those of LOUDNESS, PITCH LEVEL and DURATION are towards the upper levels of their graded systems. For both tone groups (// *mum* // and // *dad* //), the voice quality is relatively [loud] in the onset and sustain, then drops towards [soft] in the termination, in what is sometimes described as a 'sing-song' voice. In DURATION, the word *dad* is articulated over 0.65 seconds). These selections, along with that of [tense] can be interpreted as intensifying the voiced affect in (11), in this case as desperate [misery]. The intensity is visually supported by the tears in Coraline's eyes as she speaks. (Intensity in PARALINGUISTIC GRADUATION is further discussed in Section 5.6.)

(11)
phonology   //1 *mum* //1 *dad* //
VOICE AFFECT   [misery]
voice quality   relatively high, loud, wide, long, breathy, nasal
Praat visualization

Coraline's expression of [misery] in (11) is additionally realized through [wide] PITCH RANGE and is [breathy] and [nasal]. The light grey area of the spectrogram in (11) records the mixture of air with voice that produces the quality of [breathy] and audio data also reveals [vibrato] and [nasal] qualities in the speech. The voice system of TENSION contrasts [misery] and [ennui] with the former selecting [tense] and the latter very [lax].

The feature [ennui] (see Figure 5.7) is generally not considered to be a basic voiced emotion in relevant literature. This may reflect the fact that [ennui] shares certain voice qualities or reveals subtle degrees of difference with [misery] (e.g. slow, low, smooth). There is also little to distinguish [ennui] and [misery] in accompanying FACIAL AFFECT choices. Where voiced instances were compared against the baseline data of Coraline's neutral speech, a picture of subtle difference emerges in PITCH LEVEL; [misery] is measured as a little higher than Coraline's baseline data, while [ennui] shares the same maximum pitch level as her 'neutral' speech. In Coraline's expressions of [ennui] there is a more sustained loudness, while those of [misery] showed more variation in this regard. Expressions of [ennui] were also less [nasal] than [misery].

Example (12) captures an instance in which in order to kill time Coraline counts everything in her house which is blue. Her voice quality expresses [ennui] convergently with *one boring blue boy* in the segment of speech. Here the expression [ennui] contrasts with that of misery in (11) in PITCH RANGE ([narrow]) and LOUDNESS (sustained [loud]).

(12)

phonology	//1_ ^ one / *bor*ing blue / ***boy*** //
VOICE AFFECT	[ennui]
voice quality	narrow pitch range, sustained loudness
Praat visualization	

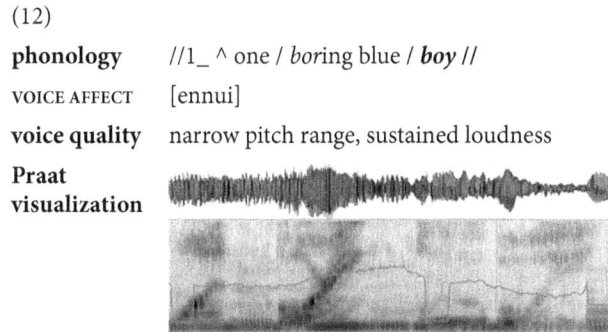

In the Praat visualization in (12), the horizontal line representing PITCH LEVEL and PITCH RANGE is mostly flattish indicating a fairly [narrow] range in the realization of [ennui], although in this instance there are 'steps up' in PITCH LEVEL on *one* and *blue*. The range in LOUDNESS is also very small in (12) compared with that in (11). Unlike the voiced expression of [misery] as [tense] in (11), [ennui] in (12) is [lax].

5.3.2.3 *Voice qualities realizing* VOICE AFFECT *as [fear], [anxiety] and [anger]*

The sets of voice qualities which differentiate VOICE AFFECT features of [fear], [anxiety] and [anger] are shown in Figure 5.9.

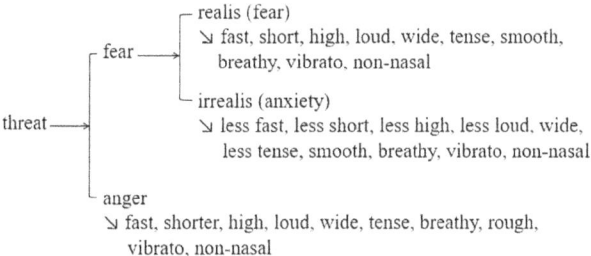

Figure 5.9 Voice qualities realizing features of [fear], [anxiety] and [anger].

Example (13) captures an instance of voiced [fear]. It occurs when Coraline suddenly hears a soft moaning voice emerging within a dark room into which she has been locked by the Other Mother. In response to this sound Coraline turns sharply to ask *Who's there?* The voice quality in this instance is relatively [fast], [high], [loud], [wide], [smooth], [breathy] and [vibrato].

(13)
phonology //1 ^ who's / ***there*** //
VOICE AFFECT [fear]
voice quality fast, high, loud, wide, smooth, breathy, vibrato and non-nasal

Praat visualization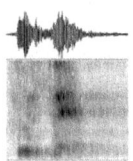

An important distinction in the AFFECT system in language (Table 5.1) is between realis (an emotional response triggered by a present or past happening) and realis (an emotional response triggered by what might happen). Where the response is irrealis positive this is glossed as 'desire' and where it is negative as 'fear'. However, in the VOICE AFFECT system [fear] is a feature (not simply a gloss) and its realizations are restricted to qualities of voice. Nonetheless the intersemiotic convergence of voiced [fear] with the language and action of the unfolding storyline in Coraline can support an interpretation of the voiced negative emotion as a response to what might happen, or in the case of (13) to whom the voices might belong.

The values of acoustic measures for [fear] and [anxiety] (i.e. time and frequency measures) are not consistently reported in psychological studies. However, a perceptual examination of the data reveals that they are most clearly differentiated in terms of LOUDNESS. The VOICE AFFECT feature [fear] compared with [anxiety] is realized through voice quality that is relatively less [loud], [fast], [short], [high] and [tense]. At the same time, the two features share qualities with respect to [smooth], [breathy], [vibrato] and [non-nasal].

The VOICE AFFECT feature of [anxiety] is illustrated in (14), which captures an incident in which Coraline comes upon the Ghost Children trapped in the dark room in the Other World. Coraline's questioning in *Who are you?* is voiced as much less [loud], more [slow], less [high] and less [tense] in comparison to [fear].

(14)

phonology	//1 ^ who/ *are* **you** //
VOICE AFFECT	[anxiety]
voice quality	less fast, less short, less high, less loud, wide, less tense, smooth, breathy, vibrato, non-nasal
Praat visualization	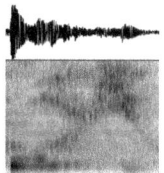

In contrast to voiced [fear], the intersemiotic convergence of voiced [anxiety] with the language and action of the unfolding storyline in Coraline can support an interpretation of the voiced emotion as a response to seeing the Ghost Children, that is, a realis happening.

There is broad agreement across acoustic and psychological studies that a voice quality contour that is relatively fast, short, high, loud, wide, vibrato, tense and rough constitutes an expression of the emotion of anger. This interpretation concurs with the realizations of [anger] in the VOICE AFFECT system in Figure 5.7. Perception analyses of the data suggest that strong [anger] in speech is also [non-nasal] and [clear]. Features of [clear] and [non-nasal] distinguish [anger] from [fear] (Figure 5.9).

An instance of voice qualities realizing extreme [anger] is illustrated in (15). At this point in the storyline, Coraline first sees the Cat, which has been chasing her. Her voiced response to this trigger is an exclamatory *urgh*. The voice quality selects for [clear], visible in the sharp and consistent darkness of the partials throughout the Praat spectrogram. It also selects for [rough] which is visible in the very dense partials spreading throughout the visualization, both in the spectrogram and waveform.

(15)

phonology	//13 *urgh* //
VOICE AFFECT	[anger]
voice quality	fast, short, high, loud, wider, vibrato, tense, rough, non-nasal, non-breathy (clear)
Praat visualization	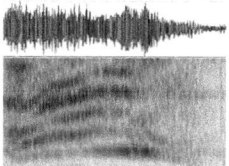

5.3.2.4 Voice qualities realizing [surprise]

The voice qualities realizing [surprise] when compared with those realizing other features in the VOICE AFFECT system (Figure 5.7) are relatively [fast] in TEMPO (articulation rate), relatively [short] in DURATION, [high] in PITCH LEVEL, [wide] in PITCH RANGE, more [loud] [vibrato] and [breathy].

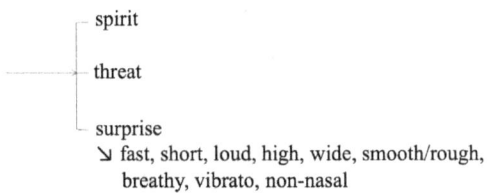

↘ fast, short, loud, high, wide, smooth/rough, breathy, vibrato, non-nasal

Figure 5.10 Voice quality realizing [surprise].

Example (16) illustrates a voiced expression of surprise in an incident in which Coraline emerges through a small door in her own apartment to find herself in a mirror apartment. The Praat visualization shows lighter partials spread relatively evenly throughout the spectrum of *haah*?, indicating a [breathy] quality.

(16)

phonology	//2 ***haah*** //
VOICE AFFECT	[surprise]
voice quality	relatively fast, short, high, loud, wide and vibrato
Praat visualizations	

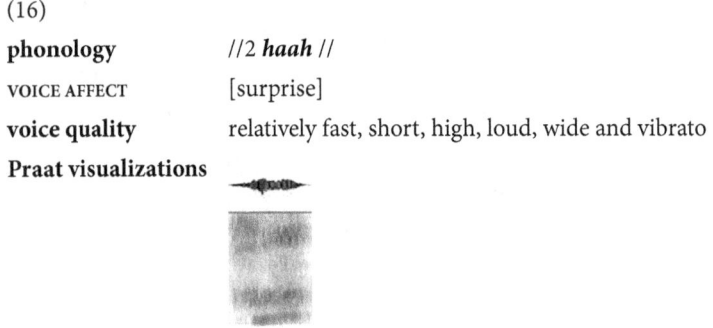

The voice quality realizing [surprise] is very [short]; it often quickly transitions to another emotion the nature of which will depend on what triggered the response of [surprise] (see discussion of example (8)). If the response to the trigger is positive, for example, [surprise] may quickly transition to a feature of [spirit:up]. In most such transitions the spectrogram shows more exaggerated voice qualities than those expressing only [surprise] or only [spirit:up], although [surprise] alone is much more [breathy] than when it transitions into [cheer]. Example (17) compares these vocal differences in relation to shifts in of FACIAL AFFECT – the first of facial [surprise], the second of [surprise] transitioning to [cheer] and the third of facial [cheer] corresponding.

(17)

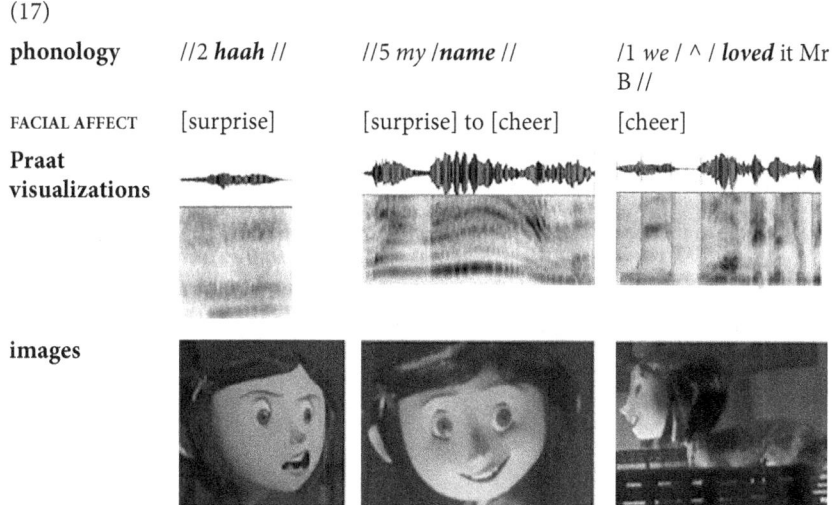

phonology	//2 **haah** //	//5 my /**name** //	/1 we / ^ / **loved** it Mr B //
FACIAL AFFECT	[surprise]	[surprise] to [cheer]	[cheer]
Praat visualizations			
images			

5.3.3 Resonance in expressions of FACIAL AFFECT and VOICE AFFECT in animation

To this point we have described two equally significant paralinguistic systems relevant to the expression of emotion: FACIAL AFFECT and VOICE AFFECT. The latter has fewer major opposing features, lacking any equivalent to the FACIAL AFFECT as [disdain]. However, it does include a number of more delicate oppositions. While animated facial expressions vary in the configurations of only three major expressive regions, that is, eyes, eyebrows and mouth, the voice offers variation across a greater range of expressive resources (vocal qualities), resulting in a wider variety of potential configurations.

If we accept that natural (i.e. not performed) vocal and facial expressions of emotion are biological in nature (Darwin, 1872; Barlow, 2002), this would suggest resonance across the systems of FACIAL AFFECT and VOICE AFFECT (in the absence of intentional divergence such as in expressions of sarcasm). In actual human interaction a reliance on FACIAL AFFECT analysis to enhance the accuracy of VOICE AFFECT analysis is a common practice. However, in film which presents an acted reality with imperfections in acting techniques, influence from background music and other sounds and distances of voice actors from a microphone, this practice cannot be entirely relied upon.

In *Coraline*, options in FACIAL AFFECT and VOCAL AFFECT are frequently found to resonate with each other, although this is not always the case. A divergence between expressions of AFFECT in voice and face is evident in (18). In convergent speech, Coraline tells her real mother about having almost fallen down a well and that she could have died. Her FACIAL AFFECT expresses [misery] as realized through raised and drawn-together eyebrows and downward lips and eyes.

(18)
phonology	//13 *I* almost / *fell* down a / ***well*** yesterday / ***mum*** //
FACIAL AFFECT	[misery]
VOICE AFFECT	[anger]
Praat visualization	
images	

We might well expect her voice to also realize [misery]. However, in this instance, her speech rate (0.472/second) and maximum pitch level (254 Hz) are the same as for her neutral utterances, and her maximum intensity (74 dB) is even louder than high-level [cheer]. There is no evidence of [breathy] and [nasal] qualities in her voice, and the voice quality on *well* is slightly [rough]. Her speech is more akin to mild [anger] than [misery]. Where such disjunction is not readily interpreted as meaningful it may simply be attributed to a slip in the production of animated film.

5.3.4 Negotiating bonds in paralanguage

From a systemic functional perspective the co-instantiation of an evaluative meaning with an ideational one constitutes a kind of 'coupling', one that can be applied to expressions of affect with accompanying ideational triggers. When such couplings are tendered in interaction with others and reciprocated they are said to constitute bonds, and it is through the sharing of multiple bonds that we build affiliating communities (Knight, 2013; Zappavigna, 2018, 2019). Here we are concerned with how selected features of FACIAL AFFECT and VOICE AFFECT couple with their ideational triggers in the negotiation of bonds in the service of affiliation. Figure 5.11 presents options and realizations in a system of BONDING adapted from Zappavigna (2018, 2019) with realizations for PARALINGUISTIC AFFECT.

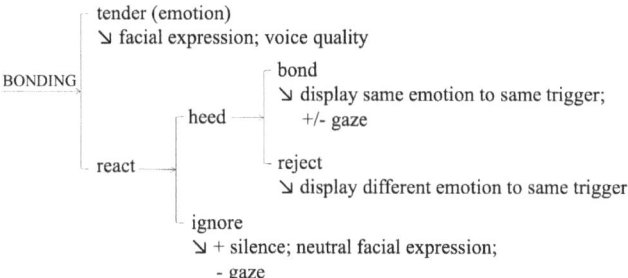

Figure 5.11 The system of BONDING.

In the system of BONDING in Figure 5.11 the first opposing features are [tender], that is, to put forward or table a coupling of ideational trigger and PARALINGUISTIC AFFECT, and [react], that is, to respond to the tendered coupling. If [react] is selected, then the opposing features are [heed] or [ignore]. The feature [heed: bond] is realized through the paralinguistic display of the same emotion to the same trigger (e.g. trigger(x) plus [positive happiness]). The feature [heed: reject] is realized through a display of a different emotion to the same trigger (e.g. trigger(x) plus [negative happiness]). If [ignore] is selected, realization strategies can include silence, neutral facial expression or absence of gaze.

Example (19) shows a silent response to a tendered coupling. Coraline is trapped in a chamber by the Other Mother. She is kicking furiously at a wall in an attempt to escape when she hears a low moan. It comes from the Ghost Children, who have been similarly trapped. The interaction unfolds as follows:

(19)
Coraline (gasping): //1 ^ Who's / ***there***
Ghost children: //5 *Hush* and / ***shush***
 //5 ^ For the /*Beldam* / *might* be / ***lis***tening
Coraline: //2 *You -* / ^ you / *mean* the / *Other* / ***Mot****her* //
Ghost children: [Silence]

Facial affect and voice affect converge with spoken language as shown in (19). Convergent with Coraline's turn – //2 *You –* / ^ you / *mean* the / *Other* /

*Moth*er // – she tenders a coupling of Other Mother (as trigger) plus emotion as [threat: fear] realized through both FACIAL AFFECT and VOICE AFFECT. The Ghost Children respond to this coupling with the option [react: ignore] realized through a long silence (7.8 seconds) and through a withdrawal into the dark. The response of [react: ignore] aligns with the unfolding plot of the story; this is the first time Coraline has met the Ghost Children, and their reaction to ignore the tendered coupling suggests extreme wariness on their part.

(20)

phonology	Coraline: //2 *You* – / ^ you / *mean* the / *Other* / **Moth**er //	silence and disappearance of the ghost children
FACIAL AFFECT	[fear]	
VOICE AFFECT	[fear]	
BONDING	Coraline tenders coupling of Other Mother + [fear]	ghost children ignore Coraline's coupling
Praat visualization		
images		

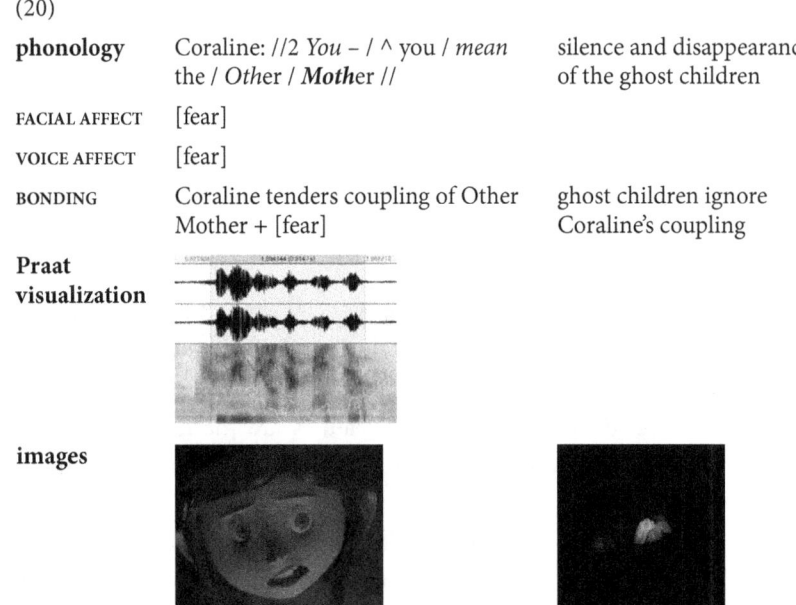

In another instance in (21), [heed: bond] is selected from the BONDING system (Figure 5.11). Coraline and her friend Wybie are watching a mouse circus. Coraline tenders a coupling of mouse circus plus high level [spirit:up]. This is realized through facial expression, gaze, voice quality and the intonation contours of a rise-fall tone 5 and a rising tone 2. (Gaze is addressed in Section 5.4.2 on PARALINGUISTIC ORIENTATION.) Wybie's response is one of [heed: bond] realized through reciprocating options in FACIAL AFFECT and PARALINGUISTIC ORIENTATION.

(21)

character		Coraline	Wybie
trigger		mouse circus	mouse circus
MOVES	phonology	//5 ^ It's / **won**derful //2 **Wy**bie //	
	paralanguage	gaze (+); smiling face; cheerful voice	smiling face
BONDING		[tender]	[heed: bond]
interpersonal meaning		FACIAL AFFECT [cheer] VOICE AFFECT [cheer] PARALINGUISTIC ORIENTATION [involved] (via gaze)	FACIAL AFFECT [cheer] PARALINGUISTIC ORIENTATION [involved] (via gaze)
images			

5.3.5 The system of PARALINGUISTIC ENGAGEMENT

The system of ENGAGEMENT in language models options in negotiating dialogic space for alternative viewpoints or 'voices' (Martin and White, 2005). An outline of the linguistic system of ENGAGEMENT is shown in Figure 5.12. The primary opposing features are [monogloss] in which other voices are ignored, and [heterogloss] in which other voices are implicitly or explicitly allowed into the discourse. If [heterogloss] is selected, the opposing features are [heterogloss: expansion], allowing space for other voices, or [heterogloss: contraction], closing down space for other voices. These features offer a rich system for dialogistic positioning (for detailed discussion, see Martin and White, 2005). The relevant section of Figure 5.1 is repeated here as Figure 5.12.

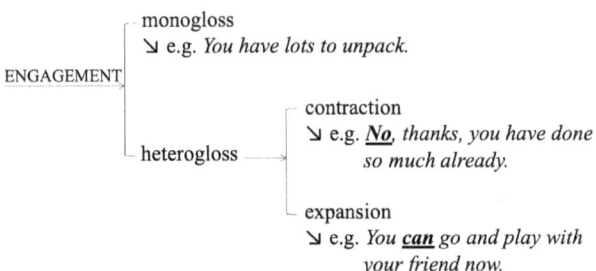

Figure 5.12 The system of ENGAGEMENT in language.

The kinds of realization strategies in Figure 5.12 would be reflective of what Kendon (2004: 158-9) refers to as 'pragmatic' gestures with a 'modal function' of hypothesizing versus asserting. From a social semiotic approach, Hood (2011) considers how embodied paralanguage resonates with linguistic ENGAGEMENT resources (see Figure 5.13). For example, a prone (palm down) hand gesture realizes [contraction] and functions to close down space for the negotiation of propositions or proposals. A supine (palm up) hand gesture realizes [expansion] and functions to open up space for negotiation. Hao and Hood (2019) and Hood and Zhang (2020) also discuss an oscillating movement of the hand as softening FOCUS in relation to the fulfilment or actualization of a propositional figure, while additionally realizing [heteroglossic: expansion]. Heteroglossic [expansion] and [contraction] are frequently realized through the positioning of the hands but can also be expressed through a more general open or closed posture of the body torso or the positioning of the head. An open face (tilted upwards) realizing [expansion] will also display relaxed rather than compressed facial muscles.

Instances of gesture and posture realizing PARALINGUISTIC ENGAGEMENT options are shown in (22).

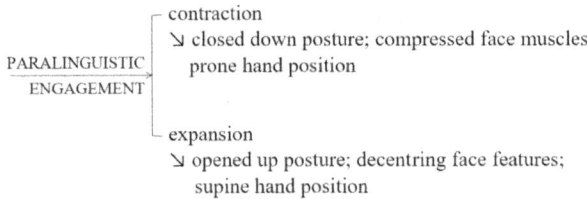

Figure 5.13 The system of PARALINGUISTIC ENGAGEMENT.

(22)

	PARALINGUISTIC ENGAGEMENT					
	[contraction]		[expansion]			
phono-logy	//4 *oh* / *no* thanks //1 ^ *ah* you - / *you've* done / *so* much al- / *read*y //	//13 be / **strong** / **Cor**aline //	//4+ ***dad*** //5 ^ I'm / *not* / *five* any-/ *more* //	//1 ^ it was / *all* I could / *think* of //	//2 *don't* be- / ***lieve*** me	//2 ***I*** didn't / *break* it //
para-language	prone hands	compressed face	prone head; closed body	supine right hand	open face; decentred head	supine head and hands; open body
images						

5.3.6 The system of PARALINGUISTIC GRADUATION

PARALINGUISTIC GRADUATION in expressions of FACIAL AFFECT and VOCAL AFFECT is discussed earlier as limited to the adjustment FORCE as intensity only. Other parts of the body can cooperate with language in adjusting both FORCE and FOCUS (Hao and Hood, 2019; Hood and Zhang, 2020). The system of PARALINGUISTIC GRADUATION (body) (Hood and Zhang, 2020) is shown in Figure 5.14.

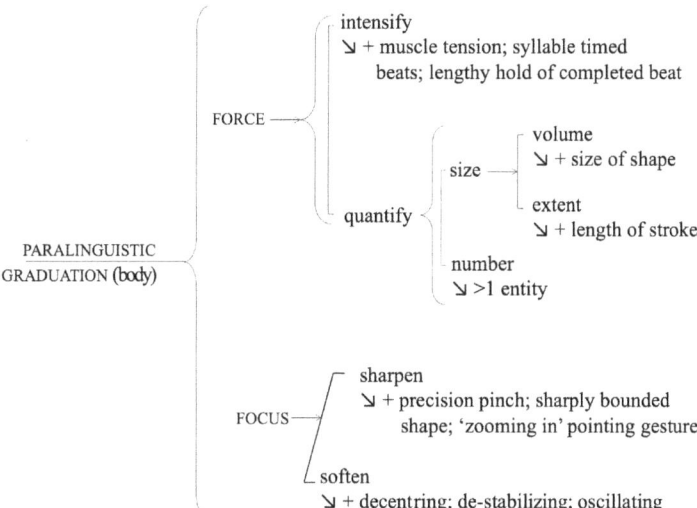

Figure 5.14 The system of PARALINGUISTIC (body) GRADUATION (Hood and Zhang, 2020).

Embodied paralanguage can adjust the FORCE of verbally expressed meanings through options of [intensify] and [quantify]. The feature [intensify] can be realized in a number of ways: through increased muscle tension in a hand-beat; in a very rapid frequency of such beats (syncing with syllable-timed rhythm in the prosodic phonology of English – see Chapter 6); or in the holding of the completed position of a beat for an extended time. FORCE as [quantify] can be expressed through adjusting [size] or [number] of phenomena (the latter realized through repetitive expressions of paralinguistic entities; see Hood and Zhang, 2020). The feature [size: volume] is realized through qualities of a depicted paralinguistic entity (see Chapter 4), and [size: extent] is realized through the length of a stroke extended horizontally or vertically from the body.

In (23), Coraline is arguing with her mother about why she has locked a tiny door. Convergent with *dreams aren't dangerous*, her left hand depicts the proposition (*dreams aren't dangerous*) as a semiotic entity (see Chapter 4) at the same time as her left arm is extended out front of her body. The expression realizes PARALINGUISTIC FORCE as [quantify:size:extent]. In this instance FORCE is expressed in the embodied paralanguage but not in convergent spoken language.

(23)

phonology	Coraline:	//1 ^ then / *why* did you lock the / ***door***
	Mother:	//5 ***oh*** I
	Coraline:	//1 ***fou****nd* some / ***rat*** crap and
		//1 ^ / I thought you'd / *feel* / ^ / ***saf***er
		//53 ^ they're / ***jump***ing mice / ***mum*** and the
		//1 *dreams* / *aren't* / ***dang***erous //
paralanguage	left arm extended	
PARALINGUISTIC GRADUATION **(body)**	FORCE [quantify:size:extent]	
image		

In (24), PARALINGUISTIC FOCUS as [sharpen] is expressed in the narrowly targeted index-finger point that zooms in towards the Other Mother. This expression of sharpened FOCUS functions to identify the target (Other Mother) in a highly specifying manner (see Chapter 6). This together with the expression of negative judgement in the spoken language in *stole* serves to amplify the expression of [disdain] in FACIAL AFFECT.[4]

(24)
phonology   //1+ ^ you / *stole* them //
paralanguage   more stretched pointing
PARALINGUISTIC GRADUATION   FOCUS [sharpen]
(body)
image

As presented in Hao and Hood (2019), embodied expressions of FOCUS as [sharpen] can also be realized through a 'pinch' gesture in which the tips of the thumb and fingers are pressed tightly together. Embodied FOCUS as [soften] is realized through what the authors refer to as decentring or destabilizing expressions, for example, when the head and shoulders tip to one side in a shrug or in an oscillating hand. For further elaboration of embodied PARALINGUISTIC GRADUATION, see Hood and Zhang (2020).

5.4 Social relations realized through body movement/positioning, gaze and voice quality

Depictions of human interaction have been analysed from a social semiotic perspective in Kress and van Leeuwen's (2006) study of images and by Painter et al. (2013) with a specific focus is on images in children's picture books. Their contributions have been foundational to the systems presented in this section. Three paralinguistic systems from Painter et al. (2013) relevant to our data are PROXIMITY (related to Kress and van Leeuwen's SOCIAL DISTANCE), ORIENTATION (related to Kress and van Leeuwen's INVOLVEMENT) and POWER.

5.4.1 The system of PARALINGUISTIC PROXIMITY

Kress and van Leeuwen's system of SOCIAL DISTANCE (2006) relates to the constructed social relation between viewer and depicted person and is realized through shot size (e.g. close-up versus long shot). Painter et al. (2013) adapt this notion of relative distance to refer to the constructed social relation between depicted characters within images as PROXIMITY. Opposing features in the system of PARALINGUISTIC PROXIMITY are: [personal], realized through close body positioning of characters vis-à-vis one another; [social] as realized through greater separation of the characters within a picture frame; and [impersonal] through distanced separation of the characters. These features are presented along a cline of PARALINGUISTIC PROXIMITY in Figure 5.15.

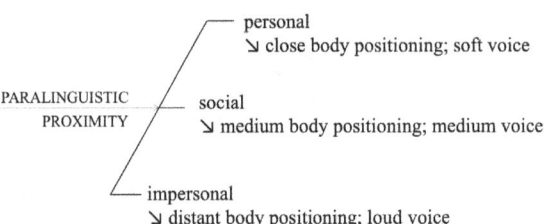

Figure 5.15 The system of PARALINGUISTIC PROXIMITY.

In *Coraline*, PARALINGUISTIC PROXIMITY resources contribute to viewers' interpretations of the relations between characters. Example (24) occurs at the beginning of one event sequence. At first the Other Mother moves very close to Coraline, expressing PARALINGUISTIC PROXIMITY as [personal] (see image 1). As Coraline, the Other Mother and the Other Father sit down at a table, the Other Mother reveals that she wants to sew buttons on Coraline's eyes. Coraline's immediate response is to stand and distance herself from the Other Mother with the excuse that she wants to go to sleep. She moves even further away when the Other Mother offers to tuck her into bed, moving to PARALINGUISTIC PROXIMITY as [impersonal] (see image 2).

(25)

phonology	Ø speech	//4 ^ I'd be / *happy* to tuck you / *in* //
PARALINGUISTIC PROXIMITY	[personal]	[impersonal]
images		

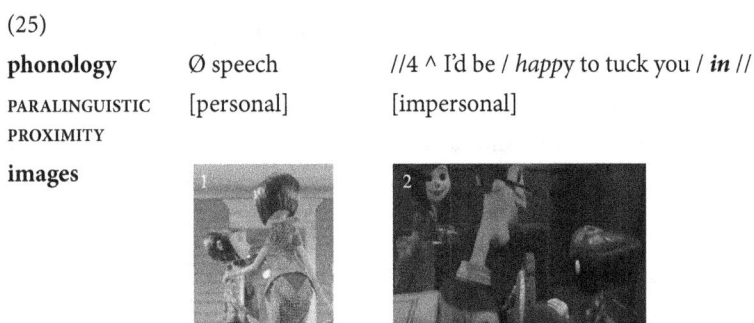

Van Leeuwen (1999) discusses the potential of relative loudness of voice to also signify degrees of social distance; whispering, for example, signalling intimacy, a soft voice signifying personal matters or confidentiality and a loud voice when projected to a large audience as signifying an impersonal relationship. This system is not further explored in instances from *Coraline*. We make the point, however, that given that [loudness] is also a feature of the VOICE AFFECT system where it functions to distinguish kinds of voiced emotion, interpreting the interpersonal meaning of loudness will be reliant on a process of abduction from meanings in the multimodal co-text.

5.4.2 The system of PARALINGUISTIC ORIENTATION

Analogizing from Kress and van Leeuwen's account of viewer/depiction relations referred to as INVOLVEMENT, Painter et al. (2013) propose a system of body ORIENTATION as an additional means for interpreting relations between depicted characters in images. Figure 5.16 shows options in a system of PARALINGUISTIC ORIENTATION and how they are relatively positioned as degrees of involvement. Greater or lesser involvement is realized through the horizontal angle between the characters and the presence or absence of accompanying gaze. At one end the features [involved] indicates maximum involvement though face-to-face orientation accompanied by mutual gaze. At the other end of the continuum there is an absence of involvement; the interlocutors share no gaze and have a widely oblique or even back-to-back orientation in relation to each other. Between these endpoints, body (and head) angle varies and involvement with the other may be enhanced by direct gaze or weakened by a lack of it. An oblique angle to another realizes a [less involved] or relatively detached orientation, while face-to-back indicates [involvement sought] or a desire to engage and back-to-back indicates [uninvolved] or thorough disengagement. A side-by-side orientation on the other hand realizes a solidarity relation but yet [less involved]. Note that the head and the body can be angled relatively independently so there are more points on the continuum than actually specified here.

In (26) three shifts in PARALINGUISTIC ORIENTATION are identified as an event unfolds; each is related to Coraline's apparent neglect by her parents. Dad is working on his computer as Coraline enters his office. He has his back to her and does not change this postural orientation even as he hears her greeting. Image 1 displays the feature [uninvolved] on Dad's part and [involvement sought] on Coraline's. Dad's involvement changes from [uninvolved] to [partial involvement] in image 2. He still has his back to her but now turns his head to look at the doll that Coraline is holding (visible in first image). In image 3 he turns 180 degrees to be face to face with Coraline. Holding a notebook he tells her to go away and write down everything that is blue in colour in the house,

```
                          ┌── involved
                          │    ↘ face-to-face;
                          │      + gaze
                          │
                          ├── less involved
                          │    ↘ oblique orientation
                          │
PARALINGUISTIC ───────────┼── solidarity
ORIENTATION               │    ↘ side-by-side
                          │
                          ├── involvement sought
                          │    ↘ front-to-back orientation
                          │
                          └── uninvolved
                               ↘ back-to-back orientation;
                                 - gaze
```

Figure 5.16 The system of PARALINGUISTIC ORIENTATION.

in other words to leave him alone. At this point he is also sharing her gaze so displaying [full involvement] in the system of ORIENTATION.

(26)

phonology	Coraline: //3 ^ Hey / **Dad** //4 ^ / ^ how's the /**writ**ing going //	Dad: //3 ^ he- / *llo* Cora- / *line* //2 and / Coraline / *doll* //	Dad: //1 *list* / everything that's / ***blue*** just //1 *let* me / **work** //
PARALINGUISTIC ORIENTATION	[involvement sought]	[less involved]	[involved]
images	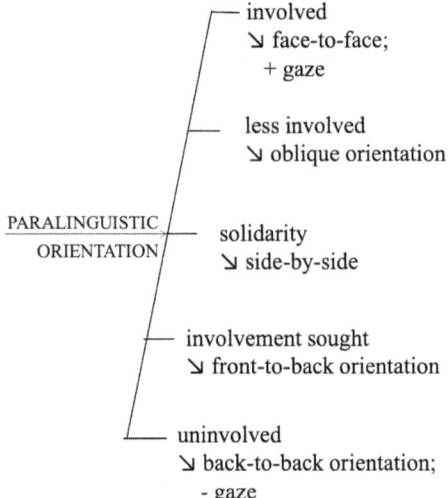		

5.4.3 The system of PARALINGUISTIC POWER

Social relations of relative POWER in images relate to the vertical angle of viewing in Kress and van Leeuwen (2006). In Painter et al. (2013) it relates to the vertical positioning of one character's body in relation to another. In van Leeuwen (1999), POWER is also discussed as an aspect of interpersonal meaning afforded by the

Interpersonal Paralanguage 151

voice; the higher in pitch and the louder the voice is, the more dominant the speaker. The system of PARALINGUISTIC POWER in Figure 5.17 opposes features of equal and unequal on a cline and realized through the vertical positioning of bodies in relation to each other. The features of relative pitch and loudness are not identified as realizations in Figure 5.17.

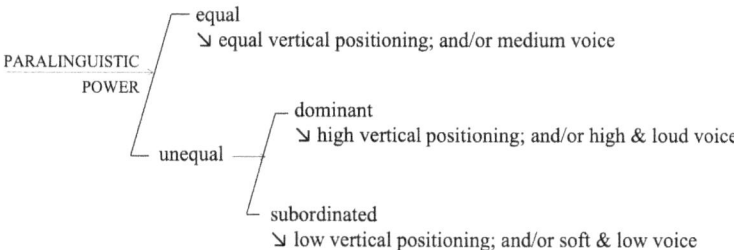

Figure 5.17 The system of PARALINGUISTIC POWER.

In *Coraline*, shifts in the relative vertical positioning of characters in the course of the storyline reveal shifts in relations of PARALINGUISTIC POWER. This is illustrated in (27). At the beginning of the complication stage of the film's narrative, both Other Parents are trying to convince Coraline that the Other Family is happy, as in image 1. Both Other Parents are positioned as [equal] to one another on the vertical plane of PARALINGUISTIC POWER and as [unequal] and [dominant] in relation to Coraline, whom they are looking down upon. Conversely Coraline's is positioned as [unequal: subordinated] as she looks up to them. Towards the latter part of the storyline the Other Mother discards her disguise to reveal her true nature. In image 2, her body positioning remains high on the vertical plane and so [dominant] with respect to Coraline, but now the vertical positioning of the Other Father is lowered to that of Coraline. Both he and Coraline are now depicted as [unequal: subordinated] to the Other Mother.

(27)

PARALINGUISTIC POWER	[equal] (parent to parent); [unequal] (parents to Coraline)	[unequal] (Other Mother to Other Father and Coraline)
images		

5.5 Intrasemiosis: The orchestration of interpersonal paralinguistic resources

To this point we have explored the interpersonal meaning potential of multiple semiotic resources of the body as they relate to language sonovergently and semovergently. We now consider how these paralinguistic resources can interact with each other, that is, intrasemiotically, to realize interpersonal meaning in the flow of multimodal text. To foreground intrasemiosis we focus on one event from *Coraline* that unfolds without the expression of spoken language. The event features an interaction between Coraline and the Cat. Immediately prior to the action played out in example (28), Coraline had been exploring the neighbourhood when a rock fell onto her path from a cliff above. She looked up but saw no one. Feeling a little concerned she called out but received no response. Reacting angrily, she threw the rock back up the cliff and immediately heard a loud piercing sound in response. The story continues as set out in example (28). The moves of each character are described as the incident unfolds.

In (28), the interpersonal interaction between Coraline and the Cat is set out in a sequence of numbered moves constructed by animators though changes in the characters' actions and emotions. At the beginning of the instance, the Cat's ear-piercing cry in move 1 triggers a response from Coraline in move 2 that realizes FACIAL AFFECT as [fear]. The expression of [fear] is maintained in move 4 and intensified with increased muscle tension in the face in moves 5 and 9. At the same time a relation of [unequal: dominant] POWER is realized though the Cat's relatively high vertical body positioning in relation to Coraline's in move 6. The Cat's very loud voice quality (an intensity of 80.2 dB) in move 7, intensifies the realization of [anger] in VOICE AFFECT. Coraline's emotional reactions up to and including move 8 are in response to aural triggers. The sight of the Cat in move 9 is a visual trigger for a sequence of emotion responses in which FACIAL AFFECT expresses [fear], then [surprise], then [anger] in moves 9, 10 and 11. The Cat's response to Coraline's expression of [anger] is to change his body position in move 11 from an upright higher vertical positioning realizing POWER as [unequal: dominant] to a lowered body position realizing [unequal: subordinated].

The possibility of different paralinguistic resources being instantiated simultaneously allows us to infer meanings not necessarily interpretable from an expression in a single paralinguistic mode. For example, FACIAL AFFECT has no distinct option for the expression of desire. However, when raised eyebrows and wide-opened eyes (realizing FACIAL AFFECT as [surprise]) are

Interpersonal Paralanguage 153

(28)

moves #	character	action & sound	semiosis (paralanguage)	interpersonal meaning	images
1	Cat	'meow'	voice quality: slow, long, high, loud, tense, wide, vibrato, smooth, breathy, nasal	VOICE AFFECT [misery]	
2	Coraline			FACIAL AFFECT [fear]	
3	Coraline	steps backwards, gasps		PARALINGUISTIC PROXIMITY [less social]	
4	Coraline	runs away quickly, looking back every now and again		FACIAL AFFECT [fear]; PARALINGUISTIC PROXIMITY [impersonal]	
5	Coraline	stops at the secret well to catch her breath and looks around for her pursuer. Gasps.		FACIAL AFFECT [fear]; +FORCE	

154 Modelling Paralanguage

#	Character	Action/Utterance		Voice quality	Category
6	Cat	chases and catches up with her, stands right at her back.			POWER [dominant]; PARALINGUISTIC ORIENTATION [involvement sought] (front-to-back)
7	Cat	'meow'		voice quality: very fast, short, high, very loud, wide, tense, breathy, rough, vibrato, non-nasal.	VOICE AFFECT [anger]
8	Coraline	'argh'		voice quality: fast, short, high, loud, wide, tense; smooth, breathy, vibrator, non-nasal	VOICE AFFECT [fear]
9	Coraline	turns around and sees Cat			FACIAL AFFECT [fear]; +FORCE; PARALINGUISTIC ORIENTATION [less involved] (oblique orientation)

10 Coraline

FACIAL AFFECT
[surprise]
ORIENTATION [involved]
(face-to-face;+gaze)

FACIAL AFFECT
[anger]
ORIENTATION [involved]
(face-to-face;+gaze)

PARALINGUISTIC POWER
[subordinated]
ORIENTATION [involved]
(face-to-face;+gaze)

11 Cat   'grr'   voice quality:
                   low and soft

expressed convergently with PARALINGUISTIC PROXIMITY as [personal] and PARALINGUISTIC ORIENTATION AS [involved], the emotion of desire is strongly invoked. Two such instances are described in (29).

(29)

paralanguage	raised brows, eyes wide-open (FACIAL AFFECT [surprise]); direct gaze (PARALINGUISTIC ORIENTATION [involved]); body slightly leaning forward (PARALINGUISTIC PROXIMITY [social])	raised brows, eyes wide-open (FACIAL AFFECT [surprise]); direct gaze (PARALINGUISTIC ORIENTATION [involved]); body leaning forward (PARALINGUISTIC PROXIMITY [personal])
intrasemiotic AFFECT **images**	invoked desire 	invoked stronger desire 

5.6 Intersemiosis: The interplay between language and multiple paralinguistic systems in the enactment of interpersonal meaning

In a final section, a brief instance from *Coraline* highlights the potential complexity of the intersemiotic relations that cooperate in the dynamic enactment of interpersonal meanings. In Coraline's first encounter with Wybie, a boy of her own age from the same neighbourhood, he accuses her of being a *water witch* to which she responds: //3 ^ and if / *I'm* a / **wat**er / witch //1 ^ then / *where's* the secret / **well** //. The focus in (30) is on the second tone group of this utterance, that is, //1 ^ then / *where's* the secret / **well** //. Corresponding Praat visualization and four consecutive convergent images are shown. The intersemiotic complexity is explored through a number of steps, taking into account interpersonal sonovergence and semovergence.

(30)

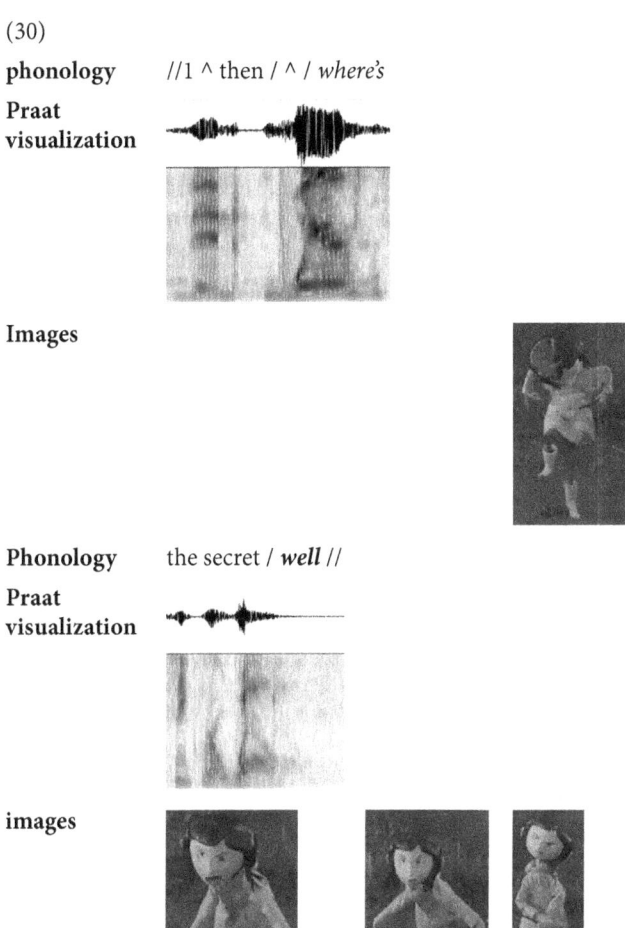

The first image in (30) captures Coraline forcefully stomping her right foot and punching down with her arms and clenched hands in an expression of PARALINGUISTIC AFFECT – [anger] with [strong] FORCE. The voice quality on *where* realizes VOICE AFFECT as [anger] – through high intensity, tension and roughness (shown as the grey area in the spectrogram in (30)). Coraline's face is not visible in the first image; but a prosody of FACIAL AFFECT [anger] is additionally realized more or less intensively in the remaining three images – as the eyebrows are drawn down and together. These expressions of PARALINGUISTIC FORCE in realizations of [anger] resonate with and amplify one another. In the spoken language of this tone group there is apparently no resonant inscribed or invoked linguistic AFFECT. However, before we assume a divergent[5] semovergent relation, there is more to be considered in the verbal and imagic co-text.

The spoken language in (30) configures a question through a wh-interrogative on a falling tone 1 (signalling 'certainty'). Taken in conjunction with the PARALINGUISTIC expressions [anger], this discourse move (*then where's the secret well*) can be interpreted as a rhetorical question, one that challenges Wybie's judgemental accusation that she is a *water witch*. From the perspective of affiliation and the negotiation of bonds (Section 5.3.4), Coraline is forcefully rejecting the coupling proposed by Wybie.

A final analytical step involves an exploration of PARALINGUISTIC ENGAGEMENT and features of [heteroglossic:contraction] and [heteroglossic:expansion]. Relevant here are shifts in body posture in the sequence of four images. In the first image (the angry stomp), the upper body and head are in a prone (closed) position. The torso remains prone in the second and third images, at the same time as the head/face is progressively raised from prone to neutral in the final image. These realizations of [contraction] are accompanied in the second and third images with realizations of [heteroglossic:expansion] – as Coraline moves her arms and hands to an open supine position by her sides, and in addition raises her eyes in the third image.

In the final image in (30), Coraline's face continues to express [anger]. Although she stands upright, her posture is prone in certain respects – her shoulders are rounded, her arms are close to her body and her hands are clasped, closing off her torso (enacting [contraction]). At the same time, however, her head and face are decentred – an expression of [heteroglossic:expansion] (Hao and Hood, 2019).

The apparently disjunctive concatenation of options in PARALINGUISTIC ENGAGEMENT needs to be interpreted in relation to the attendant semovergence. From the perspective of affiliation, as discussed earlier, the rhetorical question in the spoken text functions as a firm rejection of Wybie's tendered coupling; it is this discourse move that resonates with the prone features of Coraline's posture – those realizing [contraction]. At the same time the supine features of her posture – those realizing [expansion] – open up space for ongoing interaction and the negotiation of other potential bonds. The semiotic resources of the body negotiate relations on two fronts simultaneously – retrospective [contraction] and [prospective expansion].

This short exercise in exploring the intersemiotic enactment of interpersonal meanings in language and paralanguage points to just some of the challenges to be faced in understanding how system choices cooperate both within and between modalities – in the context of animated film. There is still much work to be done in this regard, but we hope that the emerging work on system networks in paralanguage offers a significant beginning.

5.7 Conclusion: A multimodal model of interpersonal meaning in paralanguage

Researchers from both social semiotics and linguistics (Thibault, 2004; Feng and O'Halloran, 2013; Mondada, 2016; Lim, 2019) have recently raised the challenge of developing a holistic approach to the study of social interaction. They argue persuasively that it is not sufficient to single out just one or two semiotic modes for examination (e.g. language and facial expression or language and gesture) if we are to understand the meaning of social interactions. The intention in this chapter is to respond to the challenge by providing a systemic functional social semiotic account of a number of paralinguistic systems as a framework for studying the orchestration of multiple semiotic modes in interaction in the expression of interpersonal meaning and the enactment of social relations in the context of animated film. We look forward to reports of research adapting our framework to the study of interpersonal relations in other modalities of interaction, in film, theatre, clinical, educational and forensic contexts, casual conversation and beyond, and additionally to its application in educational contexts. In relation to the latter, as an exemplary animation of its kind, *Coraline* offers a significant educational resource. Insights into the interpersonal meaning potential of facial expression, tone of voice and body positioning can all support student awareness of the construction of character and inter-character relations in what Ngo (2018) refers to as 'paralinguistic literacy', and more broadly to meeting educational goals for visual and multimodal literacy now seen as vital dimensions of the curriculum (e.g. Finnish National Board of Studies, 2016; the Australian curriculum, ACARA, 2019; British Colombia Government, 2019; Singapore Ministry of Education, 2019).

6

Textual convergence: Approaching paralanguage from the perspective of information flow

6.1 Introduction

This chapter adopts a textual perspective on embodied meaning-making. It deals with the way paralanguage cooperates with spoken language in the management of information flow – how it keeps track of entities in discourse and how it composes waves of ideational and interpersonal meaning (Martin, 1992; Martin and Rose, [2003] 2007). Two linguistic discourse semantic systems are involved: IDENTIFICATION and PERIODICITY. IDENTIFICATION has to do with the resources for introducing and tracking entities. PERIODICITY, as the term implies, has to do with resources for structuring waves of information in discourse. The discourse semantic systems are introduced in turn, together with the related paralinguistic systems that model the potential for convergence with language, those of PARALINGUISTIC DEIXIS and PARALINGUISTIC PERIODICITY. Options in the paralinguistic systems are illustrated with data from videos of face-to-face lectures from the disciplinary fields of biochemistry, health science, cultural studies and law and from academic writing classes. The study points to the significance of intermodality in pedagogic contexts – where coordinated systems support students in keeping track of information and interpreting its relative prominence, pulse by pulse, as knowledge accumulates in teaching/learning encounters.

6.2 PARALINGUISTIC DEIXIS and IDENTIFICATION: Introducing and tracking people, things and places in discourse

The management of information flow in discourse is supported by the system of textual semovergence we refer to as PARALINGUISTIC DEIXIS. Here the focus is on how paralanguage supports the introduction of people, things and places into texts and keeps track of them once there (Martin, 1992: 95). This section begins with a brief overview of the linguistic system of IDENTIFICATION. We then introduce PARALINGUISTIC DEIXIS with reference to data from live lectures. Intersemiotic convergence is explored in relation to semantically related choices from the respective linguistic and paralinguistic system networks.

6.2.1 IDENTIFICATION in language: How English is structured to keep track of people, things and places

The IDENTIFICATION system in English discourse semantics draws a basic distinction between presenting reference, which introduces entities in discourse, and presuming reference, which tracks them once there. An extract of speech from a cultural studies lecture illustrates the contrast and the linguistic resources deployed. The lecturer (L) is engaging students (St) in a discussion of 'orientalism' as they view an 'orientalist' image projected onto a screen. Signals of presenting reference are underlined in (1).

> (1)
> L: Now, <u>what</u> are <u>some</u> of the key things going on in this rather fabulous image here? <u>What</u> kind of sense does it make? <u>What</u> feeling do you have when you look at <u>an</u> image like that? Is it an upsetting image? Is it a reassuring image?[1] Okay, you're wearing <u>a</u> stripy shirt. Explain this image to me. Even tell me <u>what</u>'s going on in it.
> St: It's a harem.
> L: The famous harem. <u>What</u> was that? <u>Anyone</u> got <u>an</u> idea? (…) Up the back, you're wearing <u>a</u> beautiful green scarf. <u>What</u>'s the harem, or the harem, however you wish to pronounce it?

The types of entities (Hao, 2020a) introduced by presenting reference include people (<u>anyone</u>), concrete thing entities (<u>a</u> stripy shirt, <u>a</u> beautiful green scarf) and semiotic entities (<u>some</u> of the key things, <u>what</u> kind of sense, <u>what</u> feeling, <u>an</u> idea). The linguistic resources deployed include non-specific determiners (e.g. *a*, *an, some*), an indefinite nominal group (*anyone*) and several instances of a 'wh' entity (*what*).

Presuming reference signals to a reader/listener that an entity is assumed to be recoverable either from commonly shared knowledge, from the co-text or from the material situational setting. This brings a different set of linguistic resources into play, formatted in bold in (1') – specific determiners (e.g. *the*, *this*), a presuming adverb (e.g. *here*) and pronouns (e.g. *it, you*).

(1')

L: Now, what are some of **the** key things going on in **this** rather fabulous image **here**? What kind of sense does **it** make? What feeling do **you** have when **you** look at an image like **that**? Is **it** an upsetting image? Is **it** a reassuring image? Okay, **you**'re wearing a stripy shirt. Explain **this** image to **me**. Even tell **me** what's going on in it.

St: **It**'s a harem.

L: **The** famous harem. What was **that**? Anyone got an idea? (…) Up **the** back, **you**'re wearing a beautiful green scarf. What's **the** harem, or **the** harem, however **you** wish to pronounce **it**.

Proper names also function as presuming reference (although not instanced in 1'). When the identity of an entity is presumed there are various strategies for recovering the information presumed – as outlined in Figure 6.1.

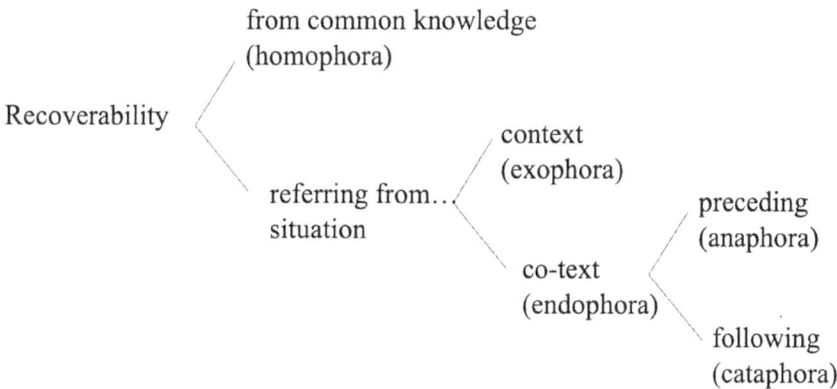

Figure 6.1 Taxonomy of recoverability strategies triggered by presuming reference (adapted from Martin and Rose, [2003] 2007: 183).

Instances of kinds of recoverability strategies from Figure 6.1 are exemplified here:

- Homophora identifies a referent as recoverable from assumed shared knowledge, as in the lecturer's reference to <u>the</u> famous harem.
- Exophora indicates recoverability from outside of the text, but in the immediate shared sensible material environment. In <u>this</u> rather fabulous image <u>here</u>, the spoken discourse 'points' to a visible entity *this* and a location in the shared space *here*.
- Endophora indicates recoverability from inside the text (i.e. from the co-text). It requires the listener (or reader) to recover the identified entity by referring either to preceding text (anaphora) or following text (catophora). A canonical example of anaphora from the preceding text would be where a speaker first presented an entity, as in *what's <u>a</u> harem*, and then followed it up with presuming reference, as in *what were some of <u>its</u> characteristics?*.

6.2.2 PARALINGUISTIC DEIXIS: How the body functions to keep track of people, things and places

Before introducing the system network for PARALINGUISTIC DEIXIS, some issues discussed in the wider gesture literature provide useful contextualization. One concern has to do with the body parts which can participate in the identification of phenomena. Reference is often made of cultural variations in what is used as a pointing gesture – contrasting, for example, the index finger in Western cultures (e.g. McNeill, 2000: 6–7) with pointing with the lips in Lao (Enfield, 2001). But all cultures employ a range of embodied pointing expressions. McNeill (2016: 16) notes that 'all kinds of gestures can be used to indicate a locus'. In our terms, the embodied identification of phenomena can be expressed in multiple ways. Fundamental to the expression of identification is the formation of a vector that indicates some direction for an observer's eye to follow. While the physiology of hands and fingers readily supports this function, the head, chin, eyes, lips or even an elbow or foot (Kendon, 2004: 199) can be called into action where contextually useful or culturally appropriate.

Reference is also made to the potential for a deictic gesture to be expressed simultaneously with gestural realizations from other paralinguistic systems. Calbris (2011: 6) refers to gestures of this kind as a 'kinesic ensemble'. In systemic functional semiotics (SFS) this is treated as the co-instantiation of choices from more than one system (Martin, 2010). For example, a speaker may configure a vector in an outstretched hand directed to a person in the shared physical space. This involves a selection from the system of PARALINGUISTIC DEIXIS. At the same time that hand might be held in a supine (palm up) position, thereby constituting a selection from the system of PARALINGUISTIC ENGAGEMENT (Chapter 5, Section 5.3.5). This particular co-instantiation of meanings in gestural expression occurs frequently in lecture data when the lecturer interacts dialogically with students – in elicitations such as *what do you think?*.

A further point of discussion relates to the directionality of embodied vectors, in particular the contrast between pointing to something present in the physical environment or something not present (e.g. Kendon, 2004: 200). Observations of pointing in storytelling (e.g. Gullberg, 1998; Haviland, 2000) note that when characters (entities) or events (occurrences) are construed in a particular position in the gesturing space they may later be identified by pointing to that space. This strategy is also widely recognized in sign language literature. Johnston (1989: 145), for example, notes how signers 'place imaginary persons or objects into the "scene of action"'. Once established they may be 'referred to as if they were actually in the assigned locations'.[2] While no instances of this kind were identified in our data, we concur with Johnston's interpretation. Where a paralinguistic entity or occurrence is first depicted in a space and that space is later pointed to, this is taken as an instance of identifying actual (as if present) phenomena.

6.2.3 PARALINGUISTIC DEIXIS: A gestural system for identifying people, things and places through paralanguage

In spoken language a primary distinction is made between the recoverability of entities from assumed shared knowledge (homophora) and from the immediately present situation (Figure 6.1). If the latter, then recovery is either from within the text (endophora) or from outside the text (exophora). In paralanguage on the other hand, options for the recoverability of entities in discourse primarily distinguish between the feature [actual] realized through a resolved vector that is directed to visibly or sensibly (as if) present phenomena, and the feature [virtual] realized through an unresolved vector – that is, one that cannot be situationally resolved. Key PARALINGUISTIC DEIXIS options are outlined in Figure 6.2 and illustrated in the following sections.

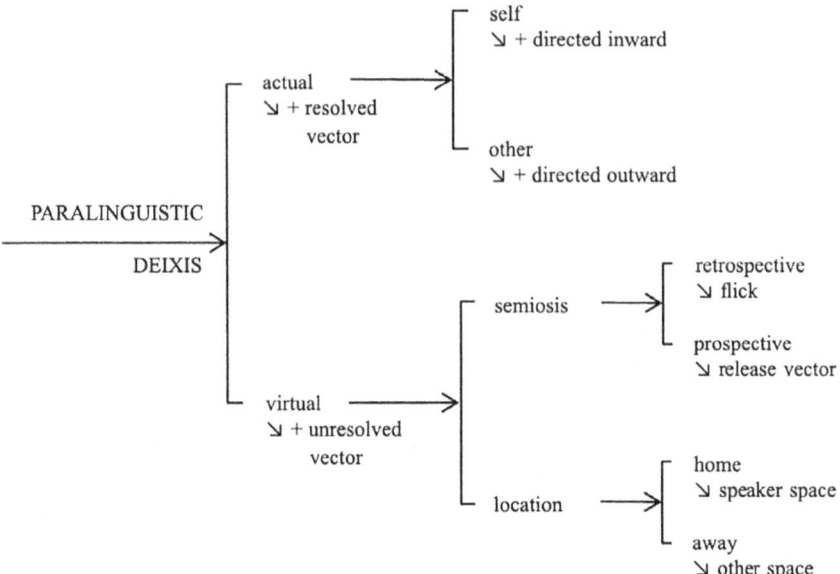

Figure 6.2 A partial system of PARALINGUISTIC DEIXIS.

6.2.3.1 PARALINGUISTIC DEIXIS: *Pointing to an [actual] referent*

As modelled in Figure 6.2, PARALINGUISTIC DEIXIS identifying an [actual] person, thing or place opens up a further choice of [self] or [other]. The feature [self] is realized through an embodied vector directed inwards towards to the speaker's body and [other] through a vector directed outwards from the body.

Example (2) illustrates contrasting instances accompanying the verbal text *you're wearing a stripy shirt – explain this image to me*. In each of the three frames a resolved vector is expressed with a hand or index finger point. Indicative arrows are added as the speed of the utterance and convergent paralanguage challenge the capturing of distinct images. In the first two frames the point is directed outwards selecting [other], first to a student and then to a projected image. In the third it is directed back to the lecturer, selecting [self]. We note that in examples of PARALINGUISTIC DEIXIS in this chapter we add an additional line 'language' in which we use underlining to locate synchronicity with pointing gestures. This avoids complicating the phonological transcription.

(2)

language	you're wearing a <u>stripy</u> shirt	explain this <u>image</u> to <u>me</u>	
phonology	//3 ^ you're / **wear**ing a / stripy / **shirt**	//1 ^ ex- /↑**plain** this / **im**age to me //	
paralanguage	extended hand point (thumb raised), in sync with *stripy*	extended hand transitions to right index finger point over left shoulder, in sync with *image* …	and curls back in a continuous movement to point to self in sync with *me*
images			

Each of the entities identified through deictic paralanguage in (2) is also tracked exophorically in the spoken text – to a student (*you*), to a thing (*this image*) and to the lecturer herself (*me*). However, as revealed in the first two images in (2), the resolution of the paralinguistic vector does not sync sonovergently with the verbal expressions of identification (i.e. *you* and *this*) but rather with the underlined lexis realizing relevant entities – specifically the *stripy* quality of a student's clothing and the thing entity *image*. In the third image the PARALINGUISTIC DEIXIS is synchronous with the presuming pronoun *me* which identifies the entity (lecturer). In this instance *me* is not salient as might be expected. This is accounted for in that the synchronous deictic gesture in image 3 is part of a gestural flow that begins on 'explain' and culminates with the completion of the tone group – in this case a tail that follows the tonic. The gestural movement maps the flow of information from 'about what' to 'to whom'. Synchronicity is discussed in detail in Section 6.3.

Note that when a speaker points to an [actual] entity in the shared material space, that entity may in fact relate indirectly to one referenced in language. Examples are presented in (3) and (4). In (3) an academic writing teacher has elicited suggestions from students on approaches to self-editing their work. Following a discussion of a contribution from a particular student the teacher remarks – *so using that approach is I think a great idea*. The verbal text endophorically tracks to the semiotic entity *approach* through the specific determiner *that* while the synchronous paralanguage points to a thing entity – a student, the student who was the source of the suggested approach.

(3)

language	so using <u>that</u> approach I think is a great idea
phonology	//4 ^ so / using / ***that*** ^ app- / roach //5 ↑I think is a / ***great*** idea //
paralanguage	an index finger points to the student as the source of the suggested approach
image	

In example (4), a biochemistry lecturer instructs students to take note of and remember a key technical term, saying *and that's a word you should encode*. Synchronous with *word* he points to his mouth (locating the source of words), and synchronous with *encode* he points to his head (as the location of memory).

(4)

language	and that's a <u>word</u> you should en<u>code</u>	
phonology	// 4 ^ and / *that's* a / *word* you / *should* en- / ***code*** //	
paralanguage	index finger points to mouth	index finger points to head
image		

*6.2.3.2 P*ARALINGUISTIC DEIXIS *identifying [virtual] phenomena*

In PARALINGUISTIC DEIXIS the selection of [virtual] is realized through an unresolved vector, that is, one that does not direct a viewer's gaze to a materially present phenomenon (Figure 6.3). Here a primary distinction in the recoverability of phenomena is made between [virtual:semiosis] and [virtual:location].

Paralinguistically, a [virtual:semiosis] entity may be identified either retrospectively or prospectively through an unresolved embodied vector. In a number of instances in the data the selection [virtual:semiosis:retrospective] is realized through a gestural flick – a small, fleeting vertically directed vector

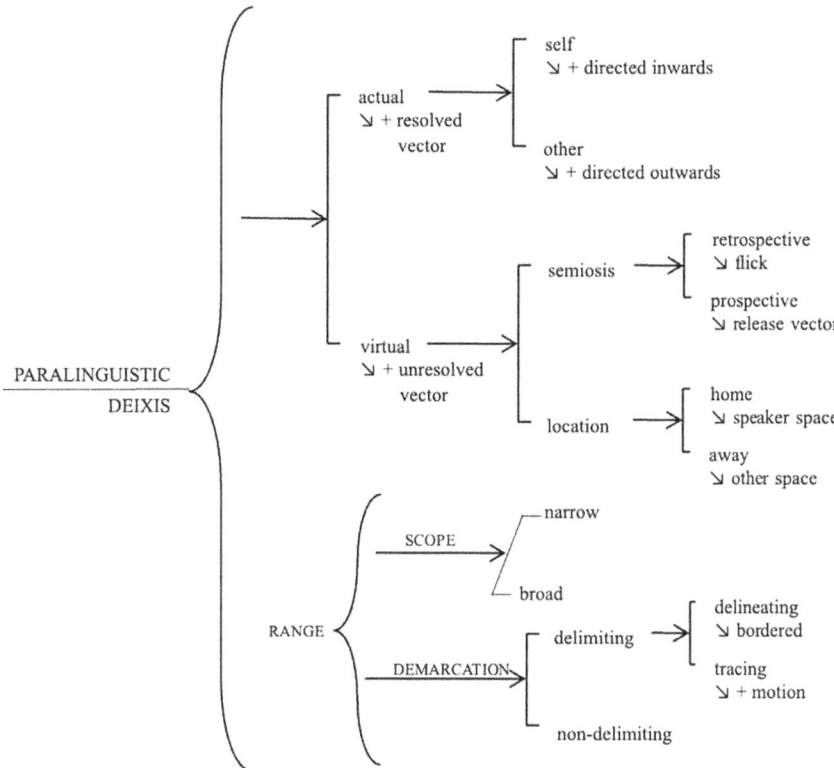

Figure 6.3 An extended system of PARALINGUISTIC DEIXIS.

expressed with an index finger or hand (body parts that facilitate speed of movement). The flick gesture synchronizes with a silent beat (^) which marks a juncture (e.g. a phase or stage boundary) in the flow of meaning in a text. The deictic gesture identifies a preceding segment of text (a semiotic entity), one that bears a logical connection to the coming phase or stage of discourse. The subsequent text is frequently initiated with an internal connector such as *so*.

Example (5) shows one such instance from the data. It comes from a lecture on commercial law in which the lecturer explains a relevant legal principle with reference to a specific case, *British Airways v. Taylor*. The case is introduced through a legal exemplum which unfolds from the perspective of the various participants – including the plaintiff (Edmonds), the airline, Edmonds's legal counsel and the judge. Following presentation of a phase of argument from the airline's legal counsel, the plaintiff's argument is introduced in (5). As the phonological transcription reveals, the vertical flick syncs with a silent beat (^) preceding the commencement of the last tone group, which begins with the internal connector *so*.

(5)

// 1 *Ed*monds had the / *oth*er view been
// 3 *wait*ing for / *years* for my / *hol*iday
// 3 *want*ed to get up to /***Lon***don
// 3 *now* I can't / ***go***
// 1 *ev*erything's mucked up
// ^ (flick)
// 1 ^ so you / *see* the / *log*ic of both /***arg***uments

In (6) the first image captures the conclusion of Edmonds's argument *everything's mucked up*. Image 2 shows the vertical flick (circled), realized in sync with the culminative silent beat (^). It retrospectively identifies the preceding semiotic entity – in this case a stage of the storytelling in which both parties (British Airways and Edmonds) put their arguments to the court. The conclusion of that stage converges with the lecturer closing his eyes and dropping his head. In image 3 the lecturer reorients his body to his left in sync with the internal connector *so* as he commences a new stage of the lecture in which he discusses the logic of the preceding arguments.

(6)

language	everything's mucked up		so you see the logic of both arguments
phonology	// 1 *ev*erything's mucked up	// ^	// 1 ^ so you / *see* the / *log*ic of both /***arg***uments //
paralanguage	faces to front	right index finger vertical flick (circled), closes eyes and drops head	re-orients his body to his left
images			

The selection [virtual:semiosis:prospective] is realized through a release vector (cf. Arnheim, 1982) – that is, an unresolved vector in which an arm is directed up and away to an 'unoccupied' space (typically to the speaker's left).[3] In example (7) an academic writing teacher is guiding students to jointly edit a draft of a text on the topic of changing work practices.

(7)

language	we could always .... bring in something here	(…) we could look at 'they could work at home and have flexible time'	'However, yeah, there are a number of disadvantages or serious disadvantages …'
phonology	//5 ^ we could / always ^ / ^ / bring in / something / **here**	//3 ^ we could / **look** at //4 they could / work at / home and have / flexibly / **time**	//4 ^ how- / **ev**er //2 **yeah** //3 there are a / **num**ber of disad- / **van**tages //3 ^ or / serious disad- / **van**tages //
paralanguage	pointing to an actual location in sync with underlined pause in speech	pointing to actual wording synchronous with underlined verbiage	pointing to virtual semiosis synchronous with underlined verbiage
images			

In the first image of (7) the teacher's point is to an [actual: other], a space between wordings on the projected text, in sync with a pause in speech. In the second image, she again points to an [actual:other], this time a sequence of words that precede the previously identified space. This syncs with *they could work at home and have flexible time*. In the third, she proposes wording that could improve the draft – *However, yeah, there are a number of disadvantages or serious disadvantages*. In sync with the proposed wording she extends her left arm and hand, pointing up and away to her left instantiating a release vector that realizes [virtual:semiosis:prospective].

The selection [virtual:location] is also realized paralinguistically through an unresolved vector. The more delicate choice [home] is realized by identifying a space occupied by the speaker; and the opposing choice [away] is realized by pointing to a space other than the space occupied by the speaker (Figure 6.2). Paralinguistic expressions of [home] and [away] can converge with the identification of both time and space in verbal discourse. The feature [home] can accordingly converge with both 'here' and 'now'. As noted by Calbris (2011: 128), past time may be pointed to as a location behind a speaker. Where the past is expressed in language in relation to the future, synchronous PARALINGUISTIC DEIXIS typically points to a space to the left of the speaker then to the right.

These choices are illustrated in the commercial law lecture in (8). The lecturer is discussing the distinction between a statement of fact and a statement of opinion. He retells an illustrative instance from a relevant case in which a plaintiff, Edmonds, has been assured by British Airways at a certain point in time that he will have a seat on an upcoming flight. In (8) verbal references to time are underlined – in the first image the linguistic reference is to present time, *today*, and in the second to time after today, *future*.

(8)

language	you told me <u>today</u>	there was a seat for me in the <u>future</u>
phonology	// ...you //4 *told* me to- / *day*	//3 *there* was a / *seat* for me in the / *fu*ture //
paralanguage	pointing down in front of body with pinched tips of left thumb and index finger	right hand and forearm extend out pointing to a location to the right as the left index finger points outwards from the body and slightly to the speaker's left.
images		

Opposing features of [home] and [away] are illustrated in the two images in (8). In the first image, synchronous with *today*, the lecturer's pinched left thumb and index finger configures a vector pointing down in front of the lecturer's body, in an expression of [home]. In the second image, synchronous with *future*, the right hand and forearm extend from the body pointing to a location to the right, expressing [away]. The second image additionally shows the left index finger pointing outwards from the body and slightly to the speaker's left. The completion of this point synchronizes with the completion of that to the right. The simultaneity of the two points delineates a space between present and future – a critical issue with respect to questions of fact or opinion. (These images are discussed further in terms of RANGE in (15) and (16).)

6.2.4 Range in paralinguistic deixis

To the partial system network of PARALINGUISTIC DEIXIS presented in Figure 6.2 we now add a simultaneous system of RANGE in Figure 6.3. Simultaneous systems are represented diagrammatically with a brace bracket, meaning that selections need to be made in [actual/virtual] and in RANGE. However, certain restrictions apply with respect to features of [virtual] PARALINGUISTIC DEIXIS. These will be commented upon as the choices in RANGE are explained and illustrated.

RANGE itself involves choices in two simultaneous systems, SCOPE and DEMARCATION. SCOPE concerns the relative mass (volume or quantity) of phenomena identified in an expression of PARALINGUISTIC DEIXIS. The slanted square bracket indicates a graded (rather than an either/or) system – a pointing gesture can be relatively [narrow] or [broad] in SCOPE.

6.2.4.1 SCOPE as [narrow/broad]: Identifying relative mass

The selection of SCOPE as relatively [narrow] or [broad] can support the identification of the quantity or volume of entities encompassed in a deictic gesture – for example, as a single entity among others or as an entire group of entities. In (9), from our cultural studies lecture, the lecturer is eliciting responses from students in relation to a projected orientalist image.

(9)

language	anyone got an idea?	up the back ...
phonology	//2 *any*one / *got* an i- / *de*a	//3 ^ up the / **back** //
paralanguage	forearms and supine hands extended in front of body – angling outwards at roughly 45°	specifying index finger point out from body
images		

In the first image in (9), the lecturer verbally refers non-specifically to any student as a potential respondent (*anyone*). In paralanguage synchronous with underlined spoken language she extends both forearms with supine hands in front of her body – angling them outwards at roughly 45°. The deictic gestures select for relatively [broad] in SCOPE – the two diverging vectors effectively identify the whole class. In the second image, synchronous with the lexical construal of a location in *up the back*, the lecturer points with an index finger, narrowing the SCOPE of identification to a specific student.

The three images in (10) show variations in SCOPE of PARALINGUISTIC DEIXIS through vectors expressed with hand or fingers. SCOPE varies from relatively [broad] via the palm of the hand in image 1, to relatively [narrow] via an index finger in image 2, to maximally [narrow] via a little finger in image 3.

(10)
images

Alongside hands and fingers, lecturers frequently rely on laser pointers to identify phenomena on presentation slides. The device readily realizes [narrow] SCOPE but is less effective for [broad] SCOPE – which is often construed by the pointer wriggling around erratically, trying in vain to colour in the region in question.

6.2.4.2 DEMARCATION as [delimiting]: Identifying parts or features of phenomena

As a first option the selection of DEMARCATION affords a distinction between [delimiting] or [non-delimiting], that is, between restricting parts or features of identified phenomena or not. Choosing [delimiting] opens up the distinction between [delineating] or [tracing].

6.2.4.2.1 DEMARCATION as [delimiting:delineating]: Embodied vectors that configure borders

The feature [delineating] is realized through an embodied vector that configures one or more borders – as in example (11). The image shows a number of lists of thematic categories on the whiteboard. In sync with the underlining in language, the teacher's left hand is angled at the wrist with fingers straightened to configure PARALINGUISTIC DEIXIS as [delineating]. She is identifying the border between the category heading *work* and the related list of words underneath.

(11)

language	(we've got a lot of words centring on work) which are related <u>to the theme of work</u>
phonology	//1 *which* are re- / *lated* to the / *theme* of / **work** //
paralanguage	delineating vector realized through the edge of hand and straightened fingers.
images	

Elsewhere in the data we find a [delineating] vector configuring boundaries with a bent finger and thumb – as in example (12). In both images the [delineating] deixis identifies segments of a projected written text. (See also example (8).)

(12)

images

It is important to note here the similarity between the expressions of PARALINGUISTIC DEIXIS in (12) and some depictions of ideational entities realizing PARALINGUISTIC IDEATION (see Chapter 4; Hood and Hao, 2021). The difference is illustrated in the two images in (13). In image 1 the teacher delineates an [actual] entity – a written text. The expression syncs with the verbal specific determiner *this* in *We need some sentences that link <u>this</u>*. In image 2 the teacher sculpts a paralinguistic entity with her left hand in the gestural space. This expression syncs with the figure *<u>How does that sentence link back to the first one</u>?*. The semiotic entity realized in *sentence* in image 2 is depicted (Chapter 4) rather than pointed to.

(13)

language	we need some sentences that link <u>this</u>	how does that sentence link back to the first one?
phonology	//1 ^ we / *need* some / *sent*ences that / *link* / **this** //	//2 *how* does / *that* sentence / *link* back to the / **first** one //

paralanguage	PARALINGUISTIC DEXIS identifying phenomena through delineation	PARALINGUISTIC IDEATION depicting a bounded entity
images		

6.2.4.2.2 DEMARCATION as [delimiting:tracing]: Dynamic vectors that identify parts or qualities

The feature [tracing] is realized through a dynamic vector which identifies a part or quality (e.g. shape) of an entity through movement. In (14), a biochemistry lecturer is describing the structure of a water molecule. He traces with his index finger[4] a 90° angle on a projected image of the atoms which compose a water molecule. The tracing motion is shown in arrows in the three sequential images as his index finger moves from right to left and then down. This movement is retraced multiple times in sync with the duration of underlined wordings. The retracing is interrupted in sync with the verbal reset (*I'm sorry*).

(14)

language	So, for example with water <u>it's got a – almost like a perpendicular stru – sh –</u>, I'm sorry, <u>like a ninety-degree sort of shape</u>.
phonology	//4 *so* for ex- /*am*ple with /*wat*er //3 ^ it's / got a – ^ / *al*most like a perpen- / *dic*ular ^ stru – sh – //1 *I'm* sorry //3 *like* a / *nine*ty de- / *gree* sort of / **shape** //
paralanguage	a tracing vector begins as shown, moves horizontally to this point, then vertically to this point.
images	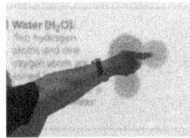 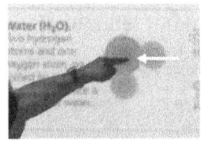 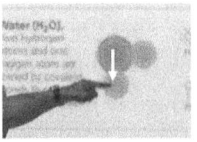

6.2.4.3 Limits to RANGE in identifying [virtual] phenomena

So far, the discussion of options in RANGE has focused on instances of identifying [actual] phenomena. The identification of [virtual] phenomena gives rise to certain restrictions. In the context of the law lecture, a discussion of fact versus opinion foregrounds contrastive time in *today* and *the future*. In example (15) the PARALINGUISTIC DEIXIS identifies time as [virtual:location] and selects for both SCOPE and DEMARCATION.

(15)

language	you told me <u>today</u>	there was a <u>seat for me in the future</u>
phonology	//...you //4 told me to- / *day*	//3 *there* was a //1 *seat* for me in the / *fut*ure //
paralanguage	The left index finger and thumb point down in front of the lecturer's body in sync with *today*	The left index finger points out in front of the body in sync with *a seat for me in the future*, as the right hand extends in an unresolved vector to the right in sync with *future*
images		

In image 1 in (15), the 'pinch' point of left thumb and index finger selects for SCOPE as [narrow], as does the left index finger point in image 2. Both these vectors contrast with the right-hand vector in image 2 where an open palm with spread fingers and thumb configures SCOPE as relatively [broad]. The narrow pinch point in image 1 syncs sonovergently with *today* and semovergently with the meaning of the narrowly defined time reference. The relatively broad right-hand point in image 2 syncs sonovergently with *future* and semovergently with the relatively open time reference.

The PARALINGUISTIC DEIXIS in (15) also selects for DEMARCATION as [delineation]. In the second image, the left index finger extends outwards from the body, sustaining its semovergence with *today*. The left index finger delineates a boundary line, a [virtual:location] from which time stretches into the future, the [virtual:location] identified to the right. Our data suggest that the selection of [virtual:semiotic], whether [prospective] or [retrospective], does not select for either relative SCOPE or DEMARCATION.

6.2.5 Co-instantiating PARALINGUISTIC DEIXIS with features from other paralinguistic systems

The potential for a deictic gesture to be expressed simultaneously with one or more gestural realizations from other paralinguistic systems was noted in the introduction to this chapter. This is further exemplified in (16) where we zero in once again on the example discussed as (8) and (15) earlier. In (16) the focus of attention is the deictic gesture realizing [virtual:location]. In this instance the realization of [home] converges with the verbal expression of time – *today*. The pinching of the thumb and index finger in image 1 selects [narrow] from the SCOPE system – but simultaneously expresses interpersonal semovergence in selecting [sharpen] in PARALINGUISTIC FOCUS (see Figure 5.14 on PARALINGUISTIC GRADUATION; Hao and Hood, 2019). Interpersonally the expression flags maximum exactitude or precision, in this instance flagging definitiveness in relation to the claim *you told me today*. Upscaled PARALINGUISTIC FORCE is also enacted through the marked muscle tension involved in the pinching point in image 1 in (16) and a forceful long downward trajectory of forearm and hand indicated by the arrow in image 2 in (16). Here the systems of PARALINGUISTIC DEIXIS and PARALINGUISTIC GRADUATION interact to invoke the significance of the claim.

(16)

language	you told me <u>today</u>	
phonology	// …you //4 *told* me to- / ***day***	
paralanguage	narrow pinch point	forceful long downward trajectory of forearm and hand
images	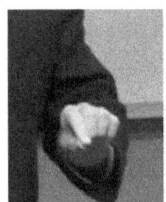	

6.2.6 PARALINGUISTIC DEIXIS coordinating meanings and participation in live lectures

The discussion of textual semovergence to this point explores the cooperation of language and paralanguage as they keep track of people, things and places in the flow of discourse. PARALINGUISTIC DEIXIS is realized through an embodied vector which directs a viewer's gaze to either [actual] or [virtual] phenomena. In the context of the multimodal lecture theatre or classroom, the lecturer's PARALINGUISTIC DEIXIS plays a highly significant role in coordinating multiple sources, locations and kinds of information in ways that support sense-making by the co-present students. At the same time the gestures invite and coordinate participation from students in the goings-on and in the unfolding of knowledge through the flow of meaning in the lecture. As vectors, the expressions of PARALINGUISTIC DEIXIS direct students' gaze, and thus their attention, to particular [actual] and [virtual] phenomena.

6.3 PARALINGUISTIC RHYTHM and PARALINGUISTIC PERIODICITY: Composing intermodal waves and junctures in the flow of sound and information

In this section we introduce two additional paralinguistic systems – PARALINGUISTIC RHYTHM and PARALINGUISTIC PERIODICITY. PARALINGUISTIC RHYTHM deals with the sonovergent synchronicity of paralanguage with waves of sound in the prosodic phonology of speech. PARALINGUISTIC PERIODICITY deals with the semovergent coordination of paralanguage with waves of information in unfolding discourse. The metaphor of 'waves' references the peaks and troughs of textual prominence as texts unfold (Martin, 1992; Martin and Rose, [2003] 2007: 189). From the perspective of sound, waves in prosodic phonology compose peaks of prominence heard as salient and tonic syllables. From the perspective of meaning, waves of information at clause level configure into longer waves of indefinite extent (for phases in register and stages in genres) – in what has been referred to as a 'hierarchy of periodicity' (Pike, 1982; Thibault, 1987; Martin, 1992; Martin and Rose, [2003] 2007).

While higher levels of PERIODICITY are especially characteristic of reflective written text, they are also relevant to the spoken mode of live lectures where there are significant phases of planned or rehearsed reflective content. This section focuses first on convergence of paralanguage with the smaller waves of sound in prosodic phonology (sonovergence) then with longer wavelengths of meaning in discourse (semovergence).

In the gesture literature there is a tendency to privilege the representational meaning of gestures, which McNeill (1992) refers to as imagistic – and what in SFL would constitute ideational paralanguage. Other kinds of gestural meaning, including embodied beats, are placed in the non-imagistic (non-representational) category by McNeill (1992). In later work, McNeill (2016: 8–9) describes beats as rhythmic hand movements that 'rather than embodying meaning … appear to synchronize with speech rhythm'. He also notes, however, that they 'arise from meanings on the discourse level', such as beating time with 'what is new in each speech unit'. His discussion does not elaborate on the notion of speech rhythm or the linguistic identification of new information.

Kendon (2004: 100–3) comments on beats and their relation to speech in a brief review of other contributions to defining and categorizing gestures (including that of McNeill, 1992). A more significant contribution is found in Kendon (1972), which references the influence of earlier work by Condon and Ogston (1967). In a study that draws on data from one speaker in an unstructured interview mode, Kendon (1972: 182) observes how movements of multiple body parts are synchronized with each other in 'a sort of hierarchy in the organisation of movement'. He notes that changes in the organization of movements occurred 'synchronously with the articulation of ... sounds'. Referencing the contribution of Halliday (1963) amongst others, Kendon (1972: 184) suggests this synchronicity with sound begins with the tone group, which he labels prosodic phrase. From there he proposes a set of higher-level units with certain indicative speech-related features, including pitch and pausing. He describes phrases as potentially combining into locutions (akin to clause complexes in SFL) and locutions into locution groups (whose shared features differ from those of neighbouring groups). Finally, locution groups combine into locution clusters, the 'highest level speech units below the level of *discourse*' and likened to 'the paragraphs of discourse' (Kendon, 1972: 187–8, italics in original). For Kendon, 'discourse' appears to mean a speaker turn in the interaction rather than the entirety of a dialogic text.

Turning to SFL perspectives, van Leeuwen (2005: 181) notes the synchronicity of how 'we act together and talk together', tracing this back to basic human biology. He foregrounds the significance of this rhythmic cooperation in the composition of multimodal texts, suggesting that it provides the 'scaffolding to keep the text from collapsing' (2005: 181) – which plays its part in getting the message across. Rhythm is explained as alternations that are realized in regular measures of time. An example from spoken English is the alternation of salient and non-salient syllables – which vary with respect to sonority, loudness, pitch and/or duration. Perceived rhythm in spoken English is built on the regularity in the timing of the salient and non-salient syllables in a tone group. It is on this basis that English is referred to as a stress-timed or foot-timed language (as introduced in Chapter 3).[5] In the discussion on intermodal synchronicity to follow, we elaborate on how body movement converges with the prosodic phonology of English (sonovergence) and with longer wavelengths of meaning in discourse (semovergence).

Martinec (2000a, 2002) shares with Kendon's (1972) earlier work an interest in the hierarchical structuring of the synchrony of body movements with speech. He is particularly influenced by van Leeuwen (1985). Martinec (2002) focuses on the potential for rhythm to function simultaneously in phonology in tandem with layers of content – including paragraph-like units and generic stages (referencing Martin, 1992).

Martinec also notes that there can be 'both rhythmic regularity and irregularity' at different levels in the hierarchy and that this can account for the 'different degrees of rhythmicality of different types of texts' (Martinec, 2002: 39). Mode and genre are likely to be significant variables. With respect to mode, the more reflectively composed the spoken discourse, the more likely we are to find high-level waves of meaning that alternate in peaks and troughs of prominence in the discourse, and predictively, the more likely we are to find phases of rhythmic regularity at these wavelengths. Martinec (2002: 43) also makes the point that the 'regularity of occurrence of accents does not have to be exact for them to be perceived as regular' and that the higher the level in the hierarchy, the greater the tolerance in perceiving regularity.

In the SFL social semiotic account of textual convergence in this chapter, we touch base with Kendon's (1972) early contributions and build upon van Leeuwen's and Martinec's studies of hierarchies of rhythm. Synchrony within the tone group (sonovergence) draws on the model of prosodic phonology developed by Halliday and his colleagues in SFL (as introduced in Chapter 3). This model grounds our descriptions of intermodal synchronicity, rhythm and intonation in spoken language. Synchrony with waves of meaning in texts (semovergence) extends Martinec's account by identifying prominence with respect to choices in discourse semantic systems, that is, abstracting beyond the stratum of lexicogrammar.

6.3.1 Sonovergence: Synchronizing prominence in sound and paralanguage

As explained in Chapter 3 and summarized in the phonological and transcription conventions at the beginning of this book, the notation system used in the book for describing prosodic phonology follows Halliday (1967, 1970a) and Greaves (2007).

6.3.1.1 Prominence in speech

As outlined by Halliday (1967, 1970a), English grammar and phonology structure textual meaning as waves of information. One peak of prominence is realized grammatically through Theme at the beginning of an English clause.

It functions as the point of departure for the message by encoding an angle on the field. A complementary peak of prominence, termed New, is realized phonologically in the unmarked case through the major pitch movement on the final salient syllable of a tone group – its Tonic segment (Halliday, 1970a; Martin and Rose, [2003] 2007: 189–92). A secondary peak of informational prominence is realized through a salient syllable, which in SFL notation begins each foot. As noted in Chapter 3, Section 3.6, a salient syllable can be made super-salient where there is a significant jump in pitch, usually upwards, which does not involve a choice of tone. Super-salience is indicated via a vertical arrow, '↑', before the syllable.

The successive feet within a tone group of spoken English are, in the unmarked case, perceived as relatively isochronous. This foot-timed regularity is maintained over a tone group, even though the number of non-accented syllables in successive feet can vary considerably. In (17), the non-accented syllables (not italicized) in each tone group vary from one to five. The perceived rhythm is maintained through reductions in the articulation of the non-accented syllables. Once a rhythm is instantiated it can be maintained even when an expected beat is not articulated; this is referred to as a silent beat.

(17)

// 4 *following* Fou- / **cault**

// 4 ^ Sa- / *id* de- / *scribes* / *dis*courses as a / *form* of knowledge that is / *not* – that is / *not* used instru- / *ment*ally in the / **serv**ice of power

// 1 ^ but / *is* it- / *self* a / **form** of power //

In the unmarked case, salient syllables highlight content words (not grammatical ones) and assign a secondary degree of prominence to that information in the discourse. However, in (17) there are two marked instances where grammatical words are made salient: *not* in the second tone group and *is* in the third. These marked choices give prominence to contrastive positions in the discourse (in this case, that which *is* and is *not* knowledge). In the first two tone groups the tonic syllables (in bold) carry tone 4 pitch contours. This falling-rising tone movement indicates *pending* meaning. The tone 1 of the third tone group signals *completion*.

6.3.1.2 *Synchronous prominence in paralanguage*

An analysis of intermodal synchronicity focuses on the convergence of peaks of prominence in language and paralanguage and their expression at multiple levels in discourse. In this section we limit the focus to convergence of paralanguage with the prosodic phonology of language. The source of (17) is a cultural studies lecture on language and power; it discusses key knowers[6] in the humanities and the values they project. The underlining in (17') indicates rhythmic synchronicity of phonological accents with paralinguistic beats.

(17')

// 4 *following* Fou- / ***cault***

// 4 ^ Sa- / *id* de- / ***scribes*** / *dis*courses as a / ***form*** of knowledge that is / *not* – that is / *not* used instru- / *ment*ally in the / ***serv***ice of power

// 1 ^ but / *is* it- / ***self*** a / ***form*** of power //

In (17") we present a sequence of images and descriptions of the lecturer's paralanguage. She begins by reading aloud from a written text on a computer screen situated on the desk in front of her. Her gaze shifts at two points from the written text to the students. A momentary gaze to the students converges with a false start on //… that is / *not*…// in the second tone group, after which she returns her gaze to the written text. She looks up again for the duration of the final tone group ('//1 ^ but /*is* it/*self* a ***form*** of power //'). The images in (17") display the timing of the downward sonovergent beats of her left hand and arm.

(17")

phonology	Fou-/ ***cault***	de- / ***scribes***	/ ***serv***ice of power	it- / ***self***	/ ***form*** of power
hand beats converge with	tonic syllable	salient syllable	tonic syllable	salient syllable	tonic syllable
giving textual prominence to	interpersonal expansion via supine hand		interpersonal contraction (negation) via out-facing palm	ideational entity via hand shape	interpersonal expansion via supine hand
images					

The sonovergent beats highlighted with arrows in (17") are noteworthy in two respects. First, the hand beats are synchronous with each tonic syllable in (17") and with some of its salient syllables – thereby amplifying the prominence of synchronous wording and the meaning they construe. Second, there are notable variations in the way they are expressed. They vary in relative size and duration of time held and in the orientation and shape of the beating hand. In terms of size, the beat synchronous with the first tonic on (*Fou<u>cault</u>*) and the last (*<u>form</u> of power*) extends the furthest, with the stroke of the latter extending maximally downwards from shoulder height. The final beat is also extended in duration as it is held beyond the completion of the tone group. Variation in the shape of the beating hand is noted in image 4 and magnified in (17''') to reveal the co-instantiation of a depicted paralinguistic entity. In this instance the gestural beat synchronizes with *self*; the pronoun refers anaphorically to the semiotic entity *form of knowledge*. The paralinguistic beat thus assigns textual prominence to an ideational meaning.

(17''')

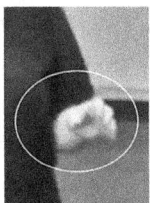

A paralinguistic beat can also give prominence to interpersonal meaning. The hand beat in image 5 of (17'') not only syncs with the final tonic segment *form*, but its low-falling trajectory is interpersonally 'in tune with' the major pitch contour of a falling tone 1 (see Chapters 3 and 5) – prominence is thus added to the meaning of this tone (here, providing information). Interpersonal meaning is additionally co-instantiated in the orientation of the hand. In images 1 and 5 of (17'') the supine (open) orientation of the hand beats invites negotiation of the relevant propositions. More technically it enacts heteroglossic expansion as opening space for negotiation (see Chapter 5; Martin and White, 2005; Hao and Hood, 2019).[7] The alternative, a prone hand with a downward orientation of the palm, would have enacted heteroglossic contraction, closing down space for negotiation. These variations are illustrative of the way textual meaning in both language and paralanguage coordinates ideational and interpersonal prominence in unfolding discourse.

The density of beat gestures convergent with the short phase of text in (17'') is not uncommon in contexts of face-to-face teaching, although the density of this synchrony will no doubt vary with particular stages or phases of lectures or lessons. It reflects the effort on the part of lecturers to support students in recognizing key content in the flow of talk, ultimately contributing to their successful induction into knowledge and values in a particular academic field.

6.3.2 PARALINGUISTIC PERIODICITY: Coordinating prominence in longer and longer wavelengths of meaning

In the system of PARALINGUISTIC PERIODICITY the focus shifts to the mapping of paralanguage onto longer wavelengths of meaning – the 'hierarchy of periodicity' modelled in Figure 6.4.

To the left, Figure 6.4 models a hierarchy of thematic prominence which extends up from clause-level Theme through hyper-Theme to an indefinite number of layers of macro-Theme. This succession of crests of predictive prominence in discourse composes the method of development in a text (Fries, [1981] 1983; Martin and Rose, [2003] 2007). To the right of Figure 6.4, the accumulation of New information is modelled as a progression from the crest of New information realized by the Tonic syllable in a tone group, to the potential for a hyper-New at phase level and indefinite layers of macro-New. As information is consolidated in higher-level News the point of the discourse is composed and regularly charged with significance of one kind or another, depending on the field.

We can consider a long text such as a lecture as waves within waves within waves. As a matter of course we expect the curriculum genre of a lecture to commence with some initiating orientation to what is to come (an orienting preview for students) and conclude with some culminating aggregation of key content (the take-away message for students). The lecture as a whole constitutes one long wavelength of meaning; and looking 'up' it may sit within yet higher waves of information – for

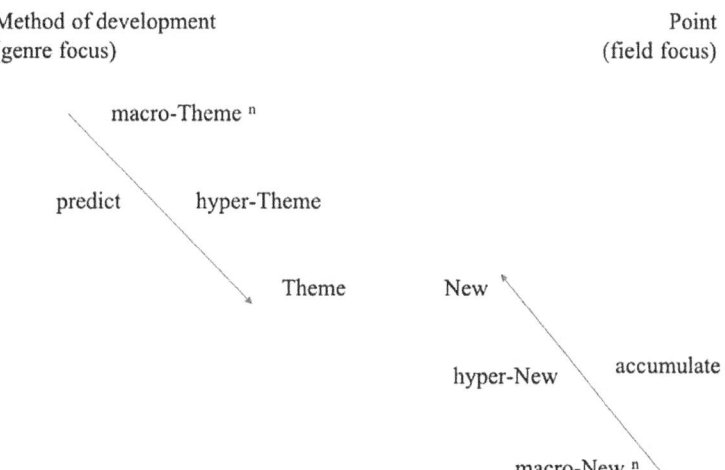

Figure 6.4 Modelling the hierarchy of periodicity in language (Martin and Rose, [2003] 2007: 199).

example, a module of content or a whole course of study. Looking 'down' the lecture is itself composed of smaller and smaller waves that structure stages and phases of discourse and ultimately clauses and tone groups within phases.

Movements of different parts of the body converge with these wavelengths of meaning. As observed in the literature (e.g. Kendon, 1972: 182; Martinec, 2000a; Hood, 2011), smaller body parts such as fingers and hands can move faster and so tend to synchronize with shorter wavelengths. Larger body parts (arms, legs, torso), that move more slowly, synchronize more readily at longer wavelengths. The movement and relocation of the whole body in space synchronizes naturally with prominence at longer wavelengths still. Where peaks of prominence at one wavelength line up with those at another we are likely to find different parts of the body in simultaneous synchrony. In other words, the beat of a hand at one wavelength may sync with a footfall at another and repositioning of the body at yet another.

The first step in exploring semovergent synchronicity is to establish where language constructs peaks of prominence for different wavelengths of information in a text. Analysis might begin at the level of whole texts (or substantial segments therein), in order to explore how long waves of meaning are composed of smaller and smaller ones. Alternatively it can begin at the level of clause and work up through phases to longer and longer wavelengths of meaning. The latter path is taken here.

The data we use to illustrate PARALINGUISTIC PERIODICITY in this section are drawn from a health science lecture on the topic of urine formation, in particular from a segment on the process of reabsorption. This technical term names a final stage of activity in the production of urine. In short, reabsorption occurs after certain waste products have been filtered out of the blood into what is called the filtrate. However, along with these waste products, the filtrate also retains some nutrients. These nutrients need to be reabsorbed back into the blood so that only waste and water remain as urine. A sequence of activities and several parts of the body are implicated in the process of reabsorption. The phase transcribed in (18) and analysed as a hierarchy of periodicity in (18') concerns the final stage of reabsorption.

(18)
The last one is the distal convoluted tubule. Now by the time the filtrate has reached the distal convoluted tubule most of the good stuff has gone. Most of the glucose is back in the bloodstream. Most of the vitamins are back in the bloodstream. Most of the ah – amino acids are back in the bl– back in the bloodstream. Lots of water is back in the bloodstream. So by this time it's pretty close to what urine ends up being, a dilute material with not a lot of– not a lot of good stuff in it and full of a lot of waste.

(18')

macro-Theme[8]
The last one is the distal convoluted tubule.
>**hyper-Theme**
>Now by the time the filtrate has reached the distal convoluted tubule most of the good stuff has gone.
>>**clause-level Theme** (underlined) (with New discussed below)
>>Most of the glucose is back in the bloodstream.
>>Most of the vitamins are back in the bloodstream.
>>Most of the ah – amino acids are back in the bl– back in the bloodstream.
>>Lots of water is back in the bloodstream.
>
>**hyper-New**
>So by this time it's pretty close to what urine ends up being – a dilute material with not a lot of– not a lot of good stuff in it and full of a lot of waste.

6.3.2.1 PARALINGUISTIC PERIODICITY *and clause-level Themes*

(19)

Most of the glucose is back in the bloodstream.

Most of the vitamins are back in the bloodstream.

Most of the ah – amino acids are back in the bl – back in the bloodstream.

Lots of water is back in the bloodstream.

(19')

// ^ / ^ /

//3 *most* of the / **gluc**ose is

// 3 *back* in the / **blood**stream

// 3 *most* of the / **vit**amins are / *back* in the / **blood**stream

// 3 *most* of the / *ah* a- / *min*o / **ac**ids are / *back* in the / *bl* – / *back* in the / *blood*stream

// 1+ *lots* of / **wat**er is

// 1 *back* in the / **blood**stream

// ^ / ^ //

It is important to recall here that clause and tone group may or may not map onto each other (Chapter 3), as evident in (19) and (19'). In (19) the underlining in each clause specifies Theme. However, New is specified in the tone group as the tonic syllable that composes phonological prominence through the major pitch movement of the tone group. This is shown in bold italics in (19').

Each of the four figures in (19") is realized by a single clause that repeats a particular grammatical pattern. However, they vary phonologically. The first and fourth clauses each map onto two tone groups with two crests of tonic prominence (formatted in bold) and hence two News; the second and third clauses each map onto a single tone group with one crest of tonic prominence and so one New. This prompts an interesting question about where intermodal convergence might occur. In this instance, as shown in (19"), each of the lecturer's hand beats syncs sonovergently with a tonic syllable, in just those cases where the tonic falls on one of the named nutrients in the phase / *gluc*ose, / *vit*amins, a- / *min*o / *ac*ids or / *wat*er. At the same time each of these named nutrients is given prominence as the Theme of a clause (see (19)). The lecturer's hand beat thus reinforces informational prominence both sonovergently and semovergently.

(19")

language	most of the glucose is back in the bloodstream	most of the vitamins are back in the bloodstream	most of the ah – amino acids are back in the bl – back in the bloodstream	lots of water is back in the bloodstream
phonology	//3 *most* of the / *gluc*ose is // 3 *back* in the /*blood*stream	// 3 *most* of the / *vit*amins are / *back* in the / *blood*stream	// 3 *most* of the / *ah* – a- / *min*o / *ac*ids are / *back* in the / bl – / *back* in the / *blood*stream	// 1+ *lots* of / *wat*er is // 1 *back* in the / *blood*stream //
paralanguage (beats)	hand beat falls on tonic in *gluc*ose and is sustained to clause completion (underlined)	hand beat falls on tonic in *vit*amins and is sustained to clause completion (underlined)	hand beat falls on tonic in *ac*ids and is sustained to clause completion (underlined)	hand beat falls on tonic in *wat*er and is sustained to clause completion (underlined)
paralanguage (whole body movement)	See 1 in Figure Figure 6.5	See 2 in Figure Figure 6.5	See 3 in Figure Figure 6.5	See 4 in Figure Figure 6.5
images				

From a discourse semantic perspective, in (19″) we have a sequence of four state figures, each construed by the same (relational circumstantial) grammatical structure – *most of the [X] / lots of [X] is back in the bloodstream*. To what extent does the regularity in this sequence synchronize with PARALINGUISTIC PERIODICITY?

The lecturer's movement is schematized in Figure 6.5 (adopting the perspective of the students). The vertical lines to left and right denote the peripheries of the space, and the black rectangle denotes a centrally located desk towards the back of the space. The arrows show direction of movement; and the orientation of the foot indicates whether the lecturer is stepping forward or backwards in a given direction (it is always forward in (19″)). The figures and movement in Figure 6.5 are correlated as follows:

Most of the glucose is back in the bloodstream.	Movement 1 (Figure 6.5)
Most of the vitamins are back in the bloodstream.	Movement 2 (Figure 6.5)
Most of the ah – amino acids are back in the bl – back in the bloodstream.	Movement 3 (Figure 6.5)
Lots of water is back in the bloodstream.	Movement 4 (Figure 6.5)

The movement in Figure 6.5 involves a regular three-step rhythm synchronous with each figure. The first step always falls on the intermodally prominent entity that construes the nutrient (i.e. *glucose, vitamins, amino acids* or *water*). The waltz-like synchrony is maintained for this phase of discourse, with a proviso that at the point of hesitation in the third figure, *ah- amino*, the lecturer loses his speech rhythm and has to stop his body rhythm (stepping) momentarily until speech rhythm is recovered. Similarly, with the repetition in <u>back</u> *in the bl -* <u>back</u> *in the* an additional (fourth) step is taken to maintain the sonovergence. Both instances highlight the close intermodal coordination of language and body rhythms.

As modelled in Figure 6.5, the sequence of verbal figures and whole-body movements begins at a point midway between the right peripheral space and the centre. At the juncture of the first and second figures, the lecturer passes the central desk. He then moves further to the left of the space and midway through

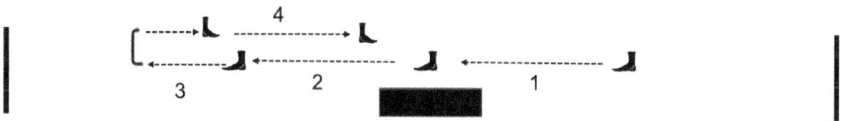

Figure 6.5 The circuit of body movement synchronous with four-figure sequence.

the articulation of the third figure makes a U-turn to head back to the right. At the completion of the fourth figure the lecturer arrives back at the centrally located desk.

While there are no explicit linguistic connectors linking the sequence of figures in the verbiage, there is an implicit additive relation that accumulates the nutrients (*glucose, vitamins, amino acids* and *water*) removed from the filtrate. The synchrony of paralinguistic beats on the nutrients and the progressive movement of the body in space suggests a sequence akin to regularly adding goods to a supermarket trolley – but in reverse, since it involves progressively returning goods to the shelves.

6.3.2.2 PARALINGUISTIC PERIODICITY *and higher-level Themes*

The Themes (underlined in (20)) in the sequence of figures explored earlier compose a method of development which is predicted by its hyper-Theme. In this instance, *the good stuff* generalizes the ideational meanings given thematic prominence in the waves which follow – that is, *glucose, vitamins, amino acids* and *water*.

(20)
>
> **hyper-Theme**
> Now by the time the filtrate has reached the distal convoluted tubule most of the good stuff has gone.
> **Themes** (underlined)
> Most of the glucose is back in the bloodstream.
> Most of the vitamins are back in the bloodstream.
> Most of the ah – amino acids are back in the bl – back in the bloodstream.
> Lots of water is back in the bloodstream.

Hyper-Themes function in this way to punctuate meaning in unfolding discourse; they can be understood as marking a periodic boundary. This boundary is scaffolded in various ways in (20). Phonologically there are two silent beats prior to the commencement of speech (as notated in (21)).

(21)

//1 ^ / ^ / ***now*** by the

//4 *time* the / *fil*trate has / *reached* the distal convoluted / ***tub***ule

//1 *most* of the / *good* stuff has / ***gone***

// ^ / ^ //

In addition the hyper-Theme begins with the internal additive connector *now*, which signals a shift in the flow of meaning and is in fact assigned prominence as the Tonic syllable of its own tone group. The shift of gears is further reinforced by a marked Theme (an ideational unit preceding the Subject; Halliday and Matthiessen, 2014) *by the time the filtrate has reached the distal convoluted tubule*. Marked Themes of this kind typically reset unfolding discourse in terms of place or time. The underlined text in (22) resets time.

(22)

<u>by the time the filtrate has reached the distal convoluted tubule</u>, most of the good stuff has gone.

How does paralanguage support this foregrounding? At the beginning of this phase the lecturer is positioned to the far right of the lecture theatre. This in effect sets up an empty physical space to the left – a space about to be filled with meaning. His body rocks back on *time* and forward on *filtrate* in Figure 6.6, presaging his take-off from this position into the space to the left. In terms of body movement, his position for the hyper-Theme thus functions quite literally as 'point of departure' for his message – as paralinguistic movement through space is coordinated with language unfolding through time.

In example (23) we move up one level in the hierarchy of periodicity from the hyper-Theme to the macro-Theme that immediately precedes it.

(23)

    macro-Theme
    The last one is the distal convoluted tubule.
    hyper-Theme
    Now by the time the filtrate has reached the distal convoluted tubule most of the good stuff has gone.

The macro-Theme is foregrounded phonologically by three silent beats, followed by a jump up in pitch on its first salient syllable (coded as ↑ in (24)).

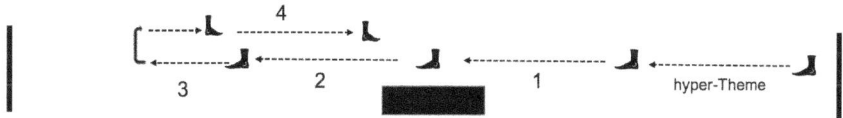

Figure 6.6 Extended circuit of body movement, beginning with hyper-Theme.

(24)

// ^ / ^ / ^

// 3 ^ the / ↑*last* one is the / *distal* /*con*voluted / **tub**ule //

In addition, the text reference in *the last one* positions this macro-Theme as culminating a series of macro-Themes (shown in (25)), each of which anticipates one stage in the reabsorption process (25).

(25)

So let's look at the individual parts of re-absorption.

The proximal convoluted tubule is the what what what? The wiggly little tube closest to the glomerulus. (…)

Moving along to the loop of Henle. (…)

The last one is the distal convoluted tubule. (…)

Sonovergently, the lecturer takes three steps in sync with three silent beats prior to the commencement of the macro-Theme in (24). This takes him from a space on the left to reach the central desk. Synchronous with the commencement of the macro-Theme, *the last one is the distal convoluted tubule*, he takes off from this central position, moving to the right. On completion of the macro-Theme, he rotates his body 180° to face left and continues stepping backwards in sync with the two silent feet that precede the hyper-Theme. This sequence of movement and body orientation is depicted in Figure 6.7. The lecturer ends up on his 'launch pad', the position from which he delivers his hyper-Theme before taking off in sync with a new phase of discourse.

The body movement and thematic development are well coordinated. Footfalls in Figure 6.6 synchronize with clause-level Themes and anticipatory positioning scaffolds higher levels of Theme – the lecturer's positioning to the

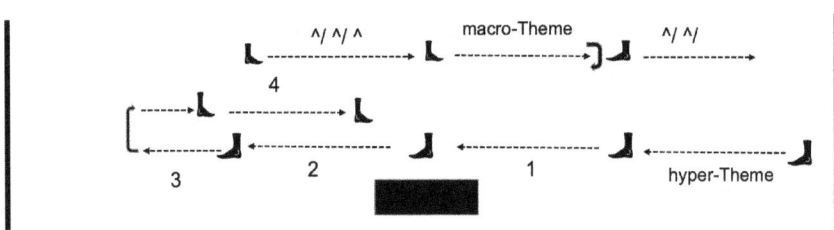

Figure 6.7 Circuit of body movement convergent with macro-Theme, hyper-Theme and four-figure sequence.

right of the lecturing space syncs with the hyper-Theme and centre-stage (desk) positioning syncs with the macro-Theme.

6.3.2.3 PARALINGUISTIC PERIODICITY *and News*

As a final step we consider the crest of prominence in the hyper-New for the same phase of discourse. The information in the hyper-New is an aggregation of the information in the New of each tone group, shown in (19′′′).

(19′′′)

// 3 *most* of the / **gluc**ose is

// 3 *back* in the / **blood**stream

// 3 *most* of the / **vit**amins are / *back* in the / *blood*stream

// 3 *most* of the / *ah* – *a-*/ *min*o / **ac**ids are / *back* in the / bl – / *back* in the / *blood*stream

// 1+ *lots* of / **wa**ter is

// 1 *back* in the / **blood**stream //

The hyper-New in (26) is preceded by two silent beats and begins with the internal causal connector *so*. The news of preceding tone groups (i.e. that most of the glucose, vitamins and amino acids and lots of water are back in the bloodstream) is distilled by declaring that by now we have a dilute material with *not a lot of good stuff in it*.

(26)

// ^ / ^

//3 *so* by / *this* / **time**, it's

//1 *pretty* / *close* to / *what* / *ur*ine / *ends* up / **be**ing

//3 ^ a / *di*lute ma- / **ter**ial with

//3 *not* a / *lot* of / *not* a lot of / **good** stuff in it and

//1 *full* of a lot of / **waste** //

Prior to the commencement of the hyper-New the lecturer has completed a full circuit of the lecturing space, arriving at the left edge of the central desk (as depicted in Figure 6.8). He sustains this central position, moving behind the desk and around its right edge as he delivers the hyper-New. Note that this is the same central position from which he launched the macro-Theme.

In effect what the body movement does here is more than culminate what has been presented. It affirms the authority of the lecturer's declaration by positioning him at the 'control centre' of the meanings in play (e.g. Lim et al.,

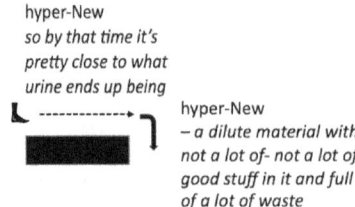

Figure 6.8 Body position and movement synchronous with hyper-New.

2012). Martin (1992: 489) uses the metaphor of an excursion to describe the complementarity of method of development and point in unfolding discourse: 'A text is a trip: method of development is the route taken, while point is why you went there in the first place – what you've seen/learned/experienced/taken away. Method of development is the plan; point is the holiday.' The biology lecturer's paralanguage enacts this metaphor quite literally as he sets off thematically, tours around and brings his message home.

6.3.2.4 Impact and implications of intermodal RHYTHM *and* PERIODICITY *in live lectures*

The exploration of intermodal RHYTHM and PERIODICITY in live lectures foregrounds a concern with prominence – what meanings are made prominent in spoken language and how. Rhythm is tied in this way to the potential for noticeability on the part of students and its implications for modes of expression in pedagogic discourse.

In spoken English, prominence is composed through the TONALITY, TONICITY and RHYTHM systems of prosodic phonology. It is also composed in multiple layers of predictive prominence in discourse, from clause-level Theme to hyper-Theme to layer upon layer of macro-Theme, and in layers of aggregating prominence from clause-level New to hyper-New and so on.

In the face-to-face discourse of live lectures we have noted the potential for expressions of prominence at multiple layers in discourse to synchronize aurally with prosodic phonology and visually with PARALINGUISTIC PERIODICITY. Such intermodal convergences amplify the prominence of the meanings involved. Face-to-face pedagogic interactions typically afford students a much greater frequency and range of expressions of paralinguistic prominence than are available through online modes. The synchronous intermodal signals in face-to-face lectures tune students in to predictive peaks of information which orient them to what is to come, and to culminative peaks of prominence which aggregate new information – thereby allocating 'their attention to important information ... in the message' (Dimitrova et al., 2016: 1255). Ultimately, as textual meaning in language and paralanguage gives prominence to and supports the noticeability of ideational and interpersonal meanings, students are guided to attend to the key knowledge and values of their disciplinary fields.

There is of course much more to be explored in relation to prominence and noticeability in different modes of lecturing. We might consider, for example, variations in intermodal expressions of prominence on the part of a lecturer when videoed lecturing to camera in contrast to lecturing to visible co-present students, or when lecturing through recorded voiced-over presentation slides (Hood and Lander, 2016). Recognition of the significance of the paralinguistic periodicity synchronous with spoken language is the driving force.

7

Afterword: Modelling paralanguage

In this chapter we reflect briefly on the model of paralanguage developed in this book – in relation to the scope of our study and its contribution to research on non-verbal communication. Our goal has been to show how our functional theory of language and semiosis can be used to interpret paralanguage, taking into account gesture, body movement, facial expression and voice quality.

7.1 Developing our model

An early step in our work involved drawing a distinction between somatic and semiotic behaviour (Figure 7.1), drawing on functional studies of language development – where the distinction bears critically on the emergence of protolanguage (our focus in Chapter 2).

We accept in drawing this distinction that all behaviour has the potential to be treated as meaningful or not by speakers. A clear example comes from the data underpinning Chapter 5, as Coraline swings rhythmically back and forth several times on a squeaky door, staring at her father who is busy at this desk as she does so (example (1)) – until he responds verbally and paralinguistically to this behaviour as a request for attention.

(1)

We can further illustrate this point anecdotally to show that it is not just human behaviour that can be construed as meaningful. In 2018 one of our

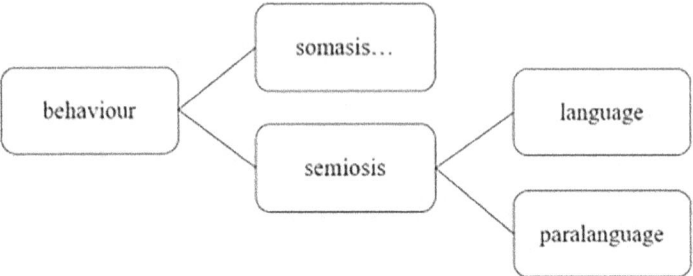

Figure 7.1 Semiotic versus somatic behaviour.

authors, along with her sister-in-law and her partner (another of our authors), participated in an informal memorial ashes ceremony on the edge of a reef in South Australia – pouring the sister-in-law's partner's ashes into the ocean there where that couple, keen divers, had spent many weekends and holidays exploring the reef together. As they did so a large ray swam slowly by. This was interpreted by all involved as a remarkable meaningful event, retold and enjoyed on many occasions with close relatives and friends – with the ray construed as a dear loved one saying goodbye. In cases such as these somasis is recontextualized as semiosis by the meaning-making interlocutors involved. What is crucial from the perspective of discourse analysis is the uptake of what went on, or not, by meaners.

We then moved to build a general model of paralanguage, drawing on the concept of stratification (levels of abstraction) and metafunction (kinds of meaning) in systemic functional linguistics (SFL) theory.[1] We used stratification to distinguish between paralanguage that converges with the prosodic phonology (intonation and rhythm) of spoken language and paralanguage that converges with its discourse semantics (IDEATION, APPRAISAL, IDENTIFICATION and PERIODICITY) – sonovergent versus semovergent paralanguage, respectively (Figure 7.2). With the exception of mime (discussed later in the chapter) and some pointing deixis (discussed in Chapter 6), paralanguage converges with the intonation and rhythm of spoken language in our data. This argues for a linguistically informed model of prosodic phonology as a prerequisite for the analysis of paralanguage. It also provides one useful criterion for distinguishing somasis from semiosis (since somatic behaviour is not coordinated with prosodic phonology). Note that in relating paralanguage to discourse semantics rather than lexicogrammar, we are suggesting that the grammatical structure of a spoken language (specifically, the nature of its syntagms) is not relevant to its paralanguage. In this respect paralanguage resembles the 'language-neutral' sign

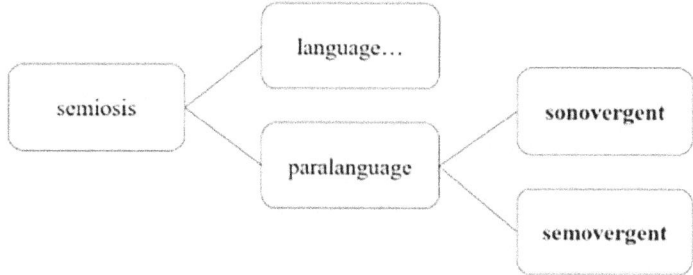

Figure 7.2 Sonovergent versus semovergent paralanguage.

language of the North American Plains Indians, but not the sign languages of Australia's indigenous communities (Kendon, 2004: 299–303), at least for their more proficient signers.

We used metafunction to distinguish between paralanguage systems converging with ideational, interpersonal or textual meaning (Figure 7.3). Seen in these terms, sonovergent paralanguage resonates with interpersonal meaning and syncs with textual meaning; there is no sonovergent concurrence with ideational meaning.[2] Semovergent paralanguage on the other hand resonates with interpersonal meaning, coordinates with textual meaning and concurs with ideational meaning.

Our final step, for this book, was to map the meaning potential of each of these five paralinguistic systems. Ideational resources were presented in

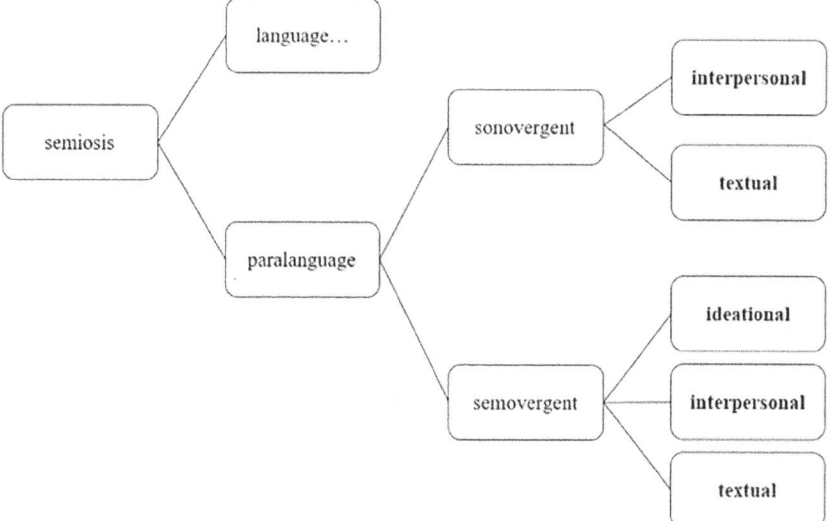

Figure 7.3 Paralanguage in relation to metafunction.

Chapter 4, focusing on the construal of paralinguistic entities and paralinguistic figures (both static and dynamic). Interpersonal resources were presented in Chapter 5, focusing on the enactment of FACIAL AFFECT, VOICE QUALITY and a range of attendant social relations. Textual resources were presented in Chapter 6, focusing on PARALINGUISTIC DEIXIS and PARALINGUISTIC PERIODICITY. The affordances of each resource were formalized in system networks, outlining the range of meanings involved and their relation to one another (i.e. their valeur).

We have not attempted in this volume to formalize realization statements specifying the realization of each choice in these networks, relying simply on verbal descriptions and imagic illustrations. Formalization of these realization statements, drawing perhaps on an expression form notation developed for deaf sign language (e.g. Johnston and Schembri, 2007: Chapter 4), is an important avenue for future research. However this proceeds, there remains the issue of representing the dynamics of facial expression, gesture and body movement in a static two-dimensional image. We adopted the well-worn strategy of including vectors and sequences of images at various points in our presentation. Fortunately most of our illustrations are from sources available online – free (the 'Random Chatty Vlog' on YouTube) or for purchase (the film *Coraline*). And comparable face-to-face lecture data is presumably readily available for most of our readers. Ideally each example in studies of this kind would be linked to a clip online, a practice to be encouraged in future publications (finance, copyright and anonymity considerations permitting).[3]

As noted in Chapter 1, although presented as a simple taxonomy in Figure 7.3, all five subtypes of paralanguage can combine with one another in support of a single tone group. Several examples of multiple dimensions of paralanguage converging on the same tone group were presented in Chapter 1, for example, the combination of a motion occurrence figure and pointing deixis in Example (14'''') of Section 1.5.2.1 (for a combination of a motion occurrence figure, paralinguistic affect and pointing deixis, see example (9'') here). It is probably fair to say that when semovergent paralanguage is deployed, it will almost always be coordinated with TONALITY, TONICITY and RHYTHM; this argues that semovergence implies sonovergence. Sonovergent paralanguage on the other hand can be deployed without semovergence, through gestures and body movement in tune with or in sync with prosodic phonology (but no more).

An important exception to these principles is what is commonly referred to as mime. In terms of our model mime is semovergent paralanguage that does not accompany language, an apparent contradiction in terms. To explore this further we will return to a miming segment in our vlogger's 'Parking Lot' phase. She sets up what happened as follows:

(2) Oh another thing that has been really annoying this summer is you know when you go to a parking lot and it's a busy place. You get in your car and you – you don't necessarily want to leave immediately. Like you might wanna – I might want to have Henry test his blood sugar, give the kids snacks. [editing cut] Or if we were at the pool, like change or look at my phone or send a text message or whatever. [editing cut] It drives me crazy when a car is like sitting there following you through the parking lot and then they just wait for you to leave. I cannot stand that. And that has happened so many times. And I was just at the mall of America and I got back to my car and I wanted to – and I met up with a YouTube mum Kimmy from the Dodge family and I went to – I wanted to like um Instagram a picture of us and Facebook whatever. [editing cut] And as I was doing that I – I had...

This is followed by a specific parking lot incident, presented in tone groups below.

(3)   // just got in my **car**,
(4)   // got my **phone** and
(5)   // as I was **do**ing that
(6)   // some / **guy** was
(7)   // **sitt**ing there and there was
(8)   // cars be**hind** him and he was like
(9)   // [mimics man's gesture and expression]
(10) // like waving me **out**. And I was
(11) // so up**set**. Like I i-
(12) // mmediately got **up**,
(13) // put my **phone** down. I i-
(14) // mmediately drove a**way** but - I
(15) // wasn't even **think**ing I
(16) // **should**n't have done that. I
(17) // should not have **done** that. But –
(18) // [editing cut]
(19) // but it was just like '**what**!' There's a
(20) // guy **sitt**ing there
(21) // waving and **ang**ry at me because I was
(22) // sitting in my **car**. It's like I am //

In this sequence, there is a miming segment where tone groups might have been, as the vlogger mimes the paralanguage of her parking spot assailant. She first mimes his exasperation.

(9')

paralinguistic affect   exasperation

image

She then mimes his ideational paralanguage as he twice gestures for her to leave (including a deictic pointing gesture).

(9")

paralinguistic   from behind shoulder to high right, pointing with index
occurrence Figure   finger; from chest to high right, pointing with index finger
Images

The third time his motion gesture is mimed in fact concurs with language.

(10')

phonology   //1 ^ like / *waving me* / ***out*** and I was //

paralinguistic   from face to high right, pointing with index finger
occurrence Figure
Images

As we can see, the two miming segments are heavily co-textualized by language that makes explicit what is going on. The orientation to the narrative introduces the recurrent problem of someone following the vlogger in a parking lot and waiting for her to leave. The miming segments are introduced with an incomplete tone group //3 cars be- / **hind** him and he was like // [mimics man's gesture and expression] //, with a missing Tonic segment. The vlogger then mimes the expected information before making it linguistically explicit in a tone group converging with the third iteration of the gesture.

Setting aside the mime performances of mime artists (the 'art of silence' Marcel Marceau referred to), we can predict that co-textualization of this kind is a generalizable pattern as far as semovergent paralanguage (in the absence of language) is concerned. What the moment of mime does not provide as far as language is concerned, the immediately preceding and following co-text does. The convergent nature of semovergent paralanguage as a recurrent pattern is clear.

This pattern of convergence underscores the importance of a linguistically informed model of prosodic phonology, covering rhythm and intonation, for work on paralanguage. Fortunately for us, SFL has provided us with the rich model introduced in Chapter 3 (a model Kendon (1972) also drew on in his early work). In this regard we would caution against the use of linguistically uninformed models of 'pausing' and 'emphasis' such as those commonly deployed in Conversation Analysis (cf. Walker's (2013: 469–72) critique of Jefferson's widely adopted notation). What is needed is a model that respects the prosodic phonology of specific languages and its convergence with paralanguage – if what makes paralanguage 'para-' is to be properly understood.

In reviewing our proposals for sonovergent and semovergent systems, it is important to keep in mind that we are treating emblems as part of the expression form of language and not as paralanguage (Figure 7.4) – and thus excluded thumbs-up or thumbs-down (as praise or censure), index finger touching lips (for 'quiet please'), hand cupped over ear (for 'I can't hear') and so on from our description. Our reasoning was presented in Chapter 1, Section 1.6. This was the basis of our argument that semovergent paralanguage cannot be used to support NEGOTIATION by distinguishing move types in dialogic exchanges (although sonovergent paralanguage can of course support TONE choice in relation to these moves).

This raises a question of how we might position onomatopoeia (e.g. animal noises such as *meow, woof, neigh, baa*) and phonaesthesia (e.g. **slinky, slimey, slinky, slippery, slither, slurp, slushy**) were we to further develop our description of language and paralanguage. This would involve bringing relevant

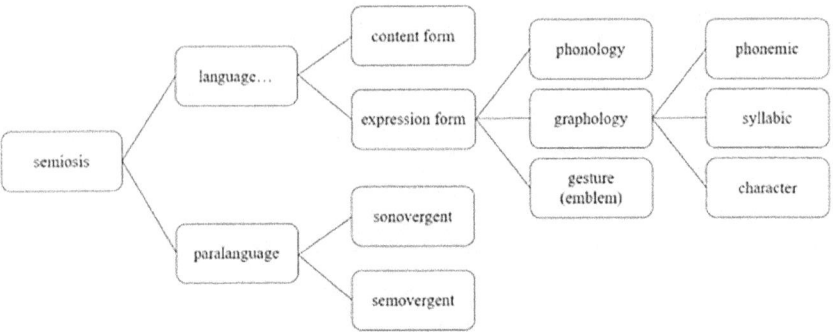

Figure 7.4 The place of emblems in our model of language and paralanguage.

dimensions of voice quality (outlined in Chapter 5) to bear, as well as exploring the potential for human articulatory resources to imitate sounds (arguably an ideational resource) and attitudinally 'colour' phonaesthetic series (arguably an interpersonal one). Our expectation is that these resources could be brought into a model of paralanguage based on further research (cf. Chapter 5, Section 5.5, on voice quality differentiation between miserable and angry meows).

7.2 A note on interdisciplinarity

What we are calling paralanguage can be approached from a number of different perspectives. McNeill's (2000, 2006) psycholinguistic studies are well known; Kendon (2004) draws heavily on both linguistic and anthropological research; and Heath and Luff (2013) survey Conversation Analysis initiatives. Our approach has been deliberately intradisciplinary, informed by SFL theory. We eschew eclecticism. There are two main reasons for this. First, as outlined in Chapter 1, there is an ever-increasing catalogue of SFL-inspired work on modalities other than language – triggered by Kress and van Leewuen (1990, 1996), who focused on single static images. This work has now been extended to the study of diagrams, PowerPoint slides, webpages, comics, picture books, animations, film, sound and music, architecture, sculpture, toys and even somatic behaviour. With so many texts involving one or more of these modalities, it is advantageous when studying intermodal relations to be able to draw on descriptions informed by the same theoretical principles.

Our second motivation has to do with our conception of interdisciplinarity and what makes productive dialogue possible. In our experience (e.g. Martin,

2011a; Maton et al., 2016) working across disciplines is most effective when there is a shared object of inquiry, a problem to be redressed and shared politics informing this redress. In addition it is important that each of the disciplines involved has something to say which deals substantively with something the other discipline or disciplines are interested in. This means that if we as functional linguists are going to contribute to an understanding of paralanguage, then we need a comprehensive description of paralanguage, formulated in systemic functional semiotic terms, before we can start talking. For us, productive interdisciplinary dialogue is not a matter of 'you do your bit and I'll do mine'. Rather it involves distinct theories and descriptions of comparable phenomena and ways of making explicit to one another what complementary theories and descriptions afford. It is only on this basis that attention can be drawn to patterns that matter but have not been noticed or are poorly described from another point of view. And this may mean revising theory so that such patterns can be brought into view. It might be wise to secure the term 'transdisciplinarity' (in place of interdisciplinarity) for dialogue of this kind.

We are also motivated in our enterprise by what we consider an alarming trajectory in multimodal studies, generally referencing Kress and van Leeuwen (2001). This involves the trend in conferences and publications celebrating multimodality to set aside the analysis of language as 'logocentric' and focus on some somatic or semiotic phenomenon that has not been much described before and/or adopt a new relatively implicit theoretical and descriptive perspective on this phenomenon. Typically, almost no analysis of the kind promoted in the various editions of Kress and van Leeuwen's *Reading Images* (1990/1996/2006/2020) is involved (i.e. no system networks or function structures are deployed). And typically there is no discussion of intermodality, since the focus is on one particular phenomenon or another. The conferences are multimodal; but the presentations are not. Let us stand back a moment and consider what is going on here from the perspective of Maton's Legitimation Code Theory (LCT).

Maton (2014: 174) notes that knowledge practices involve 'epistemic relations between knowledge claims and their objects of study; and social relations between knowledge claims and their subjects'. He continues: 'One can … analytically distinguish *ontic relations* (OR) between practices and that part of the world towards which they are oriented' (i.e. the degree to which knowledge practices bound and control legitimate objects of study) 'and *discursive relations* (DR) between practices and other practices' (i.e. the degree to which knowledge practices legitimate procedures for constructing objects of study) (Maton, 2014: 175, italics in original).

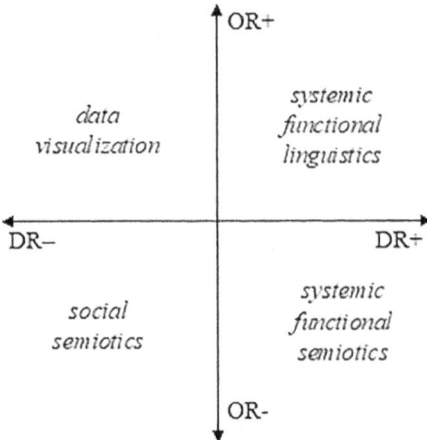

Figure 7.5 Approaches to multi/modality (ontic vs discursive relations).

This enables Maton to establish the topological parameters deployed in Figure 7.5. There the vertical axis refers to the strength of ontic relations – how strongly a knowledge practice restricts what can be studied; and the horizontal axis refers to the strength of discursive relations – how strongly a knowledge practice limits the way in which something is studied. Taking multimodal studies as our focus, we have populated the topology as follows: SFL is positioned as bearing a relatively strong ontic relation to its object of study (since its singular focus is language) and a relatively strong discursive relation to other knowledge (since it is one particular theory of language). What we are calling systemic functional semiotics on the other hand has a relatively weak ontic relation to its objects of study (since it welcomes work on semiotic systems other than language) but maintains its relatively strong discursive relation to other approaches (since it continues to draw on SFL theory to model non-linguistic semiosis). What we are calling social semiotics involves relatively weak ontic and discursive relations (since it embraces the study of an ever-increasing range of phenomena from an ever-wider range of perspectives). As an example of a knowledge practice with relatively strong ontic relations and weak discursive ones we have proposed data visualization, since its focus is well-defined, but it can draw on a range of relevant knowledges to achieve its goals.

Seen in these terms the general drift in multimodal studies has been towards ever-weaker ontic and discursive relations (a move from social science to the humanities one might say). Wildfeuer et al. (2019) explore this trajectory and others with respect to the status of multimodality studies as a discipline. Needless to say, our approach to paralanguage fits snugly into an alternative weak ontic relations, strong discursive relations trajectory – because of our concern with modelling intermodality and fostering transdisciplinary dialogue, as outlined earlier.

7.3 A note on intermodality

As reviewed in Section 7.1, our project involves developing paralanguage as a semiotic system alongside language. We adopted our model of the relation of paralanguage to language from earlier work on the convergence of language and image in children's picture books (Painter et al., 2013). As outlined in Table 7.1, sonovergence was explored in terms of how linguistic and paralinguistic systems resonate with one another (interpersonal meaning) and sync with one another (textual meaning).

And, as outlined in Table 7.2, semovergence was explored in terms of how linguistic and paralinguistic systems concur with one another (ideational meaning), resonate with one another (interpersonal meaning) and sync with one another (textual meaning).

Table 7.1 Sonovergence – language and paralanguage

Verbiage	*Sonovergent*	Paralanguage ('prosodic')
Interpersonal: TONE	*Resonance*	Interpersonal: IN TUNE
Textual: TONALITY, TONICITY, RHYTHM	*Synchronicity*	Textual: IN SYNC

From the perspective of instantiation (the system to text relation in SFL), this raises the central challenge of intermodal studies, namely, the ineffable process whereby systems from different modalities end up seamlessly instantiated as coherent text. As in film (van Leeuwen, 1985, 2005), textual meaning has a critical role to play, as the 'beat' of feet and tone groups (TONALITY, TONICITY, SALIENCE and RHYTHM) coordinates the convergence of linguistic and paralinguistic resources (the focus of Chapter 6).

Modelling concurrence and resonance is more of a challenge. One response would be to quantify the semantic 'weight' of the contributions from alternative modalities in terms of degrees of commitment – where commitment refers, following Martin (2010), to the number of optional systems taken up and the degree of delicacy of selections from both optional and obligatory systems.

Table 7.2 Semovergence – language and paralanguage

Verbiage	*Semovergent*	Paralanguage ('articulatory')
Ideational: IDEATION	*Concurrence*	Ideational: 'mimetic'
Interpersonal: APPRAISAL	*Resonance*	Interpersonal: 'expressive'
Textual: IDENTIFICATION/PERIODICITY	*Synchronicity*	textual: 'coordinating'

Figueredo and Figueredo (2019) outline a quantitative model for measurements of this kind. This would offer us a gauge of how much meaning language and paralanguage were committing but not tell us much about the kinds of meaning involved. Another response, perhaps better suited to this shortcoming, would be to turn to a higher-order semiotic such as register (Matthiessen, 2007) or genre (Bateman, 2008) and assign it responsibility for the distribution of meaning across modalities. Models of this kind take advantage of work on the relation of hierarchically organized categories in language (i.e. system realized in structure, higher ranks realized by lower ones and more abstract strata realized through more concrete ones) to explore intermodality – in effect treating co-instantiation across modalities as if it were realization within a modality.

Our suggestion on the basis of the model of paralanguage developed in this volume would be to explore models of intermodal relations one metafunction or stratum at a time – taking care to specify which strata or which metafunctions are in focus and, where relevant, which ranks (e.g. levels of constituency such tone group, foot, syllable or phoneme).

7.4 A note on altermodality

Kendon (2004: chapter 14) distinguishes between primary sign languages which develop in communities of deaf people and alternate sign languages which develop in certain speaking/hearing communities. Of the latter he reviews crane driver guider gestures, a sawmill system, monastic sign languages, North American Plains sign language and Central Australian sign languages. What is the relation of paralanguage, we might ask, to some or any of these?

In order to explore this question we need to first ask why paralanguage came to be regarded as in some sense 'outside' language proper in the first place – a position which has been challenged by specialists such as Fricke (2013), who argue for a more unified approach to gesture and speech. To understand this we probably have to appreciate the privileged position of the phoneme in influential linguistic paradigms such as the American structuralism documented in Joos (1957). This work founds a phonemics, morphology and syntax approach to language description which continues to shape introductions to linguistics, at least in the English-speaking world and its compliant intellectual dominions. The approach is fundamentally a combinatorial one, with clauses (ultimately) composed of morphemes and morphemes composed of phonemes – all of which is presented as linguistic form, arbitrarily related to meaning. Since paralinguistic signs are not composed of phonemes (or arguably of comparable entities) and do make meaning, paralanguage gets positioned as something to be studied alongside language, not as part of it.

Working from a functional paradigm we of course have to approach the relation of 'sign languages' to one another differently. In essence this means adopting a paradigmatic perspective and formalizing their meaning potential as far as possible in system networks specifying the relation of one sign (in Saussure's sense of the term) to another. The crucial question we then need to ask is whether meanings combine with one another. To what extent, for example, do we simply have an inventory of signs, distinct from, but not combining with, one another – as in protolanguage or Kendon's (2004) crane driver gesture system (a list of 'emblems' we might say)? And if meanings do combine, is that because ideational choices distinguish themselves from say interpersonal ones and combine freely with one another – as with the emergence of language in SFL studies of language development (e.g. Halliday, 1975; Painter, 1984)? And/or do combinations of meanings involve structural configurations, with both the parts and their whole distinguishing the meanings involved (as in Halliday, 2003; Painter, [1999] 2005)? The paralinguistic systems we describe in this volume do combine ideational, interpersonal and textual meanings but apparently without involving syntagmatic relations (i.e. parts configuring as wholes).

Ultimately then, comparing paralanguage with primary or alternate sign systems involves specifying the meaning potential of these systems. Thanks to Rudge's (2017, 2021) SFL work on British Sign Language we are now in a position to compare one primary sign system with English paralanguage. And as part of this research we can begin to ask about the distinction between language and paralanguage in such systems (cf. Johnston, 2013, 2018) – a politically sensitive issue in relation to the recognition of primary sign languages as bona fide languages in many communities. Even more sensitive might be consideration of the genesis of sign languages around the world, and the possibility of a pidgin/creole continuum involving the range of speakers who had the opportunity to learn sign in childhood as a 'native language' and those who came to it at various stages later on in life as a first or additional language. How might such studies bear on the hypothesis that sign languages emerged as creolized paralanguages among communities of deaf speakers?

If we are to ask these questions, then it is important to approach each primary and alternate modality by specifying its meaning potential and then considering the complementarities among the different meaning potentials at play. Matthiessen and Halliday (2009) and Martin et al. (2013a, to appear) outline how this kind of analysis can be pursued from the perspective of SFL.

In the interest of balance, one might up the ante here. How many modalities other than language can be conceived as creolized paralanguage? Is paralanguage drawing in the air or turning this around – is drawing or painting actually inscribed ideational paralanguage? Would analysis of concert conducting be a useful stepping stone for imagining music as creolized interpersonal and textual paralanguage? Is dance creolized paralanguage along similar lines? As flagged in Section 7.2, in an era when presentations on multimodality so often ignore language (for fear of 'logocentrism') and regularly focus on one modality other than language rather than intermodality, these seem usefully challenging questions to pose.

7.5 A closing note on register variation and beyond

It might seem anticlimactic to end on a note of caution. But our work on paralanguage from an SFL perspective is still embryonic, especially with respect to the range of registers we have considered. As noted in Chapter 1, our work emerged in studies of New South Wales Youth Justice Conferencing (Zappavigna and Martin, 2018) – and so involved fairly formal interactions between younger offenders, support persons, police officers, youth workers and a convenor. For this volume we concentrated on one vlog (Chapters 1, 3 and 4), one animated film (Chapter 5) and a range of face-to-face lectures (Chapter 6). This made it easier for us to co-textualize and contextualize our examples and for readers to access our data in the case of the vlog and the film.

Probably the biggest gap in our work so far has been work on casual conversation. A paralinguistic supplement to Eggins and Slade's (1997) classic study is urgently required. Attention also needs to be given to registers in which speakers have been instructed to perform – in theatre or music schools or for debating and public speaking. Our expectation is that each new register will lead to reconsideration of the details of the specific paralinguistic systems proposed in Chapters 4, 5 and 6. We do hope on the other hand that our general model of sonovergent and semovergent systems will stand a longer test of time and prove a productive framework for exploring the contribution of gesture, body orientation, position and movement, facial expression, gaze and voice quality to face-to-face interaction. Go online, sample any animation, film or vlog and take in all the meaning going on (not just the meaning that linguists typically describe). That is our challenge. As functional linguists, we have been sidelining paralanguage for far too long.

Appendices

Appendix A: 'Chatty Vlog' transcript

Intro

Hi everybody it is August first and I'm going to do just a random chatty vlog for you guys.[1] [editing cut] I had a video for today. I filmed it and I was going to edit it. It was a type one Tuesday. I was showing all the diabetes supplies – like the extra supplies we brought on vacation but I had bent down like before I started filming and my shirt got caught in my bra so it was like sitting – it just – it's all I could see the whole time so I was like 'I'm not posting this video' 'cause that's all people would be looking at. [editing cut] So this is what you get today. [editing cut] So many of you actually love these sit-down chatty videos so I thought it would be kind of fun. [editing cut]

'National Night Out' phase

It is two twenty and I just got out of the shower and I just put some makeup on because it is National Night Out – and I put a fancy shirt on. I like never wear this. I think I have worn this one time since I got it. I'm usually in like a tank top with sports bra with these like yoga pants. So. But it is national night out like I said and our neighbourhood gathers together and we have like a potluck and the police come and the fire truck come and there are neighbours that I see like once a year and I wanted to look – I wanted to look presentable. Different than they normally probably see me every single day walking with the kids. I wanted to look nice. [editing cut] So that's kind of exciting. I'm bringing two big macaroni and cheeses just like the Stouffer's brand I think. Andy went and got it, um yesterday at the store. Yeah, I got two big ones. I

'Hair Dye' phase

… [I] thought that'd be really good for the kids and myself since I'm a picky eater. [editing cut] Oh and you're probably seeing how dark my hair is. Well, one it's wet. But I could not find the hair dye that I bought previously when I dyed my hair which I loved – I loved the first time, so I ended up having to do like a different shade that I didn't use previously and it's so dark, I hate it! I hate the – the colour of it so I've tried washing it out – it's lighter than it was a few days ago but yeah it's such a bummer, and then I went to Target like two days later and there was a whole stack of them so I bought three of them. So hopefully next time I will get my hair colour back, [handclap] um but for now this will do.

'Caring for Children' phase

What else can we talk about? I hear children coming. They're gonna ask for more food. I just gave them Chex Mix and applesauce squeezes. What's up? [editing cut] I'm back. [laughs] So my kids just came upstairs and of course asked me for more food which – they had a big lunch. Then they had a snack. I gave them each a bowl – like a heaping bowl full of Chex Mix and an applesauce squeeze and they want more food, but they cannot have more food.

'Dermatologist Visit' phase

I was going to vlog the day – I went to the dermatologist because I have these like marks on my feet. I'll show you. Let's see if I can show you from here. [lifting up leg] Ooh. I don't know if you can see that. I have that mark and then there's another one and then another one on my other feet and it was all like bumpy and stuff. And it was spreading, and it had like tripled – quadrupled in size in a year. It actually was there for two years. Anyway, it was some granuloma [out-breath] something I don't know – it's called – it's some sort of skin thing. And so, the dermatologist um took like this needle and under each like bump and injected this like steroid and it would like all bubble up. It was really gross and it hurt so bad [handclap] but I didn't film it because there's like feet people out there that like are obsessed with feet and I didn't want to – you know. I didn't want those people attracted to my videos, so I did – I decided not to film it. But it was really itchy. [editing cut] And the bumps are supposed to go away and it shouldn't spread anymore but the discolouration might stay there for a really, really long time so … Yeah. But that was good to get checked out. [editing cut]

'Parking Lot' phase

Oh another thing that has been really annoying this summer is you know when you go to a parking lot and it's a busy place. You get in your car and you – you don't necessarily want to leave immediately. Like you might wanna – I might want to have Henry test his blood sugar, give the kids snacks. [editing cut] Or if we were at the pool, like change or look at my phone or send a text message or whatever. [editing cut] It drives me crazy when a car is like sitting there following you through the parking lot and then they just wait for you to leave. I cannot stand that. And that has happened so many times. And I was just at the mall of America and I got back to my car and I wanted to – and I met up with a YouTube mum Kimmy from the Dodge family and I went to – I wanted to like um Instagram a picture of us and Facebook whatever. [editing cut] And as I was doing that I – I had just got in my car, got my phone and as I was doing that some guy was sitting there and there was cars behind him and he was like [mimics man's gesture and expression] like waving me out. And I was so upset. Like I immediately got up, put my phone down. I immediately drove away but – I wasn't even thinking I shouldn't have done that. I should not have done that. But – [editing cut] but it was just like 'what!' There's a guy sitting there waving and angry at me because I was sitting in my car. It's like I am sitting in my car – I shouldn't have to leave. Mad at myself that I did that but – from now on I am not moving. I don't care if they follow me around the whole parking lot to get to my car. I am not moving. [editing cut]

'Social Media' phase

I don't want this video to like ramble on. I want it to be kind of short. But I do want to start going live either on Instagram, Facebook, YouTube, I don't know. I don't know what exactly. Um I started doing like Instagram stories for like three days but then I lost a huge chunk of people that were following me, so I don't know if people like hated it or I was really annoying. So, I stopped doing that and I did – I'd posted like four little clips of videos so I don't know if people just realized and didn't know who I was or didn't like me in their feed or whatnot. So that like tur – totally turned me off from Instagram. [editing cut] Then I thought 'well maybe I'll do it on my Facebook page' but only about two hundred of you follow me there and I feel like so many of you would miss out. And then on YouTube, if I go live on YouTube, the only thing I don't like is, you know, you have all the comments and stuff but when you play it back people watching can't see the comments so I just think it's kind of weird, I don't know. 'Cause I would be talking to the people in the comments and the replay viewers would be like 'what?' you know. Like I don't know. I don't know but I really think it would be fun to go live and answer questions and things. I have not done a

Q and A, years. It's been years and all the one's that I've done prior, like many, many years ago, Andy and I used to do them all the time. I for some reason deleted them all. Every single one. Every Q and A I have deleted. So, when I hit twenty thousand subscribers. That is my goal. That's always been my goal. I just hit nineteen although I just lost like thirty-eight subscribers yesterday. So, I was like at nineteen thousand and one. So, I don't even know if I'm there – if I'm at nineteen thousand anymore.

'Caring for Children' phase

[talking to child] Just a second honey. [editing cut] I totally forgot what I was just saying. Charlie just came up here and was talking to me [laughs]. [editing cut] I remember what I was talking about. So when I hit twenty thousand subscribers I am going to do a big Q and A with the family – with Andy or whoever has questions and I'm gonna to do that for you guys. Clock is dinging, Charlie needs me, kids are hungry, so I better go.

Outro

Thank you for watching guys. [editing cut] I will see you Thursday for a day in the life video. It will be live at two p.m. Eastern Standard Time. [editing cut] So don't miss it. Thanks for watching guys. Bye. [child walks in] Mummy I need a drink. You need a drink. OK. [reaches to turn off camera]

Appendix B1: Phonological analysis of Intro

[0:00–0:38]²

1. //3 ↑*hi* every- / **bod**y it is
2. //3 *aug*ust / **first** and
3. //3 *I'm* going to / **do**
4. //1_3 ^ just a / *ran*dom / *chat*ty / **vlog** for you / **guys**
5. // [editing cut]
6. //3 *I* had a / *vid*eo for to- / **day** I
7. //3 **filmed** it and I was
8. //3 *go*ing to *ed*it it it was a
9. //3 *type* one / **Tues**day I was

10. //3 *show*ing all the / *di*abetes supp- / **lies** – like the
11. //2 **ex**tra supp- / *lies* we
12. //2 *brought* on va- / **cat**ion
13. //3 ^ but I had / *bent* / **down** like be-
14. //2 *fore* I / *start*ed / **film**ing and my
15. //3 *shirt* got / *caught* in my / **bra** so it was like
16. //3 *sit*ting – it / *just* – / ^ it's / *all* I could / *see* the / *whole* / **time** so I was like
17. //1 *I'm* not / *post*ing this / **vid**eo 'cause that's
18. //1 *all* people would be / **look**ing at
19. // [editing cut]
20. //3 ^ so / ↑*this* is what you / *get* to- / **day**
21. // [editing cut]
22. //3 ^ so / *man*y of you / *act*ually / *love* these / *sit* down / *chat*ty / **vid**eos
23. //3 so ^ I / *thought* it would be / *kind* of / **fun**
24. // [editing cut]

Appendix B2: Phonological analysis of 'National Night Out' phase

[0:38–1:26]

1. //4 *it* / **is**
2. //3 *two* / **twent**y and I
3. //3 *just* got out of the / **show**er and I
4. //3 ↑*just* put some / **make**up on be-
5. //1 *cause* it is / *national* night / *out* / *and* I put a / *fancy* / **shirt** on
6. //1 I like / *nev*er / **wear** this
7. //3 ^ I / *think* I have / *worn* this / *one* / *time* since I / **got** it
8. //1 ^ I'm / *us*ually in like a / *tank* / *top* with / *sports* / *bra* with these like / **yog**a pants
9. //1 **so**
10. //3 ^ / *but* it is / ↑*national* night / *out* like I / **said**
11. //3 *and* our / *neigh*bourhood / *gathers* to- / **geth**er and we
12. //3 *have* like a / *pot* / *luck* and the po-
13. //4 **lice** / *come* and the

14. //3 *fire* truck / *come* and
15. //3 *there* are / *neigh*bours that I
16. //3 *see* like / once a / *year* and I
17. //3 *wanted* to / *look* – ↑I / *wanted* to look pre- / *sent*able
18. //3 *different* than they / *normally* / *probably* / *see* me / *every* / *single* day / *walk*ing with the / *kids* I
19. //1_ *wanted* to look / *nice*
20. // [editing cut]
21. //3 ^ ↑so / *that's* kind of ex- / *cit*ing I'm
22. //3 *bringing* / *two* big / *macaroni* and / *chees*es just like the
23. //2 *Stouff*er's brand I / *think*
24. //1 *Andy* went and / *got* it um / *yest*erday at the
25. //4 *store*
26. //3 *yeah* I got / *two* / *big* ones I //

Appendix B3: Phonological analysis of 'Hair Dye' phase

[1:26–2:01]

1. //…[I]
2. //3 *thought* that'd be / *really* good for the / *kids*
3. //3 *and* my- / *self* since
4. //13 *I'm* a picky / *eat*er
5. // [editing cut]
6. //5 ↑*oh* and you're
7. //1 *probably* / *seeing* how / *dark* my / *hair* is well
8. //1_ *one* it's / *wet*
9. //4 *but* I could / ↑*not* / *find* the / *hair* dye that I
10. //2 *bought* / *prev*iously when I
11. //3 *dyed* my / *hair* which I
12. //3 *loved* – I
13. //3 *loved* the / *first* time
14. //3 ^ so I / *ended* up having to / *do* like a / *different* / ^ / *shade* that I
15. //3 *didn't* use / *prev*iously and it's
16. //1 *so*:: / *dark* I
17. //1 *hate* it I
18. //3 *hate* the – the / *col*our of it so I've

19. //1 *tried* washing it / **out** it's
20. //3 *ligh*ter than it / *was* a few / ***days*** ago
21. //1 ^ but / ↑***yeah*** it's
22. //1 *such* a / ***bumm****er* and then I
23. //2 *went* to / ***Targ****et*
24. //3 ^ like / *two* days / *lat*er and there was a
25. //1_ *whole* / ***stack*** of them so I
26. //1 *bought* / ***three*** of them so
27. //3 ↑*hopefully* next / ***time*** I will
28. //1 *get* my / ***hair*** colour / *back*
29. //3 [handclap] / *um* / *but* for / ↑***now***
30. //3 *this* will / ↓***do*** //

Appendix B4: Phonological analysis of 'Caring for Children (A)' phase

[2:02–2:26]

1. //1 *what* else can we / ***talk*** about
2. //1 ^ I / *hear* children / ***com****ing*
3. //1 ^ they're / *gonn*a ask for more / ***food*** I
4. //3 *just* gave them / ***Chex*** Mix and
5. //3 *app*lesauce / ***squeez****es*
6. //1 *what's* / ***up***
7. // [editing cut]
8. //1 ^ I'm / ***back***
9. //3 [laughs] so my / *kids* just / *came* up- / ***stairs*** and of
10. //4 *course* / *asked* me for / *more* / ***food***
11. //3 ^ which they / *had* a big / ***lunch***
12. //1 ^ then they / *had* a / ***snack*** I
13. //4+ *gave* them / *each* a / *bowl* – like a / ↑*heaping* / ***bowl***
14. //3 *full* of / ***Chex*** Mix and an
15. //4 *app*lesauce / ***squeeze*** and they
16. //1_ *want* more / ***food*** but they can-
17. //1_ *not* have more / ***food*** //

Appendix B5: Phonological analysis of 'Visit to the Dermatologist' phase

[2:27–3:26]

1. //1 ^ I / *was* going to / *vlog* the / **day** I
2. //3 *went* to the / derma- / **to**logist because I
3. //2 *have* these like / **marks** on my / **feet** I'll
4. //1 **show** you let's
5. //1 *see* if I can / *show* you from / **here** [lifting up leg]
6. //1 **ooh**
7. //3 *I* don't know if you can / **see** that I have
8. //3 **that** mark and then there's an-
9. //3 **oth**er one and then an- / *other* one on my / **oth**er feet and it was
10. //3 *all* like / **bump**y and / *stuff*
11. //3 *and* it was / **spread**ing and it had like
12. //3 *tripled* – quad- / *rup*led in / *size* in a / **year** it
13. //3 *actually* was there for / **two** years
14. //4 **an**yway it was
15. //3 *some* / *granu*- / *loma*:: / ^ [out-breath] / **some**thing
16. //1_ *I* don't know – it's / *called* – it's / *some* sort of / **skin** thing
17. //3 *and* so the / *derma*tologist um / *took* like this / **need**le and
18. //3 *under* / *each* like / **bump** and in-
19. //3 *jected* this like / **ster**oid and it would like
20. //3 *all* / **bubb**le up it was
21. //1 *really* / **gross** and it
22. //4 *hurt* / **so** bad
23. //4 [handclap] but I / ↑**did**n't / *film* it be-
24. //2 *cause* there's like / **feet** people / *out* there that like
25. //3 ^ are ob- / *sessed* with / **feet** and I
26. //4 *didn't* want to – / **you** know I
27. //1_ *didn't* want / *those* people a- / *ttract*ed to my / **vid**eos so I / *did* – I de-
28. //3 *cided* / *not* to / **film** it but it was
29. //1 *really* / **itch**y
30. // [editing cut]
31. //3 *and* the / **bumps** are supposed to go a- / *way* and it
32. //3 *shouldn't* / **spread** any- / *more* but the
33. //3 *discolour*- / **ati**on might

34. //1_ *stay* there for a / *really* really long / **time** so
35. //1+ ^ / **yeah** but
36. //3 *that* was / **good** to get checked / **out**
37. // [editing cut]

Appendix B6: Phonological analysis of 'Parking Lot' phase

[3:27–4:51]

1. //4 ↑*oh* an- / **oth**er / *thing* that has been
2. //3 *really* a- / **nnoy**ing this / **summ**er is you
3. //3 *know* when you / *go* to a / **park**ing lot and it's a
4. //3 *busy* / **place**
5. //3 ^ *you* / *get* in your / **car** and you – you
6. //3 *don't* necessarily / *want* to / **leave** immediately like you
7. // *might* wanna – / ^ I
8. //3 *might* want to have / *hen*ry test his / **blood** sugar
9. //3 *give* the kids / **snacks**
10. // [editing cut]
11. //4 ^ *or* if / *we* were at the / *pool* like / **change** or
12. //2 *look* at my / **phone** or
13. //4 *send* a / **text** message or what-
14. //3 **ev**er
15. // [editing cut]
16. //3 ^ it / ↑*drives* me / **craz**y when a
17. //3 *car* is like / **sitt**ing there
18. //2 *following* you through the / **park**ing lot and
19. //3 *then* they just / *wait* for you to / **leave** I
20. //4+ *can*not / **stand** that and
21. //3 *that* has happened / *so* many / **times**
22. //3 ^ and I was / *just* at the / *mall* of a- / **mer**ica and I
23. //1 *got* back to my / **car** and I
24. //2 *wanted* to – / ^ and I / *met* up with a / *You*Tube / *mum* / **Kimm**y from the
25. //4 **Dodge** / *fam*ily
26. //3 *and* I / *went* to – I / *wanted* to like um / *In*stagram a / **pic**ture of us and
27. //2 *Facebook* what- / **ev**er

28. // [editing cut]
29. //2 ^ and / *as* I was / *do*ing that I – I had
30. //3 *just* got in my / **car**
31. //3 *got* my / **phone** and
32. //3 *as* I was / *do*ing that
33. //3 *some* / **guy** was
34. //3 ***sitt***ing there and there was
35. //3 *cars* be- / ***hind*** him and he was like
36. // [mimics man's gesture and expression]
37. //1 ^ like / *waving* me / ***out*** and I was
38. //5 ↑*so* up- / ***set*** like I i-
39. //3 *mmed*iately got / ***up***
40. //1 *put* my / ***phone*** down I i-
41. //1 *mmed*iately / *drove* a- / ***way*** but – I
42. //1 *wasn*'t even / ***think***ing I
43. //2 ***should***n't have / ***done*** that I
44. //1 *should* not have / ***done*** that but –
45. // [editing cut]
46. //2 ↑*but* it was / *just* like / "***what***" there's a
47. //5 *guy* / ***sitt***ing there
48. //5 *wav*ing and / ***ang***ry at me because I was
49. //1 *sitt*ing in my / ***car*** it's like I am
50. //2 *sitt*ing in my / ***car*** – I / *should*n't have to / ***leave***
51. //1 ^ / *mad* at my- / ***self*** that I / ***did*** that
52. //4 *but* – from / ↑***now*** on I am
53. //4 ***not*** moving I don't
54. //1 *care* if they / *foll*ow me around the / *whole* / ***park***ing lot to
55. //1 *get* to my / ***car***
56. //1 ^ I am / *not* / ***mov***ing
57. // [editing cut]

Appendix B7: Phonological analysis of 'Social Media' phase

[4:52–6:24]

1. //1 ^ I / *don't* want this video to like / *ramble* / ***on*** I
2. //3 *want* it to be kind of / ***short***

3. //4 ***but*** I
4. //3 ↑***do*** want to start / going / ***live*** either on
5. //1 *In*stagram / *Face*book / *You*Tube / *I* don't / ***know*** I
6. //2 *don't* know / ***what*** ex- / ac*tly*
7. //3 ^ / *um* I / *start*ed / *do*ing like / *In*stagram / ***stor***ies for like
8. //3 ***three*** days but
9. //2 *then* I / *lost* a / ↑*huge* / *chunk* of / *peo*ple / *that* were / ***foll***owing me so
10. //3 *I* don't know if / *peo*ple like / ***hate***d it or
11. //3 *I* was / *really* a- / ***nnoy***ing
12. //2 ^ / *so* I / *stopped* / ***do***ing that and I
13. //1_ *did* – I'd / *posted* like / ↓*four* little / *clips* of / ***vid***eos so
14. //3 *I* don't / ***know***
15. //3 ^ if / *people* just / *realized* / ^ and / *didn't* know who I / ***was*** or
16. //3 *didn't* / *like* me in their / *feed* or / *what* / ***not***
17. //4 ^ so / *that* like / *tur* – / ↑*to*tally turned me / *off* from / ***In***stagram
18. // [editing cut]
19. //3 *then* I thought "well / *may*be I'll do it on my / *Face*book / ***page***" but
20. //2 *only* about / *two* hundred of you / ***foll***ow me / *there* and I
21. //3 *feel* like / *so* many of you would / *miss* / ***out***
22. //4+ ^ and / *then* on / ↑***You***Tube if I go
23. //2 *live* on / *You*Tube the / *only* thing I / *don't* like / *is* / *you* know / *you* have / *all* the / ***comm***ents and / *stuff* but
24. //4 *when* you / ***play*** it / *back*
25. //1 *people* watching / *can't* see the / ***comm***ents so I
26. //1 *just* think it's / *kind* of / ***weird***
27. //4 ***I*** don't / *know*
28. //4 ^ 'cause I would be / *talk*ing to the / *peo*ple in the / ***comm***ents
29. //2 ^ / and the / *replay* viewers would be like / ***what*** you
30. //3 ***know*** like
31. //1 ***I*** don't know
32. //4 ↑***I*** don't / *know*
33. //4 ^ but I / *really* think it would be / *fun* to go / *live* and answer / ***quest***ions and / *things*
34. //3 ↑***I*** have / *not* done a / *q* and / ***a***
35. //1 ^ / ***years*** it's been
36. //1 ***years*** and
37. //3 *all* the / *one's* that I've done / ***pri***or like
38. //1 *many* many / ***years*** ago

39. //1 *Andy* and I used to / *do* them / **all** the time I for
40. //3 *some* reason de- / **lete**d them
41. //1 ↓ **all**
42. //1 *every* single / **one**
43. //3 *every* q and / ***a*** I have de-
44. //1↓ **lete**d
45. //4 ^ / *so* when / ↑I hit / **twen**ty thousand sub- / *scrib*ers
46. //3 *that* is my / **goal** that's
47. //3 *always* been my / **goal** I
48. //3 *just* hit nine- / **teen** al-
49. //3 *though* I just / *lost* like / *thir*ty eight sub- / *scrib*ers / **yes**terday
50. //3 ^ so / *I* was like at / *nine*teen / *thous*and and / **one**
51. //2 ^ so / *I* don't even know if I'm / *there* – if I'm at / *nine*teen / **thous**and any- / *more* //

Appendix B8: Phonological analysis of 'Caring for Children (B)' phase

[6:25–6:46]

1. //4 [talking to child] *just* a / ↑**sec**ond / *honey*
2. // [editing cut]
3. //3 ^ I / ↑*totally* for- / *got* / *what* I was just / **say**ing
4. //1_ ^ / *Char*lie just came / *up* here and was / **talk**ing to me [laughs]
5. // [editing cut]
6. //1 *I* remember what I was / **talk**ing about
7. //3 ^ so when / *I* hit / ↑*twenty* thousand sub- / **scrib**ers I am
8. //3 *going* to do a / *big* / ↑Q and / ***A***
9. //3 *with* the / **fam**ily – with
10. //4 *Andy* or / **who**ever
11. //3 *has* / **quest**ions and
12. //1 *I'm* gonna to do / *that* for **you** guys
13. //3 *clock* is / **ding**ing
14. //3 *Charlie* / **needs** me
15. //3 *kids* are / **hung**ry so
16. //3 *is* better / **go** //

Appendix B9: Phonological analysis of Outro

[6:46–7:01]

1. //4 *thank* you for / **watch**ing guys
2. // [editing cut]
3. //2 *I* will see you / **Thurs**day
4. //3 *for* a / *day* in the / *life* video it will be
5. //4 *live* at / ↑**two** p / m
6. //1_ ↓*eas*tern / **stand**ard time
7. // [editing cut]
8. //4 ^ so / ↑*don't* / **miss** it
9. //3 *thanks* for / **watch**ing guys
10. //4 **bye**
11. //2 [child walks in] *mummy* I need a / **drink**
12. //1_ *you* need a / **drink**
13. //4 *ok*
14. // [reaches to turn off camera]

Appendix C: The visual display and measurement of aspects of voice quality in Praat

The widely used speech analysis in phonetics software, Praat, visualizes voice quality in terms of the three acoustic measures of **time, frequency** and **intensity/energy** in a visualization combining a spectrogram (below) with a waveform (above). If we match these acoustic features with van Leeuwen's (1999) account of the semiotic parameters of voice quality, it is obvious that time relates to 'fast/slow', intensity or energy relates to 'loud/soft' and fundamental frequency relates to 'high/low'. The three acoustic measures can be seen in a visualization produced by Praat as in Figure C1.

The visualization Figure C1 represents the voice quality of the word 'Mum' in three dimensions: time, frequency and energy (or intensity). **Time** is presented on the horizontal axis, measured in seconds and also shown as a (doubled) waveform. The articulation rate is calculated as the number of recognized sounds per second. In this diagram, the duration of the whole recording is 3.5 seconds, in which the duration of the utterance 'Mum' is 0.59 seconds. **Frequency** (pitch) is represented on the vertical axis of the spectrogram, measured in Hertz (Hz)

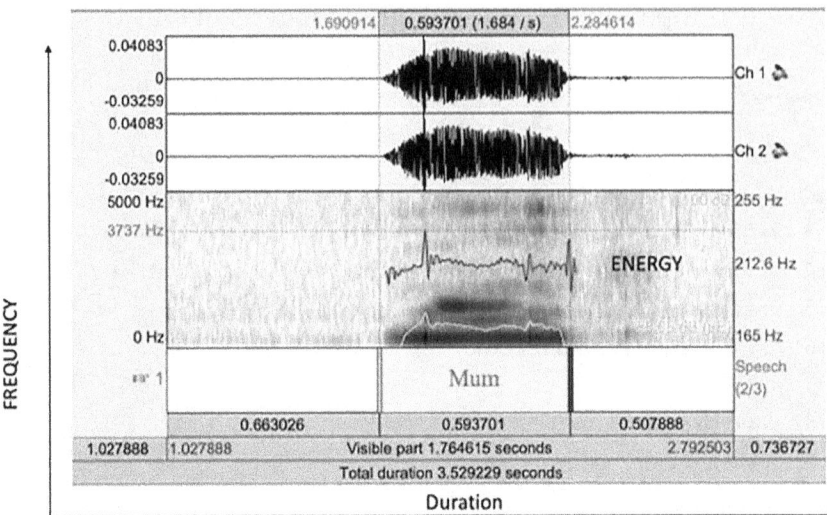

Figure C.1 Praat visualization showing time, frequency and energy (or intensity).

ranging from 0 to 5,000 Hz. The highest pitch in this segment of speech is 3,737 Hz and the lowest is 1,772 Hz. The pitch contour is shown by the upper line (coloured blue in Praat) in the spectrogram (this area comprises paler and darker 'partials'). **Energy** (indicating loudness) is represented by the lower line (coloured yellow in Praat) in the same area of the spectrogram. Energy is measured in dB on the right-hand axis with the common top value of 100 dB and bottom of 50 dB. The top level of energy of 'Mum' here is 59.33 dB, which is relatively soft. The level of darkness of the colour within the grey area also corresponds to the level of energy – the greater the energy, the darker the colour. The darkness of the partials in the greyish areas can be used impressionistically to compare the loudness of segments of speech when the dB value is not informative because of background noise (as is often the case when analysing film).

Vocal qualities related to energy, including tenseness (tense/lax), breathiness (breathy/clear), roughness (rough/clear) and vibrato, can also be interpreted from the spectrogram. Tense speech has stronger high-frequency energy than lax speech, which means the colours of the upper bands (or harmonics) in the grey area are darker in tense speech compared with lax speech. Figure C2 contrasts the 'tenseness' of two utterances of the same word 'Mum'. On the right, the voice is seen to be more tense due to the harmonics spreading from the bottom to the top of the voice range – making the harmonic bands sharper, the colour of the bands darker and the spread of darkness all the way from the right

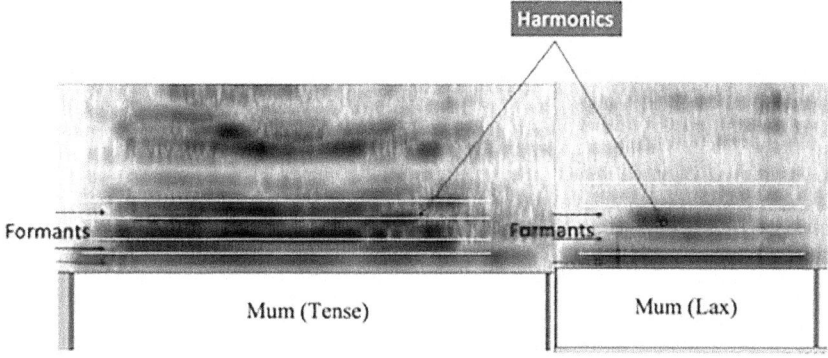

Figure C.2 Visual representation of harmonics showing voice 'tenseness'.

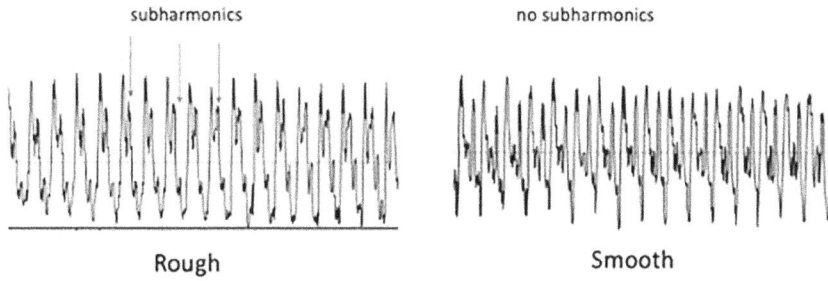

Figure C.3 Visual representation of rough and smooth voice quality.

to the left, representing the strong energy of the formants.[3] The opposite is seen in the diagram on the right for the lax speech.

Rough voice sounds 'uneven and bumpy, appearing to be unsteady short-term, but persisting over the long-term' (NCVS, 2019). Acoustically, rough voice is related to irregular vocal fold vibrations (Omori et al., 1997) and has an intimate correlation with the appearance of subharmonics (or the lower frequency peak) in speech. This means rough voice is related to all the three components of 'energy', 'time' and 'frequency'. Figure C3 contrasts a rough and smooth voicing of the same word 'Mum', with the rough speech having subharmonics that are absent in the smooth speech.

Breathy voice is perceived as 'voice mixed in with breath' due to some 'turbulent airflow through the glottis' as a result of the vocal cords being fairly abducted (relatively to the constricted glottis as in creaky voice) with 'little longitudinal tension' (Gordon and Ladefoged, 2001: 385). Acoustically, breathy voice happens when the energy drops as the frequency increases. In a

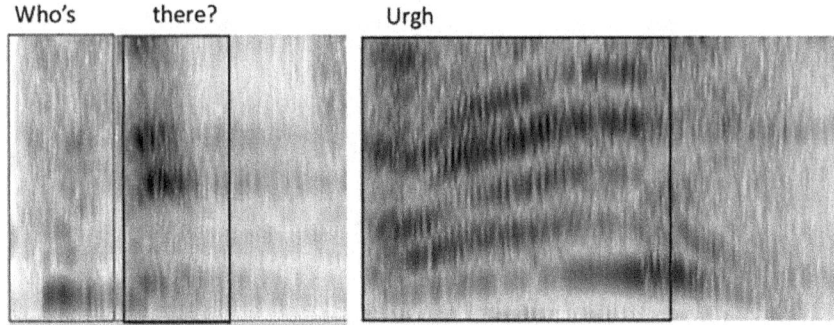

Figure C.4 Visual representation of breathy and clear voice qualities.

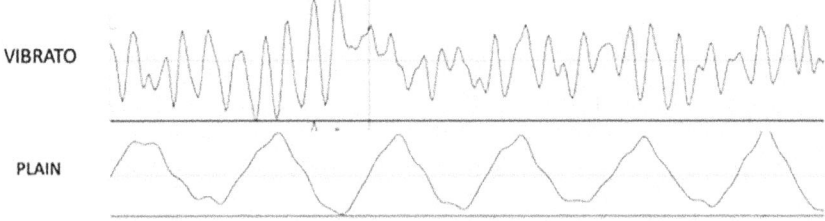

Figure C.5 Visual representation of vibrato and plain voice qualities.

spectrogram this means that the partials in the upper part (higher frequency) of the voice range are lighter (less energy) while the lower part (lower frequency) is darker (higher energy). A visual representation of breathiness (breathy/clear) is provided in Figure C4.

In the box corresponding to 'Who's', the partials are darker and denser in the bottom part, indicating stronger energy being released, but lighter and thinner in the rest of the box, indicating a mixture of sources of energy on the same segment, which is typical of breathiness. In the box corresponding to 'there?' a similar phenomenon can be seen but the amount of breath reduces, hence the dark area is larger than in the first box. In the box on the right-hand column, the 'darkness' of the partials (or sources of energy) is sharp and consistent throughout the spectrum, indicating that the voice is clear with no mixture of different sources of energy, no breathiness.

Vibrato refers to rapid variation in pitch and energy (Titze, 1994). All speech involves a certain degree of vibration in the vocal cords to produce sounds. However, overly fast vibration heard in speech can be caused by lack of vocal fold approximation or lack of support as in old people's shaking voice or an excessive level of energy in the high vocal range (Titze, 1994) as a result of certain psychological phenomena. Vibrato is visually represented by the deviation from the dotted blue line (the average room air temperature) in the middle of the spectrogram. The more the deviation and variation seen, the greater the degree of vibrato. Figure C5 shows contrasts between a vibrato speech and non-vibrato version of the word 'Mum'.

The quality of **nasality** is usually mathematically measured rather than visually represented in a spectrogram, and in our research, it is determined by empirical listening exercises.

Notes

1 Embodied meaning: A systemic functional perspective on paralanguage

1 Archie Roach is describing his wife Ruby Hunter's embodied reaction to his doubts about recording his debut album *Charcoal Lane*, produced by Paul Kelly (Boulton, 2019).
2 This chapter incorporates material previously published in Martin and Zappavigna (2019).
3 For an SFL-informed description of one of these languages, British Sign Language, see Rudge (2017, 2021).
4 A comparable multifunctional perspective has been proposed (Kok, 1996; Kok et al., 2016) within the framework of functional discourse grammar (FDG). In contrast to SFL, FDG recognizes two rather than three 'levels' – representational and interpersonal (the latter concerned with SFL's interpersonal and textual meaning); and within these levels FDG operates with its own set of semantic parameters.
5 The specific systems whereby languages organize tone groups for rhythm and intonation of course vary across languages (stress timed vs syllable timed languages being an obvious example). But recognition of the tone group (aka intonation unit or intonational phrase) as a segment of speech with a single prosodic contour (i.e. pitch and rhythm contour) is well established across languages.
6 Kendon in fact uses this example to argue that the gestures differentiate two meanings of the verb *slice*. We would argue on the other hand that the gestures are converging with the meaning of two different clause structures (distinguishing two different actions): *the hunter…sliced the wolf's head off* involves a phrasal verb (cf. *the hunter **sliced off** the wolf's head*) affecting the wolf, whereas *the hunter…sliced the Wolf's stomach open* involves the non-phrasal verb *slice*, again affecting the wolf, but this time with the effect of the action specified (as the resulting attribute *open*). Kendon's reading reflects the logocentric (word-centred) bias in much of the gesture literature.
7 In SFL names of systems are conventionally written in small caps (e.g. IDEATION), and we follow this convention throughout the volume.
8 The examples used in this section have been adapted from the 'Chatty Vlog' text introduced at the beginning of Section 1.4.

9 In the realization statements '#' indicates initial position in a unit, '+' means 'insert Function', '^' sequences Functions and ':' relates a Function to the class through which it is realized; 'P' stands for Predicator.

10 Research on paralanguage typically assumes of model of language of this kind (as reflected in Table 1.1).

11 For corresponding networks and realization statements, see Kress and van Leeuwen (2006: 74, 87, 104, 105, 149, 210).

12 The phonological (phoneme, syllable, foot, tone group) and lexicogrammatical (morpheme, word, group/phrase, clause) hierarchies noted here are referred to as ranks in SFL and represent another way in which systems bundle in SFL-informed descriptions. For further discussion of metafunction, rank and strata as bundles of features, see Martin et al. (2013a).

13 Unless otherwise noted, lexicogrammatical analyses throughout this book are based on Halliday and Matthiessen (2014).

14 The term 'CONNEXION' is taken from Hao (2015, 2018), replacing Martin's earlier term 'CONJUNCTION' in order to more clearly differentiate discourse semantic and lexicogrammatical terminology (reacting in particular to confusion invited by the use of grammatical terminology for semantic description in several SFL publications, particularly those dealing with grammatical metaphor (e.g. Halliday and Matthiessen, 1999).

15 For Hao (2020) a positioned figure is one that is in some sense attributed to a particular source.

16 The term 'congruent' is used in SFL for direct non-metaphorical realizations.

17 Martin (1992) treats text reference of this kind as textual grammatical metaphor, since it involves a nominal group referring to a phase of discourse rather than an entity (a person, place or thing). However, it is difficult to see how reference of this kind is symbolizing a phase of discourse, and there is arguably no stratal tension (i.e. there are not two meanings in play, one of which could be interpreted literally). In retrospect the concept of grammatical metaphor was being pushed too far.

18 Just as gesture and facial expression are marshalled as the expression plane of the sign language of deaf communities (cf. Johnston (2013, 2018) on the use of paralanguage alongside signing in sign language).

19 Cf. Martinec (2000b) who includes non-semiotic behaviour in his modelling.

20 For exemplary forays into this realm of inquiry, see Martinec (1998, 2000a,b, 2001, 2004), who models somasis as if it was semiosis, drawing on SFL theory to do so.

21 Zappavigna and Martin's (2018) dimension of protolinguistic body language has been subsumed in our current model as subtypes of somasis and interpersonal semovergent paralanguage. This avoids the problem of using the term 'protolinguistic' for a paralinguistic system making meaning alongside language (protolanguage, as initial emergent semiosis, by definition cannot accompany

language), and it makes room for paralinguistic systems enabled by the discourse semantic system of APPRAISAL (see Chapter 2 for further discussion of this point).
22 A 'blog' (truncated form of 'weblog') is a website comprising posts displayed in reverse chronological order. Most often they involve personal diary-style entries composed by individuals; corporations and organizations may also incorporate blogs into their online material.
23 For wavelengths longer than a tone group, whole body motion is involved.
24 SFL's interpretation of the 'beats' in Figure 1.1 was first pursued by Martinec (2000a, 2002) but is anticipated in Kendon (1972) – who in fact makes reference to Halliday's work on intonation and rhythm in his paper.
25 In our phonological analyses, drawing on Halliday (1967, 1970a; Halliday and Greaves, 2008), '//' stands for tone group boundary, '/' for foot boundary (feet begin with a salient syllable), '^' for a silent beat (where a salient syllable would have been), bold face highlights the tonic syllable, salient syllables are rendered in italics and numbers indicate tones: 1 falling, 2 rising, 3 level, 4 fall rise, 5 rise fall, 13 fall then level with no pre-tonic segment, 53 rise fall then level with no pre-tonic segment.
26 Lateral gesture movement will be named from the perspective of the vlogger.
27 Our vlogger is sitting and so her central gesturing space is a little higher relative to her body position than if she were standing (where it would correspond roughly to what in ballet is called Position 1).
28 Semovergent synchronicity is concerned with the syncing of paralanguage with periodic structure composed above and beyond prosodic phonology.
29 Our discourse semantic perspective distinguishes our work from that of Martinec (1998, 2000a,b, 2001); our metafunctional perspective distinguishes our classification from the work underpinning Kendon's Continuum (Figure 1.1).
30 To be more precise, these are paralinguistic occurrence figures, as introduced in Chapter 4.
31 The 'out-of-kilter' mouth here can be interpreted as soft focus, converging with *kind of.*
32 Martinec (1998) interprets textual meaning as realized through cohesion, following Halliday and Hasan (1976); as introduced earlier for this monograph we follow Martin (1992) who reinterprets cohesion as discourse semantics (Martin, 2014), organized metafunctionally in Martin and Rose ([2003] 2007) as ideational resources (IDEATION, CONNEXION), interpersonal resources (NEGOTIATION, APPRAISAL) and textual resources (IDENTIFICATION, PERIODICITY).
33 van Leeuwen (1985, 1992) and Martinec (2002) argue that SFL's phonological hierarchy can be pushed up several wavelengths beyond the tone group; their work suggests that higher-level rhythm would converge with higher-level periodicity in Martin's (1992) framework.

34 We are not referring to the 'iconicity' of emblems and characters here but rather to the way in which they function as the 'expression form' of meaning.

2 An ontogenetic perspective on paralanguage

1 It is important to note that the term 'sign' (also 'symbolic act' or 'act of meaning') in Halliday's usage refers to a Saussurean content/expression pair and not to sign language forms or to any subcategory of gesture. An infant sign may be primarily vocal or gestural or a combination of these, perhaps in concert with directed gaze and/or affective behaviour.
2 Hal's behaviour thus fulfils Meguerditchian et al.'s (2011: 98) three criteria for 'intentional signalling': the signal being directed to an addressee, the presence of gaze alternation and persistence if the addressee does not respond.
3 'Protolanguage' is the term coined by Halliday (1975) to describe the infant's first semiotic system, prior to the adoption of the mother tongue. It is distinct from Bickerton's (1990) later use of the term as a hypothetical stage in linguistic phylogenesis (for a discussion, see Painter, 2005).
4 Halliday ([1975] 2004b: 35) used the criterion of three distinct comparable instances while Painter ([1984] 2015: 55) required four.
5 'Iconic' is not intended here as a technical term for a gesture type in opposition to terms for other categories of gesture, such as 'metaphoric', 'referential' or 'symbolic'.
6 For some signs there was considerable random variation in vowels or initial consonants used for expression forms – but these carried no discernible variation in meaning.
7 As Acredolo and Goodwyn (1988: 71) point out: 'Although such utterances would appear to a naïve observer to be words, they simply do not function in a way which indicates that the child truly understands the representative relation true words convey. Specifically, many of these forms of prelexical utterances can be characterized as "context bound".'
8 Many descriptions of development outside the SFL case studies have also noted the pragmatic/mathetic distinction while using different terminologies. For example, Bates ([1979] 2014), Dore (1973), Greenfield and Smith (1976), Lewis (1951), McShane (1980) and Menn (1978) all distinguish 'imperative' (or 'volitional' or 'request' or 'command') utterances from 'declarative' (or 'indicative' or 'informative') ones. In many studies, it is also noted that tone contours discriminate the two functional types, with level or rising tones on early words typical for the pragmatic category (for more details, see Painter, [1984] 2015: 130–1).
9 Pizzuto and Capobianco (2005) observed that 'representational' gestures were found with children under two years, but only a few of these would count as ideational

in our scheme. Moreover, these few cases, such as opening and closing the mouth to mean *fish* or flapping hands for *bird*, may well be used by the children as part of protolanguage rather than the mother tongue given that every word-like utterance in this research is treated as a true lexical word. Mayberry and Nicoladis (2000) observed both 'iconics' (which could include ideational gestures) and 'beats' (which would include textual gesturing) in their child-subjects aged from two to three-and-a-half years but only where accompanying language had advanced to multiword utterances.

10 They found an increase in 'iconic' and 'beat' gestures compared with deictic gestures as children's language develops.
11 Or, with a corresponding shift in emotion, that it has been interrupted or sabotaged. See Murray and Threvathen (1985) for descriptions of 'still face' and other experiments demonstrating the genuineness of the infant's moment-by-moment sensitivity to the caregiver's communicative behaviour.

3 The semiotic voice: Intonation, rhythm and other vocal features

1 For alternative systemic views, see also Tench ([1965] 2015) and O'Grady (2010).
2 See Halliday ([1985] 1989) and Linell (2004) for discussion of the written-language bias in English-speaking cultures and in linguistics.
3 But see, for example, Arvaniti (2009) for discussion of rhythm, timing and the distinction between stress-timed and syllable-timed languages. We take English rhythms to be identifiable according to temporal and pitch features of the speech signal that create the perception of relative prominence.
4 At the top is the waveform, with the vertical height of the waveform showing amplitude; underneath the waveform is the spectrogram (to which we will return later); then, the two tiers below the spectrogram show the foot boundaries and the tone group boundary (to which we will return later); at bottom the time (in seconds) is shown. Further details on Praat visualizations can be found in Appendix C.
5 The divisions into feet clearly align with the peaks of intensity shown in the Praat waveform in the top row and shading in the spectrogram in the middle row of this image. The beginning of each salient syllable in fact begins where the vowel sound begins (the Nucleus of the syllable). For example, the foot containing 'Spain' actually begins on the vowel sound 'ai', not the initial consonants 'Sp'. For an introduction to Praat, see https://web.stanford.edu/dept/linguistics/corpora/material/PRAAT_workshop_manual_v421.pdf. See Ladefoged ([1975] 2001) for a discussion of the internal structure of the English syllable.

6 Thus, the foot boundaries will not correspond directly with grammatical units, where different principles of organization obtain – as mentioned earlier, the purpose here, of the phonological description, is to indicate the phonologically salient syllables, that is, the choices in phonology.

7 Praat does not allow italics, so we have capitalized the salient syllables in the Praat visualization. We avoid using capitalization in our book as the personal pronoun 'I' is already capitalized and thus capitalized initials cannot be consistently used to distinguish salient syllables.

8 There is not the space here to go into the isochrony debate (e.g. Lehiste, 1977; Abercrombie, 1965; Couper-Kuhlen, 1993). We hold to the view that the perception of rhythmic isochrony is produced through relative similarity in the temporal duration of feet.

9 Thus, syllables in beat position in an established rhythm are heard as salient regardless of what acoustic measurements might tell us: the interface between phonetics and phonology – between the material and the abstract/semiotic – is not always a straightforward one.

10 Note the caret '^' is used here to denote sequencing in function structure (as opposed to rendering for silent Ictus in phonological annotation).

11 To facilitate analysis of intonation and rhythm, it is helpful to use the 0.75 'speed' under 'Settings' (the cog symbol at bottom right of the video screen in YouTube).

12 This foot, which begins this move in the discourse, is not shown here (the purpose here is to show visually the rhythmic pattern that begins on 'probably') but will be addressed in the discussion in the chapter.

13 Compound words such as 'hair dye' have primary stress on the first lexical item, as in 'ice cream'; cf. the common jest, 'I scream for ice cream', which depends on this distinction – // ^ I / *scream* for / *ice* cream //.

14 'that I', which begins the next clause, is transcribed as part of this foot because it is non-salient, phonologically speaking, although, of course, grammatically it is part of the following clause. Note that it would make no significant difference to the length of this foot if it ended after 'dye' – such post-salient items are usually spoken quickly (leading up to first salient syllable of the next tone group) and add little to the temporal duration of a foot.

15 The Hz values to the right indicate the pitch range of the excerpt shown. As before, in Praat, the salient syllables are in upper caps, as italics are not possible; the horizontal tier at the bottom marks the Tonic with an asterisk, '*', before a forward slash, */ PLAIN, as bold type is also not possible in Praat annotation.

16 There is also visible in this Praat visualization a rising pitch on 'rain'; but this does not constitute a tone choice, as is clear from listening to the spoken source audio for this image (it is, instead, the result of the speaker's articulatory effort to reach a high pitch for the first salient syllable in this utterance). Tone identification needs

to be done by listening to the spoken text, rather than through visual analysis of the Praat representation. Praat is a useful platform for listening and annotating in the environment of the source text (as sound) and can sometimes be helpful in analysing rhythm and intonation (e.g. the waveform indicating foot boundaries). However, it is not a reliable substitute for using one's ears, particularly for pitch contour (TONE) analysis: the Praat representation of pitch is an unreliable substitute for auditory analysis, as it is subject to settings in various parameters such as the pitch range for the spectrogram and temporal window length which will influence the visual representation of pitch, creating often misleading representations. Just as there is no software for reliably performing analyses of TRANSITIVITY or AFFECT, there is as yet no reliable software for determining (abstract) phonological choices in rhythm and intonation from a physical sound signal. For this reason, except for Figure 3.4, we do not use Praat visualizations to show tone representations.

17 Pre-Tonic syllables can show variations in pitch movements (that are not pitch contours) which help to signal salience and can also prosodically form part of the overall Tonic pitch contour shape and its identification (see Halliday and Greaves, 2008: 169–84). Variation in pre-Tonic syllable height can also have other functions as discussed in Section 3.6.

18 The Remiss syllables in the final foot may show a reset of pitch anticipating the next tone group, for example, a drop low after the final salient syllable in a tone group with rising tone. Non-salient syllables have relatively little significance.

19 We discussed earlier how a speaker likewise does not need to work as hard to articulate a salient syllable that falls in beat position within an established rhythm; the analysis of phonology should always be conducted while keeping in mind both phonetics and the local context and meaning.

20 'Given' information, in Halliday's terms (for a discussion of the terms Given and New, see O'Grady, 2016).

21 It is important here to distinguish between two phenomena. One is where the speaker is doing extra phonetic work to make sure that the listener can hear a marked choice in SALIENCE. We normally expect there to be a pattern of salient and non-salient syllables (Ictus-Remiss) in English speech. Thus, if this expected pattern is overridden and there are two salient syllables in succession, then the speaker needs to do some extra phonetic work to make this marked choice clear. The other, which we discuss here, is where the speaker is adding extra salience above that needed to indicate two choices of SALIENCE in succession – which, nevertheless, does not involve a Tonic, that is, no pitch contour and choice in the system of TONE.

22 In this instance, as in the *Pygmalion* example earlier, the rising pitch is the result of the speaker reaching for a high target rather than instantiating a Tonic contour.

23 Van Leeuwen uses the terms 'accent' and 'juncture', which for reasons of space we will not go into further here, to distinguish phonological choices with textual

functions (which have varying levels of prominence) from those with interpersonal function (choice of the type of tone contour, whether rising or falling, etc.) – precisely so that these choices can be distinguished. While not always identifying the same phenomena, van Leeuwen's observations on 'accent' and 'juncture' are broadly applicable to Halliday's 'tonicity' and 'tonality'. Halliday's approach is, as with the clause, to have the mapping of meanings from different metafunctions onto the same unit, the tone group, with pitch contours serving both interpersonal and textual purposes.

24 Note that we indicate restarts by a dash. The dash is not to be confused with a hyphen which indicates that a word spreads across a foot or tone group boundary, as in Ber- / *mud*a in the law excerpt earlier.

25 Halliday uses subscript underlining for tone 1_, but this underlining is not possible in Praat, so we use 1_ (which is also consistent with tone 1+ which has the '+' sign after the numeral).

26 This consideration, from a systemic perspective, raises the issue of what it means to choose in the textual metafunction. Work on information systems has tended to be done with a structural, rather than systemic, orientation, in terms of 'Given-New' structure. However, when analysing textual systems in terms, not of structure but of choice and function, we are forced to ask what constitutes the systemic potential for choice in these textual systems (for a discussion, see Smith, 2007).

4 Ideational semovergence: Approaching paralanguage from the perspective of field

1 A full transcription of the vlog is provided in Appendix A, and phonological analyses of blog phase are provided in Appendix B1–9.

2 The combined brace and square bracket notation for the system [relative size] versus [relative position] in this network stands for an and/or relation (i.e. either one choice or the other or both); the realization statement '> one entity' means that more than one paralinguistic entity is involved.

3 We make a distinction between the movement required to represent an entity in a paralinguistic state figure and movement used to represent the entity in motion in a paralinguistic occurrence figure.

4 Deictic pointing gestures are discussed in Chapter 6.

5 This choice probably reflects the way writing unfolds in English graphology – written and read from left to right.

5 Interpersonal paralanguage: Approaching paralanguage from the perspective of social relations

1 In linguistic AFFECT, the term 'fear' is not a feature but simply a gloss to suggest a wide range of possible lexical instantiations. In linguistic AFFECT, the feature glossed as 'fear' is that of [irrealis: negative] (see Table 5.1). In PARALINGUISTIC AFFECT [fear] is a feature (a technical term in the system).
2 See Chapter 3 for explanations of voice quality information recorded in Praat visualizations.
3 It is important to note here that while the words 'cheer' and 'affection' also appear in the presentations of the system of linguistic AFFECT (e.g. Martin and White, 2005: 49), as is explained in discussion of Figure 5.7, with reference to Martin (in press), they do not constitute features in the linguistic system. They merely function as glosses for the array of potential instantiations in texts. In paralinguistic systems for VOICE AFFECT (or FACIAL AFFECT) a shared lexical choice in two systems will not be taken as indicating the same feature in a system or as entering into the same oppositions.
4 For other functions of points, see Chapter 6 and Martinec (2001: 136).
5 When referring to a divergent relationship between language and paralanguage it is always semovergent paralanguage that is at stake since sonovergent paralanguage always resonates with the phonology of language by definition.

6 Textual convergence: Approaching paralanguage from the perspective of information flow

1 Attributes in intensive attributive clauses (as in *is it an upsetting image?*, *is it a reassuring image?*, *it's a harem*) do not involve presenting reference. The Attribute does not realize a discourse semantic entity but rather classifies and/or describes one.
2 In parallel to the semiosis of gestures convergent with spoken language, Hodge and Johnston (2018: 264) discuss such pointing gestures as functioning alongside 'fully conventional semiotic signs to create unified utterances that are interpreted holistically'.
3 The directionality described here is assumed to relate to that of the prevalent writing system (in this case the left to right) of English and/or to the visual perspective of the viewer whereby what is to come is identified to the left.
4 [tracing] is also frequently realized with a laser pointer.
5 English rhythm contrasts with rhythm in syllable-timed language (e.g. Spanish or Vietnamese), where each syllable is perceived as taking the same amount of time.

6 The term is adopted here from Maton (2014), and it refers to people whose expertise is legitimated on the basis of who they are.
7 A hand beat amplified in size or muscle tension also has the potential to invoke an interpersonal evaluative meaning (see Chapter 5; Hood, 2011; Hao and Hood, 2019).
8 The macro-Theme prefaces the third stage in the activity sequence through which urine is formed.

7 Afterword: Modelling paralanguage

1 In this respect our model contrasts with the syntax, semantics and pragmatics framework assumed in most related studies. We do not oppose form to meaning (syntax vs semantics); and we do not conflate resources enacting social relations with those composing information flow (as pragmatics).
2 Phonology does not construe IDEATION (conceived as state and occurrence figures, and the entities, occurrences and qualities comprising them). Tone concord and sequence can play a part in the construal of CONNEXION (Halliday and Matthiessen, 2014: 553–4); but this is not reflected in paralanguage.
3 The vexing experience of our colleagues Gunther Kress and Theo van Leeuwen with the four editions of their acclaimed *Reading Images* is less than encouraging.

Appendices

1 Available at https://www.youtube.com/watch?v=YRx-zDoPbVw (accessed 8 January 2020).
2 For transcription conventions, see Phonological Transcription Conventions at the start of this book. Numbers in brackets refer to time in vlog text.
3 Harmonics come from vibrations of the vocal folds while formants come from the vibrations of the air inside the vocal tract. Source: https://www.voicescienceworks.org/harmonics-vs-formants.html.

References

Abercrombie, D. 1965. *Studies in phonetics and linguistics*. London: Oxford University Press.

ACARA. 2019. *Australian curriculum: English* (online). Available: http://www.australiancurriculum.edu.au/english/Curriculum/F-10?layout=1 (accessed 30 November 2017).

Acredolo, L. P., and Goodwyn, S. W. 1988. Sign language among hearing infants: The spontaneous development of symbolic gestures. *Child Development*, 59, 450–66.

Arbib, M. A. 2012. *How the brain got language: The mirror system hypothesis*. Vol. 16. New York: Oxford University Press.

Arnheim, R. 1982. *The power of the center: A study of composition in the visual arts*. Berkeley: University of California Press.

Arvaniti, A. 2009. Rhythm, timing and the timing of rhythm. *Phonetica*, 66, 46–63.

Banse, R., and Scherer, K. R. 1996. Acoustic profiles in vocal emotion expression. *Journal of Personality and Social Psychology*, 70, 614.

Barlow, D. 2002. *Anxiety and its disorders: The nature and treatment of anxiety and panic*. New York: Guilford.

Bateman, J. 2008. *Multimodality and genre: A foundation for the systematic analysis of multimodal documents*. Hampshire: Springer.

Bateman, J. A. 2007. Towards a grande paradigmatique of film: Christian Metz reloaded. *Semiotica*, 167(1–4), 13–64.

Bateman, J. A. 2014. *Text and image: A critical introduction to the visual/verbal divide*. London: Routledge.

Bates, E. [1979] 2014. *The emergence of symbols: Cognition and communication in infancy*. New York: Academic Press.

Bates, E., and Dick, F. 2002. Language, gesture, and the developing brain. *Developmental Psychobiology: The Journal of the International Society for Developmental Psychobiology*, 40, 293–310.

Bateson, M. C. 1979. The epigenesis of conversational interaction: A personal account of research development. In M. Bullowa (ed.), *Before speech: The beginning of interpersonal communication*. Cambridge: Cambridge University Press, 63–78.

Bickerton, D. 1990. *Language and species*. Chicago: University of Chicago Press.

Birdwhistell, R. L. [1970] 1990. *Kinesics and context: Essays on body motion communication*. Philadelphia: University of Pennsylvania Press.

Blake, J. 2000. *Routes to child language: Evolutionary and developmental precursors*. Cambridge: Cambridge University Press.

Boersma, P., and Weenink, D. 2019. Praat: Doing phonetics by computer [computer program]. Version 6.1.08. Available: http://www.praat.org/ (cf. http://www.fon.hum.uva.nl/praat/manual/FAQ__How_to_cite_Praat.html) (accessed 5 December 2019).

Bolinger, D. L. 1951. Intonation: Levels versus configurations. *Word*, 7, 199–210.

Boulton, M. 2019. Hope and music: How Archie Roach overcame his demons. *Sydney Morning Herald*.

Bowcher, W. L. 2004. Theme and New in play-by-play radio sports commentating. In D. Banks (ed.), *Text and texture: Systemic functional viewpoints on the nature and structure of text*. Paris: L'Harmattan, 455–93.

Bråten, S. (ed.). 1998. *Intersubjective communication and emotion in early ontogeny*. Cambridge: Cambridge University Press.

Brazelton, T. B., and Tronick, E. 1980. Preverbal communication between mothers and infants. In D. Olson (ed.), *The social foundations of language and thought*. New York: Norton, 299–315.

Brazil, D. 1975. *Discourse intonation*. Vol. 1. Birmingham: Birmingham University.

Brazil, D. 1997. *The communicative value of intonation in English*. Cambridge: Cambridge University Press.

British Colombia Government. 2019. *British Colombia's new curriculum – English language arts* (online). Available: https://curriculum.gov.bc.ca/curriculum/english-language-arts (accessed 6 December 2019).

Bullowa, M. (ed.). 1979. *Before speech: The beginning of interpersonal communication*. Cambridge: Cambridge University Press.

Butler, C. 2003. *Structure and function: A guide to three major structural-functional theories (Part 2, From clause to discourse and beyond)*. Amsterdam: John Benjamins.

Caffarel, A., Martin, J. R., and Matthiessen, C. M. I. M. (eds). 2004. *Language typology: A functional perspective*. Amsterdam: John Benjamins.

Calbris, G. 2011. *Elements of meaning in gesture*. Gesture Studies. Amsterdam: John Benjamins.

Caldwell, D. 2013. The interpersonal voice: Applying appraisal to the rap and sung voice. *Social Semiotics*, 24(1), 40–55.

Capirci, O., Contaldo, A., Caselli, M. C., and Volterra, V. 2005. From action to language through gesture: A longitudinal perspective. *Gesture*, 5, 155–77.

Carter, A. L. 1978. The development of systematic vocalizations prior to words: A case study. In N. Waterson and C. Snow (eds), *The development of communication*. New York: Wiley, 71–92.

Caselli, M. C., and Volterra, V. 1990. From communication to language in hearing and deaf children. In V. Volterra and C. J. Erting (eds), *From gesture to language in hearing and deaf children*. Berlin: Springer, 263–77.

Clark, J., Yallop, C., and Fletcher, J. [1990] 2007. *An introduction to phonetics and phonology*. Malden, MA: Wiley-Blackwell.

Cléirigh, C. 2010. *Gestural and postural semiosis*. Unpublished mss.

Cole, M., and Engeström, Y. 1993. A cultural-historical approach to distributed cognition. In G. Salomon (ed.), *Distributed cognitions: Psychological and educational considerations*. New York: Cambridge University Press, 1–46.

Colletta, J.-M., and Guidetti, M. (eds). 2012. *Gesture and multimodal development*, Amsterdam: John Benjamins.

Condon, W. S., and Ogston, W. D. 1967. A segmentation of behavior. *Journal of Psychiatric Research*, 5, 221–35.

Condon, W. S., and Sander, L. W. 1974. Neonate movement is synchronized with adult speech: Interactional participation and language acquisition. *Science*, 183, 99–101.

Corballis, M. C. 2003. *From hand to mouth: The origins of language*. Princeton: Princeton University Press.

Couper-Kuhlen, E. 1993. *English speech rhythm: Form and function in everyday verbal interaction*. Vol. 25. Amsterdam: John Benjamins.

Crystal, D. 1969. *Prosodic systems and intonation in English*. Vol. 1. London: Cambridge University Press Archive.

Danielsson, K. 2016. Modes and meaning in the classroom – the role of different semiotic resources to convey meaning in science classrooms. Linguistics and Education, 35, 88–99.

Darwin, C. 1872. *The expression of the emotions in man and animals*. London: John Murray.

Davis, B. 2011. Illuminating language origins from the perspective of contemporary ontogeny in human infants. In A. Vilain, J.-L. Schwartz, C. Abry and J. Vauclair (eds), *Primate communication and human language*. Amsterdam: John Benjamins, 173–92.

Dimitrova, D., Chu, M., Wang, L., Özyürek, A., and Hagoort, P. 2016. Beat that word: How listeners integrate beat gesture and focus in multimodal speech discourse. *Journal of Cognitive Neuroscience*, 28, 1255–69.

Doran, Y. J., and Martin, J. R. 2021. Field relations: Understanding scientific explanations. In K. Maton, J. R. Martin and Y. Doran (eds), *Teaching science: Language, knowledge and pedagogy*. London: Routledge, 105–33.

Dore, J. 1975. Holophrases, speech acts and language universals. *Journal of Child Language*, 2, 21–40.

Dore, J. 1978. Conditions for the acquisition of speech acts. In I. Markova (ed.), *The social context of language*. Chichester: Wiley, 87–111.

Eggins, S., and Slade, D. 1997. *Analysing casual conversation*. New York: Cassell.

Eggins, S., Wignell, P., and Martin, J. R. 1993. The discourse of history: Distancing the recoverable past. In M. Ghadessy (ed.), *Register analysis: Theory and practice*, 75–109.

Eisenberg, R. B. 1975. *Auditory competence in early life: The roots of communicative behavior*. Baltimore, MD: University Park Press.

Ekman, P. 2003. *Emotions revealed: Recognizing faces and feelings to improve communication and emotional life*. New York: Henry Holt.

Ekman, P. 2004. Emotional and conversational nonverbal signals. In J. M. Larrazabal and L. A. P. Miranda (eds), *Language, knowledge and representation*. Netherlands: Kluwer Academic, 39–50.

Ekman, P. 2009. Darwin's contributions to our understanding of emotional expressions. *Philosophical Transactions of the Royal Society B: Biological Sciences*, 364, 3449–51.

Ekman, P., and Friesen, W. V. 1969. The repertoire of nonverbal behavioural categories: Origins, usage and coding. *Semiotica*, 1, 49–98.

Ekman, P., and Friesen, W. V. 1971. Constants across cultures in the face and emotion. *Journal of Personality and Social Psychology*, 17, 124–9.

Ekman, P., and Friesen, W. V. [1975] 2003. *Unmasking the face: A guide to recognizing emotions from facial clues*. Los Altos, CA: Malor Books.

Enfield, N. J. 2001. Linguistic evidence for a Lao perspective on facial expression of emotion. In J. Harkins and A. Wierzbicka (eds), *Emotions in crosslinguistic perspective*. Berlin: Mouton de Gruyter, 149–66.

Faigin, G. 1990. *The artist's complete guide to facial expression*. New York: Watson-Guptill.

Farroni, T., Csibra, G., Simion, F., and Johnson, M. H. 2002. Eye contact detection in humans from birth. *Proceedings of the National Academy of Sciences*, 99, 9602–5.

Farroni, T., Massaccesi, S., Pividori, D., and Johnson, M. H. 2004. Gaze following in newborns. *Infancy*, 5, 39–60.

Fasel, B., and Luettin, J. 2003. Automatic facial expression analysis: A survey. *Pattern Recognition*, 36, 259–75.

Feng, D., and O'Halloran, K. L. 2013. The multimodal representation of emotion in film: Integrating cognitive and semiotic approaches. *Semiotica*, 197, 79–100.

Figueredo, G., and Figueredo, G. P. 2019. A systemic dynamics model of text production. *Journal of Quantitative Linguistics*, 27(4), 291–320.

Finnish National Board of Studies. 2016. *Finnish curriculum for basic education* (online). Available: http://www.oph.fi/download/47675_POPS_net_new_2.pdf (accessed 24 February 2016).

Firth, J. R. 1948. Sounds and prosodies. *Transactions of the Philological Society*, 47, 127–52.

Frick, R. W. 1985. Communicating emotion: The role of prosodic features. *Psychological Bulletin*, 97, 412.

Fricke, E. 2013. Towards a unified grammar of gesture and speech: A multimodal approach. In C. Müller, A. Cienki, E. Fricke, S. H. Ladewig, D. McNeill and S. Teßendorf (eds), *Body – language – communication: An international handbook on multimodality in human interaction. Handbooks of linguistics and communication science*. Berlin: Mouton de Gruyter, 733–54.

Fries, P. H. [1981] 1983. On the status of theme in English: Arguments from discourse. In J. S. Petöfi and E. Sozer (eds), *Micro and macro connexity of texts*. Hamburg: Buske, 116–52.

Gaiman, N. 2002. *Coraline*. London: Bloomsbury.

Goldin-Meadow, S., and Morford, M. 1990. Gesture in early child language. In V. Volterra and C. J. Erting (eds), *From gesture to language in hearing and deaf children*. Berlin: Springer, 249–62.

Goodwin, C. 2003. Pointing as situated practice. In S. Kita (ed.), *Pointing: Where language, culture, and cognition meet*. New Jersey: Laurence Erlbaum, 217–42.

Gordon, M., and Ladefoged, P. 2001. Phonation types: A cross-linguistic overview. *Journal of Phonetics*, 29, 383–406.

Goren, C. C., Sarty, M., and Wu, P. Y. 1975. Visual following and pattern discrimination of face-like stimuli by newborn infants. *Pediatrics*, 56, 544–9.

Greaves, W. S. 2007. Intonation in systemic functional linguistics. In R. Hasan, C. M. I. M. Matthiessen and J. Webster (eds), *Continuing discourse on language: A functional perspective*. Vol. 2. London: Equinox, 979–1025.

Greenfield, P. M., and Smith, J. H. 1976. *Structure of communication in early language development*. New York: Academic Press.

Gullberg, M. 1998. *Gesture as a communication strategy in second language discourse: A study of learners of French and Swedish*. Lund: Lund University Press.

Halliday, M. A. K. 1963. The tones of English. *Archivum Linguisticum*, 15, 1–28.

Halliday, M. A. K. 1967. *Intonation and grammar in British English*. The Hague: Mouton.

Halliday, M. A. K. 1970a. *A course in spoken English: Intonation*. Oxford: Oxford University Press.

Halliday, M. A. K. 1970b. Language structure and language function. In J. Lyons (ed.), *New horizons in linguistics*. Harmondsworth: Penguin, 140–65.

Halliday, M. A. K. 1985. *An introduction to functional grammar*. London: Edward Arnold.

Halliday, M. A. K. 1975. *Learning how to mean: Explorations in the development of language*. London: Edward Arnold.

Halliday, M. A. K. [1985] 1989. *Spoken and written language*. Oxford: Oxford University Press.

Halliday, M. A. K. 1996. On grammar and grammatics. In R. Hasan, C. Cloran and D. Butt (eds), *Functional descriptions: Theory into practice*. Amsterdam: John Benjamins, 1–38.

Halliday, M. A. K. [1979] 2002. Modes of meaning and modes of expression: Types of grammatical structure, and their determination by different semantic functions. In J. J. Webster (ed.), *On grammar: The collected works of M. A. K. Halliday*. London: Continuum, 57–79.

Halliday, M. A. K. [1992] 2002. How do you mean? In J. J. Webster (ed.), *On grammar: The collected works of M. A. K. Halliday*. Vol. 1. London: Continuum, 352–68.

Halliday, M. A. K. [1978] 2003. *Language as social semiotic: The social interpretation of language and meaning*. London: Edward Arnold.

Halliday, M. A. K. [1995] 2003. On language in relation to the evolution of human consciousness. In J. J. Webster (ed.), *On language and linguistics: The collected works of M.A.K. Halliday*. Vol. 3. London: Continuum, 390–432.

Halliday, M. A. K. [1975] 2004a. Into the adult language. In J. J. Webster (ed.), *The collected works of M.A.K. Halliday*. Vol. 4. 157–96.

Halliday, M. A. K. [1975] 2004b. Learning how to mean. In J. J. Webster (ed.), *The collected works of M.A.K. Halliday*. Vol. 4. 28–59.

Halliday, M. A. K. [1978] 2004. Meaning and the construction of reality in early childhood. In J. J. Webster (ed.), *The language of early childhood: The collected works of M.A.K. Halliday*. Vol. 4. London: Continuum, 113–43.

Halliday, M. A. K. [1983] 2004. On the transition from child tongue to mother tongue. In J. J. Webster (ed.), *The Language of Early Childhood: The collected works of M.A.K. Halliday*. Vol. 4. London: Continuum, 210–26.

Halliday, M. A. K. [1998] 2004. Representing the child as a semiotic being. In J. J. Webster (ed.), *The language of early childhood: The collected works of M. A. K. Halliday*. Vol. 4. London: Continuum, 6–27.

Halliday, M. A. K. 2004. *The language of early childhood: The collected works of M. A. K. Halliday*. Vol. 4. London: Continuum.

Halliday, M. A. K. [1963] 2005a. Intonation in English grammar. In J. J. Webster (ed.), *Studies in English language: The collected works of M.A.K. Halliday*. Vol. 7. London: Bloomsbury Academic, 143–69.

Halliday, M. A. K. [1963] 2005b. The tones of English. In J. J. Webster (ed.), *Studies in English language: The collected works of M.A.K. Halliday*. Vol. 7. London: Bloomsbury Academic, 264–86.

Halliday, M. A. K. [1974] 2009. Language and social man. In J. J. Webster (ed.), *The collected works of M.A.K. Halliday*. Vol. 10. London: Bloomsbury Academic, 65–130.

Halliday, M. A. K., and Greaves, W. S. 2008. *Intonation in the grammar of English*. London: Equinox.

Halliday, M. A. K., and Hasan, R. 1976. *Cohesion in English*. London: Longman.

Halliday, M. A. K., and Matthiessen, C. M. I. M. 1999. *Construing experience through meaning: A language-based approach to cognition*. London: Continuum.

Halliday, M. A. K., and Matthiessen, C. M. I. M. 2014. Halliday's introduction to functional grammar, 4th edn. London: Routledge.

Hao, J. 2015. *Construing biology: An ideational perspective*. PhD dissertation, University of Sydney, Australia.

Hao, J. 2018. Reconsidering 'cause inside the clause' in scientific discourse – from a discourse semantic perspective in systemic functional linguistics. *Text & Talk*, 38(3), 1–26.

Hao, J. 2020a. *Analysing scientific discourse from a systemic functional linguistic perspective: A framework for exploring knowledge building in biology*. London: Routledge.

Hao, J. 2020b. Nominalisations in scientific English: A tristratal perspective. *Functions of Language*, 27(2), 143–73.

Hao, J., and Hood, S. 2019. Valuing science: The role of language and body language in a health science lecture. *Journal of Pragmatics* (Special edition, Communicating Sciences, E. de Martino and D. Banks, eds), 200–15.

Haviland, J. B. 2000. Pointing, gesture spaces, and mental maps. In D. McNeill (ed.), *Language and gesture*. Cambridge: Cambridge Unversity Press, 13–46.

Heath, C., and Luff, P. 2013. Embodied action and organizational activity. In J. Sidnell and T. Strivers (eds) *The handbook of conversation analysis*. Chichester: Wiley-Blackwell, 283–307.

Hirschberg, J. 2002. Communication and prosody: Functional aspects of prosody. *Speech Communication*, 36, 31–43.

Hjelmslev, L. 1961. *Prolegomena to a theory of language*. Madison: University of Wisconsin Press.

Hodge, G., and Johnston, T. 2014. Points, depictions, gestures and enactment: Partly lexical and non-lexical signs as core elements of single clause-like units in Auslan (Australian Sign Language). *Australian Journal of Linguistics*, 34(2), 262–91.

Hood, S. 2011. Body language in face-to-face teaching: A focus on textual and interpersonal meaning. In S. Dreyfus, S. Hood and M. Stenglin (eds), *Semiotic margins: Meaning in multimodalities*. London: Continuum, 31–52.

Hood, S. 2021. Graduation in research writing: Managing the dual demands of objectivity and critique. In J. R. Martin, J. Knox and D. Caldwell (eds), *Appliable linguistics and social semiotics: Developing theory from practice*. London: Bloomsbury.

Hood, S., and Hao, J. 2021. Grounded learning: Telling and showing in the language and paralanguage of a science lecture. In K. Maton, J. R. Martin and Y. J. Doran (eds). Teaching Science: Knowledge, Language, Pedagogy. London: Routledge, 226–57.

Hood, S., and Lander, J. 2016. Technologies, modes and pedagogic potential in live versus online lectures. *International Journal of Language Studies*, 10, 23–42.

Hood, S., and Maggiora, P. 2016. The lecturer at work: Language, the body and space in the structuring of disciplinary knowledge in Law. In H. De Silva Joyce (ed.), *Language at work: Analysing language use in work, education, medical and museum contexts*. Newcastle upon Tyne: Cambridge Scholars, 108–28.

Hood, S., and Zhang, D. 2020. GRADUATION in play with other systems of meaning in the enactment of interpersonal relations. *(Chinese) Journal of Foreign Languages (外国语(上海外国语大学学报)*, 43(6), 21–41.

Jia, J., Zhang, S., Meng, F., Wang, Y., and Cai, L. 2011. Emotional audio-visual speech synthesis based on PAD. *IEEE Transactions on Audio, Speech, and Language Processing*, 19, 570–82.

Johnson, M. H., Dziurawiec, S., Ellis, H., and Morton, J. 1991. Newborns' preferential tracking of face-like stimuli and its subsequent decline. *Cognition*, 40, 1–19.

Johnston, T., and Schembri, A. 2007. *Australian Sign Language (Auslan): An introduction to sign language linguistics*. Cambridge: Cambridge University Press.

Johnston, T. A. 1989. *Auslan: The sign language of the Australian deaf community*. PhD dissertation, University of Sydney, Australia.

Johnston, T. A. 2013. Formational and functional characteristics of pointing signs in a corpus of Auslan (Australian Sign Language): Are the data sufficient to posit a grammatical class of 'pronouns' in Auslan? *Corpus Linguistics and Linguistic Theory*, 9, 109–59.

Johnston, T. A. 2018. The role of headshake in negation in Auslan (Australian Sign Language): Implications for signed language typology and the gestural substrate in signed languages. *Linguistic Typology*, 22, 185–231.

Johnstone, T., and Scherer, K. R. 2000. Vocal communication of emotion. In M. Lewis and J. Haviland (eds), *Handbook of emotions*. Vol. 2. New York: Guilford, 220–35.

Joos, M. (ed.). 1957. *Readings in linguistics I*. Chicago: Chicago University Press.

Jun, S.-A. (ed.). 2005. *Prosodic typology: The phonology of intonation and phrasing*. Oxford: Oxford University Press.

Kato, T., Takahashi, E., Sawada, K., Kobayashi, N., Watanabe, T., and Ishh, T. 1983. A computer analysis of infant movements synchronized with adult speech. *Pediatric Research*, 17, 625.

Kendon, A. 1972. Some relationships between body motion and speech: An analysis of an example. In A. W. Siegman and B. Pope (eds), *Studies in dyadic communication*. New York: Pergamon, 177–210.

Kendon, A. 1997. Gesture. *Annual Review of Anthropology*, 26, 109–28.

Kendon, A. 2004. *Gesture: Visible action as utterance*. Cambridge: Cambridge University Press.

Kendon, A. 2017. Reflections on the 'gesture-first' hypothesis of language origins. *Psychonomic Bulletin & Review*, 24, 163–70.

Kita, S. 2000. How representational gestures help speaking. In D. McNeill (ed.), *Language and gesture*. New York: Cambridge University Press, 379–415.

Knight, N. K. 2013. Evaluating experience in funny ways: How friends bond through conversational hum. *Text & Talk*, 33, 553.

Kohler, K. J. 2006. Paradigms in experimental prosodic analysis: From measurement to function. In S. Sudhoff, M. Lenertova, R. Meyer, S. Pappert, P. Augurzky, I. Mleinek, N. Richter and J. Schieber (eds), *Methods in empirical prosody research*. Vol. 3. New York: Walter de Gruyter, 123–52.

Kok, K. 1996. The grammatical potential of co-speech gesture: A functional discourse grammar perspective. *Functions of Language*, 23, 149–78.

Kok, K., Bergmann, K., Cineki, A., and Kopp, S. 2016. Mapping out the multifunctionality of speakers' gestures. *Gesture*, 15, 37–59.

Kress, G., and Van Leeuwen, T. 1990. *Reading images*. Geelong: Deakin University Press.

Kress, G., and Van Leeuwen, T. 1996. *Reading images: The grammar of visual design*. London: Routledge.

Kress, G., and Van Leeuwen, T. 2001. *Multimodal discourse: The modes and media of contemporary communication*. London: Arnold.

Kress, G., and Van Leeuwen, T. 2006. *Reading images: The grammar of visual design*, 2nd ed. London: Routledge.

Kress, G., and Van Leeuwen, T. 2020. Reading images: The grammar of visual design, 3rd ed. London: Routledge.

Ladefoged, P. [1975] 2001. *A course in phonetics*. Fort Worth: Harcourt College.

Ladefoged, P., and Maddieson, I. 1996. *The sounds of the world's languages*. Vol. 1012. Oxford: Blackwell.

Laika Studios. 2017. *LAIKA | Coraline | Biggest Smallest Movie | Coraline | Biggest Smallest Movie* (online). Available: https://www.youtube.com/watch?v=cayV MHSRHZI&list=PLIOvQw23ql2tbKIbBstoxZmOAkiUFRW7J (accessed 15 November 2016).

Lee, N., Mikesell, L., Joaquin, A. D. L., Mates, A. W., and Schumann, J. H. 2009. *The interactional instinct: The evolution and acquisition of language*. New York: Oxford University Press.

Lehiste, I. 1977. Isochrony reconsidered. *Journal of Phonetics*, 5, 253–63.

Lewis, M. M. 1951. *Infant speech: A study of the beginnings of language*. London: Routledge & Kegan Paul.

Lim, F. V. 2019. Investigating intersemiosis: A systemic functional multimodal discourse analysis of the relationship between language and gesture in classroom discourse. *Visual Communication*, doi: 1470357218820695.

Lim, F. V., O'Halloran, K. L., and Podlalasov, A. 2012. Spatial pedagogy: Mapping meanings in the use of classroom space. *Cambridge Journal of Education*, 42(2), 235–51.

Linell, P. 2004. *The written language bias in linguistics: Its nature, origins and transformations*. London: Routledge.

Liszkowski, U. 2008. Before L1: A differentiated perspective on infant gestures. *Gesture*, 8, 180–96.

Liszkowski, U. 2014. Two sources of meaning in infant communication: Preceding action contexts and act-accompanying characteristics. *Philosophical Transactions of the Royal Society B: Biological Sciences*, 369, 20130294. doi: 10.1098/rstb.2013.0292

Lock, A. J. 1978. *Action, gesture and symbols*. New York: Academic Press.

Malatesta, C. Z. 1985. Developmental course of emotion expression in the human infant. In G. Zivin (ed.), *The development of expressive behavior: Biology-environment interactions*. Orlando, FL: Academic Press, 183–220.

Martin, J. R. 1992. *English text: System and structure*. Amsterdam: John Benjamins.

Martin, J. R. 1993. Life as a noun: Arresting the universe in science and humanities. In M. A. K. Halliday (ed.), *Writing science: Literacy and discursive power*. London: Falmer, 221–67.

Martin, J. R. 2000. Beyond exchange: Appraisal systems in English. In S. Hunston and G. Thompson (eds), *Evaluation in text: Authorial stance and the construction of discourse*. Oxford: Oxford University Press, 142–75.

Martin, J. R. 2008. Intermodal reconciliation: Mates in arms. In L. Unsworth (ed.), *New literacies and the English curriculum: Multimodal perspectives*. London: Continuum, 112–48.

Martin, J. R. 2009. Discourse studies. In M. A. K. Halliday and J. Webster (eds), Continuum *companion to systemic functional linguistics*. London: Continuum, 154–65.

Martin, J. R. 2010. Semantic variation: Modelling realization, instantiation and individuation in social semiosis. In M. Bednarek and J. R. Martin (eds), *New discourse on language: Functional perspectives on multimodality, identity, and affiliation*. London: Continuum, 1–34.

Martin, J. R. 2011a. Bridging troubled waters: Interdisciplinarity and what makes it stick. In F. Christie and K. Maton (eds), *Disciplinarity: Functional linguistic and sociological perspectives*. London: Continuum, 35–61.

Martin, J. R. 2011b. Multimodal semiotics: Theoretical challenges. In S. Dreyfus, S. Hood and M. Stenglin (eds), *Semiotic margins: Meaning in multimodalities*. London: Continuum, 243–68.

Martin, J. R. 2014. Evolving systemic functional linguistics: Beyond the clause. *Functional Linguistics*, 1, 1–24.

Martin, J. R. 2015a. Cohesion and texture. In D. Tannen, H. E. Hamilton and D. Schiffrin (eds), *The handbook of discourse analysis*, 2nd ed. Chichester: John Wiley, 61–81.

Martin, J. R. 2015b. Meaning beyond the clause: Co-textual relations. *Linguistics and the Human Sciences*, 11, 203–35.

Martin, J. R. 2016. Meaning matters: A short history of systemic functional linguistics. *Word*, 61, 35–58.

Martin, J. R. 2017a. The discourse semantics of attitudinal relations: Continuing the study of lexis. *Russian Journal of Linguistics*, 21, 22–47.

Martin, J. R. 2017b. Revisiting field: Specialized knowledge in secondary school science and humanities discourse. *Onomázein*, 111–48.

Martin, J. R. 2019. Discourse semantics. In G. Thompson, W. Boucher, L. Fontaine and D. Schönthal (eds), *The Cambridge handbook of systemic functional linguistics*. Cambridge: Cambridge University Press, 358–81.

Martin, J. R. 2020. The effability of semantic relations: Describing attitude. *(Chinese) Journal of Foreign Languages*, 43(6), 2–20.

Martin, J. R., Quiroz, B. Wang, P. to appear. *Systemic functional grammar: Another step into the theory-grammatical description*.

Martin, J. R., and Rose, D. [2003] 2007. *Working with discourse: Meaning beyond the clause*. London: Continuum.

Martin, J. R., and Rose, D. 2008. *Genre relations: Mapping culture*. London: Equinox.

Martin, J. R., and Veel, R. 1998. *Reading science: Critical and functional perspectives on discourses of science*. London: Routledge.

Martin, J. R., Wang, P., and Zhu, Y. 2013a. *Systemic functional grammar: A next step into the theory–axial relations*. Beijing: Higher Education.

Martin, J. R., and White, P. 2005. *The language of evaluation: Appraisal in English*. Basingstoke: Palgrave Macmillan.

Martin, J. R., and Wodak, R. 2003. *Re/reading the past: Critical and functional perspectives on time and value*. Vol. 8. Amsterdam: John Benjamins.

Martin, J. R., and Zappavigna, M. 2013. Youth Justice Conferencing: Ceremonial redress. *International Journal of Law, Language and Discourse*, 3(2), 103–42.

Martin, J. R., and Zappavigna, M. 2019. Embodied meaning: A systemic functional perspective on body language. *Functional Linguistics*, 6(1), 1–33.

Martin, J. R., Zappavigna, M., Dwyer, P., and Cléirigh, C. 2013b. Users in uses of language: Embodied identity in Youth Justice Conferencing. *Text & Talk*, 33, 467–96.

Martinec, R. 1998. Cohesion in action. *Semiotica*, 120, 161–80.

Martinec, R. 2000a. Rhythm in multimodal texts. *Leonardo*, 33, 289–97.

Martinec, R. 2000b. Types of process in action. *Semiotica*, 130, 243–68.

Martinec, R. 2001. Interpersonal resources in action. *Semiotica*, 135, 117–46.

Martinec, R. 2002. Rhythmic hierarchy in monologue and dialogue. *Functions of Language*, 9, 39–59.

Martinec, R. 2004. Gestures which co-occur with speech as a systematic resource: The realisation of experiential meanings in indexes. *Social Semiotics*, 14, 193–213.

Martinec, R. 2005. Topics in multimodality. In R. Hasan, C. M. I. M. Matthiessen and J. J. Webster (eds), *Continuing discourse on language: A functional perspective*. Vol. 1. London: Equinox, 157–81.

Martinec, R. 2008. Review of Cienki & Müller. *Linguistics and the Human Sciences*, 4, 1–19.

Maton, K. 2014. *Knowledge and knowers: Towards a realist sociology of education*. London: Routledge.

Maton, K., Martin, J. R., and Matruglio, E. 2016. LCT and systemic functional linguistics: Complementary approaches for greater explanatory power. In K. Maton, S. Hood and S. Shay (eds), *Knowledge-building: Educational studies in legitimation code theory*. London: Routledge, 93–113.

Matthiessen, C. M. I. M. 1992. Interpreting the textual metafunction. In M. Davies and L. Ravelli (eds), *Advances in systemic linguistics: Recent theory and practice*. London: Pinter, 37–81.

Matthiessen, C. M. I. M. 2004. The evolution of language: A systemic functional exploration of phylogenetic phases. In G. Williams and A. Lukin (eds), *The development of language: Functional perspectives on species and individuals*. London: Continuum, 45–90.

Matthiessen, C. M. I. M. 2007. The multimodal page. In T. Royce and W. L. Bowcher (eds), *New directions in the analysis of multimodal discourse*. Mahwah, NJ: Lawrence Erlbaum, 1–62.

Matthiessen, C. M. I. M. 2009. Multisemiosis and context-based register typology. In E. Ventola and M. Guijarro (eds), *The world told and the world shown: Multisemiotic issues*. London: Palgrave Macmillan, 11–38.

Matthiessen, C. M. I. M., and Halliday, M. A. K. 2009. *Systemic functional grammar: A first step into the theory*. Beijing: Higher Education.

Mayberry, R. I., and Nicoladis, E. 2000. Gesture reflects language development: Evidence from bilingual children. *Current Directions in Psychological Science*, 9, 192–6.

McNeill, D. 1985. So you think gestures are nonverbal? *Psychological Review*, 92, 350.

McNeill, D. 1992. *Hand and mind: What gestures reveal about thought*. Chicago: University of Chicago Press.

McNeill, D. 2000. *Language and gesture*. Chicago: University of Chicago Press.

McNeill, D. 2006. Gesture: A psycholinguistic approach. In E. Brown and A. Anderson (eds), *The encyclopedia of language and linguistics*. Amsterdam: Elsevier, 58–66.

McNeill, D. 2012. *How language began: Gesture and speech in human evolution*. Cambridge: Cambridge University Press.

McNeill, D. 2016. *Why we gesture: The surprising role of hand movements in communication*. Cambridge: Cambridge University Press.

McShane, J. 1980. *Learning to talk*. Cambridge: Cambridge University Press.

Meguerditchian, A., Cochet, H., and Vauclair, J. 2011. From gesture to language: Ontogenetic and phylogenetic perspectives on gestural communication and its cerebral lateralization. In A. Vilain, J.-L. Schwartz, C. Abry and J. Vauclair (eds), *Primate communication and human language: Vocalisation, gestures, imitation and deixis in humans and non-humans*. Amsterdam: John Benjamins, 91–119.

Menn, L. 1978. *Pattern, control and contrast in beginning speech: A case study in the development of word form and word function*. Bloomington: Indiana University Linguistics Club.

Mittelberg, I., and Evola, V. 2014. Iconic and representational gestures. In C. Müller, A. Cienki, E. Fricke, S. L. Ladewig, D. McNeill and J. Bressem (eds), *Body-language-communication. An international handbook on multimodality in human interaction*. Berlin: Mouton de Gruyter, 1732–46.

Mohamed, F. N., and Nor, N. L. M. 2015. Puppet animation films and gesture aesthetics. *Animation*, 10, 102–18.

Mondada, L. 2016. Challenges of multimodality: Language and the body in social interaction. *Journal of Sociolinguistics*, 20, 336–66.

Müller, C. 1998. Iconicity and gesture. In S. Santi, C. C. Guatiella and G. Konopczynki (eds), *Oralité et gestualité: Communication multimodale, interaction*. Montreal, Paris: L'Harmattan, 321–8.

Muntigl, P. 2004. Modelling multiple semiotic systems: The case of gesture and speech. In E. Ventola, C. Charles and M. Kaltenbacher (eds), *Perspectives on multimodality*. Amsterdam: John Benjamins, 31–50.

Murray, L., and Threvathen, C. 1985. Emotional regulations of interactions between two-month-olds and their mothers. In T. N. Field and N. A. Fox (eds), *Social perception in infants*. Norwood, NJ: Ablex, 177–97.

NCVS. 2019. *Voice qualities* (online). National Center for Voice and Speech: Giving Voice to America. Available: http://www.ncvs.org/ncvs/tutorials/voiceprod/tutorial/quality.html (accessed 27 August 2019).

Ngo, T. 2018. Gesture as transduction of characterisation in children's literature animation adaptation. *Australian Journal of Language and Literacy*, 41, 30–43.

Ngo, T. 2019. Teaching multimodal literacy: A focus on the comprehension and representation of gesture in oral interactions. In H. De Silva Joyce and S. Feez (eds), *Multimodality across classrooms*. New York: Routledge, 115–27.

O'Grady, G. 2010. *A grammar of spoken English discourse: The intonation of increments*. London: Bloomsbury.

O'Grady, G. 2013. Choices in Tony's talk: Phonological paragraphing, information unit nexuses and the presentation of tone units. *Choice in Language: Applications in Text Analysis*, 125, 157.

O'Grady, G. 2016. Given/new: What do the terms refer to? *English Text Construction*, 9, 9–32.

O'Halloran, K. L., Tan, S., and Wignell, P. 2019. SFL and multimodal discourse analysis. In D. Schönthal, G. Thompson, W. L. Bowcher and L. Fontaine (eds), *The Cambridge handbook of systemic functional linguistics*. Cambridge: Cambridge University Press, 433–61.

Omori, K., Kojima, H., Kakani, R., Slavit, D. H., and Blaugrund, S. M. 1997. Acoustic characteristics of rough voice: Subharmonics. *Journal of Voice*, 11, 40–47.

Ouni, S., Colotte, V., Dahmani, S., and Azzi, S. 2016. Acoustic and visual analysis of expressive speech: A case study of French acted speech. *Interspeech*, 580–4.

Painter, C. 2003. Developing attitude: An ontogenetic perspective on APPRAISAL. *Text*, 23, 183–210.

Painter, C. [1999] 2005. *Learning through language in early childhood*. London: Continuum.

Painter, C. 2005. The concept of 'protolanguage' in language development. *Linguistics and the Human Sciences*, 1, 177–96.

Painter, C. [1984] 2015. *Into the mother tongue: A case study in early language development*. London: Pinter/Bloomsbury.

Painter, C., and Martin, J. R. 2012. Intermodal complementarity: Modelling affordances across verbiage and image in children's picture books. In Huang Guo Wen (ed.), *Studies in systemic functional linguistics and discourse analysis (III)*. Beijing: Higher Education, 132–58.

Painter, C., Martin, J. R., and Unsworth, L. 2013. *Reading visual narratives: Image analysis of children's picture books*. London: Equinox.

Pike, K. L. 1945. *The intonation of American English*. Ann Arbor: University of Michigan Press.

Pike, K. L. [1959] 1972. Language as particle, wave, and field. In R. M. Brend (ed.), *Selected writings*. The Hague: Mouton de Gruyter, 129–43.

Pike, K. L. 1982. *Linguistic concepts: An introduction to tagmemics*. Vol. 790. Lincoln: University of Nebraska Press.

Pizzuto, E. A., and Capobianco, M. 2005. The link (and differences) between deixis and symbols in children's early gestural-vocal system. *Gesture*, 5, 179–99.

Ramenzoni, V. C., and Liszkowski, U. 2016. The social reach: 8-month-olds reach for unobtainable objects in the presence of another person. *Psychological Science*, 27, 1278–85.

Reddy, V. 2008. *How infants know minds*. Cambridge, MA: Harvard University Press.

Reddy, V., Hay, D., Murray, L., and Trevarthen, C. 1997. Communication in infancy: Mutual regulation of affect and attention. In G. Bremner, A. Slater and G. Butterworth (eds), *Infant development: Recent advances*. Hove, East Sussex: Psychology Press, 247–74.

Roach, A. 2019. *Tell me why: The story of my life and my music*. Sydney: Simon & Schuster.

Rudge, L. 2017. *Analysing British sign language through the lens of systemic functional linguistics*. Bristol: University of Western England.

Rudge, L. 2021. Interpersonal grammar of British Sign Language. In J. R. Martin, B. Quiroz and G. Figueredo (eds), *Interpersonal grammar: Systemic functional linguistic theory and description*. Cambridge: Cambridge University Press, 227–65.

Sampson, G. 1980. *Schools of linguistics: Competition and evolution*. London: Hutchinson.

Scherer, K. R. 1986. Vocal affect expression: A review and a model for future research. *Psychological Bulletin*, 99, 143.

Sekine, K., Rose, M. L., Foster, A. M., Attard, M. C., and Lanyon, L. E. 2013. Gesture production in aphasic discourse: In-depth description and preliminary predictions. *Aphasology*, 27, 1031–49.

Selick, H. (writer/dir.). 2009. *Coraline*. DVD, Laika Studios, Pandemonium Films, United States, distributed by Focus Features.

Shaw, G. B. 1913. *Pygmalion*.

Silverman, K., Beckman, M., Pitrelli, J., Ostendorf, M., Wightman, C., Price, P., Pierrehumbert, J., and Hirschberg, J. 1992. ToBI: A standard for labeling English prosody. Second International Conference on Spoken Language Processing.

Singapore Ministry of Education. 2019. *English language and literature* (online). Available: https://www.moe.gov.sg/education/syllabuses/english-language-and-literature (accessed 28 January 2020).

Smith, B. A. 2007. The language of the heart and breath: Bridging strata, bridging discourses of INFORMATION systems. Online Conference

Proceedings for the 2007 ASFLA Congress: Bridging Discourses, Wollongong University. Available: https://www.academia.edu/1975175/information_systems_language_of_the_heart_and_breath.

Smith, B. A. 2008. *Intonational systems and register: A multidimensional exploration.* PhD dissertation, Macquarie University, Australia.

Smith, B. A., and Greaves, W. S. 2015. Intonation. In J. J. Webster (ed.), *The Bloomsbury companion to MAK Halliday.* London: Bloomsbury, 291–313.

Streeck, J. 2008. Depicting by gesture. *Gesture,* 8, 285–301.

Tann, K. 2017. Context and meaning in the Sydney architecture of SFL. In T. Bartlett and G. O'Grady (eds), *The Routledge handbook of systemic functional linguistics.* London: Routledge, 438–56.

Taylor, C. 2017. Reading images: Including moving ones. In T. Bartlett and G. O'Grady (eds), *The Routledge handbook of systemic functional linguistics.* London: Routledge, 575–90.

Tench, P. [1965] 2015. *The intonation systems of English.* London: Bloomsbury.

Thibault, P. J. 1987. An interview with Michael Halliday. In R. Steele and T. Threadgold (eds), *Language topics: Essays in honour of Michael Halliday.* Vol. 2. Amsterdam: John Benjamins, 601–28.

Thibault, P. J. 2004. *Brain, mind and the signifying body: An ecosocial semiotic theory.* London: Continuum.

Thibault, P. J. 2008. Face-to-face communication and body language. In G. Antos and E. Ventola (eds), *Handbook of interpersonal communication.* Berlin: Mouton de Gruyter, 285–329.

Tian, P. 2011. *Multimodal evaluation: Sense and sensibility in Anthony Browne's picture books.* Unpublished thesis, University of Sydney, Australia.

Titze, I. R. 1994. *Principles of voice production.* Old Tappan, USA: Prentice Hall.

Tomasello, M. 2008. *Origins of human communication.* Cambridge, MA: MIT Press.

Tomasello, M., Carpenter, M., and Liszkowski, U. 2007. A new look at infant pointing. *Child Development,* 78, 705–22.

Torr, J. 1997. *From child tongue to mother tongue: A case study of language development in the first two and a half years. Monographs in systemic linguistics no.9.* Nottingham: Department of English Studies, University of Nottingham.

Trevarthen, C. 1979. Communication and cooperation in early infancy: A description of primary intersubjectivity. In M. Bullowa (ed.), *Before speech: The beginning of interpersonal communication.* Vol. 1. Cambridge: Cambridge University Press, 321–47.

Trevarthen, C. 1987. Sharing makes sense: Intersubjectivity and the making of an infant's meaning. In R. Steele and T. Threadgold (eds), *Language topics.* Vol. 1. Philadelphia: John Benjamins, 177–99.

Trevarthen, C. 1993. The function of emotions in early infant communication and development. In J. Nadel and L. Camaioni (eds), *New perspectives in early communicative development.* London: Routledge, 48–81.

Trevarthen, C. 2005. First things first: Infants make good use of the sympathetic rhythm of imitation, without reason or language. *Journal of Child Psychotherapy,* 31, 91–113.

Trubetskoy, N. S. [1939] 1969. *Principles of phonology*. Berkeley: University of California Press.
Tuite, K. 1993. The production of gesture. *Semiotica*, 93, 83–106.
Van Leeuwen, T. 1985. Rhythmic structure of the film text. In T. Van Dijk (ed.), *Discourse and communication: New approaches to the analysis of mass media discourse and communication*. Berlin: Mouton de Gruyter, 216–32.
Van Leeuwen, T. 1992. Rhythm and social context: Accent and juncture in the speech of professional radio announcers. In P. Tench (ed.), *Systemic phonology*. London: Pinter, 231–62.
Van Leeuwen, T. 1999. *Speech, music, sound*. London: Macmillan.
Van Leeuwen, T. 2005. *Introducing social semiotics*. London: Routledge.
Van Leeuwen, T. 2009. Parametric systems: The case of voice quality. In C. Jewitt (ed.), *The Routledge handbook of multimodal analysis*. London: Routledge, 68–77.
Volterra, V., and Erting, C. J. 1990. *From gesture to language in hearing and deaf children*. Berlin: Springer-Verlag.
Walker, G. 2013. Phonetics and prosody in conversation. In J. Sidnell and T. Strivers (eds), *The handbook of conversation analysis*. Chichester: Wiley-Blackwell, 455–74.
Warren, P. 2016. *Uptalk: The phenomenon of rising intonation*. Cambridge: Cambridge University Press.
Welch, G. F. 2005. Singing as communication. *Musical Communication*, 1, 239–59.
Wignell, P., Martin, J. R., and Eggins, S. 1989. The discourse of geography: Ordering and explaining the experiential world. *Linguistics and Education*, 1, 359–91.
Wildfeuer, J., Pflaeging, J., Bateman, J. A., Seizov, O., and Tseng, C.-I. 2019. *Multimodality: Disciplinary thoughts and the challenge of diversity – Introduction*. Berlin: Mouton de Gruyter.
Zappavigna, M. 2018. *Searchable talk: Hashtags and social media metadiscourse*. London: Bloomsbury.
Zappavigna, M. 2019. Ambient affiliation and #brexit: Negotiating values about experts through censure and ridicule. In V. Koller, S. Kopf and M. Miglbauer (eds), *Discourses of Brexit*. London: Routledge, 48–68.
Zappavigna, M., Cléirigh, C., Dwyer, P., and Martin, J. R. 2010. The coupling of gesture and phonology. In M. Bednarek and J. R. Martin (eds), *New discourse on language: Functional perspectives on multimodality, identity and affiliation*. London: Continuum, 219–36.
Zappavigna, M., and Martin, J. R. 2018. *Discourse and diversionary justice: An analysis of Youth Justice Conferencing*. London: Palgrave Macmillan.

Index

accent 181
actual 165 (*see* paralinguistic deixis)
affect in language 62, 118–19, 127–8
   happiness / security /
      satisfaction 118–19
   irrealis / realis affect 118–21, 136–7
   (*see also* appraisal)
affection (*see* voice affect)
affordances 21, 112, 200
anaphora 58, 164 (*see* recoverability)
anger (*see* paralinguistic affect; voice affect)
anxiety (*see* paralinguistic affect; voice affect)
appliable linguistics 247
appraisal 4, 12, 14–16, 29, 33–8, 54, 115, 117–19
   attitude 34–5, 115, 117–18, 120
   engagement 37–8, 115, 117, 143–4
   graduation 35–6, 57, 115, 117, 145–6
   force and focus 36
articulation 48, 55, 64, 74, 77, 91, 180, 182, 190 (*see also* protolanguage)
articulation rate 138, 225
attitude (*see* appraisal)

beats (*see* paralinguistic rhythm)
behaviours 3, 15, 19–20, 47–8, 50, 53, 61–2, 64, 118, 124, 197
   affective 234 biological 19, 47–8, 50
   semiotic 20, 28, 48–50, 197
   somatic 19, 49–50, 60, 64, 116, 198, 204
body language 1, 3, 18, 35, 57, 60, 112, 116
body orientation 60, 62, 115, 149, 192, 211
body parts 164, 169, 180, 186
   arms 63, 116
   eyebrows 23, 26, 34, 116–17, 120, 122–3, 125, 139–40, 152, 157
   eyes 40, 60–2, 120, 122–3, 128, 139–40, 152, 156, 158, 164, 170

face 45, 54
forearms 60, 172–3
hands 18, 30–1, 33, 37–8, 41, 43, 47, 49, 60, 63, 74, 96–9, 106–7, 144–5, 158, 164–6, 174–5, 178, 183–4, 186, 199–200
head 36, 40, 42, 47, 54, 60, 64, 116, 144–5, 147, 149, 158, 164, 168, 170
index finger 4, 12–13, 29–31, 41–2, 91–2, 105–7, 109, 164, 169, 172, 174, 176–8, 198, 208, 202–3
lips 41, 61, 68, 122–3, 140, 128, 164, 203
mouth 34, 47, 120, 122, 125, 139
palm 60, 144, 165, 174, 184, 177, 183
body position /positioning 148, 151–2, 159, 194
bonds /bonding 16, 140–3
breathiness (*see* paralinguistic affect; voice affect)

caret symbol 71, 73
cheer (*see* paralinguistic affect)
clause 5, 7–15, 17, 58–9, 78–80, 85–6, 92, 186–8
co-instantiation 123, 140, 164, 184, 208
commitment 2, 30, 94, 207
concurrence 21 29, 91, 93, 112, 208
conjunction 80, 86, 158
   internal 17, 86
connexion 12–14, 29, 33, 91, 112
consonants 68, 70
   initial 234–5
context 46, 52, 56, 61, 74, 77, 88, 176, 178, 184
contraction 37, 143–5, 158, 183
convergence / convergent / converging 3, 21–3, 28–30, 33, 36–8, 41, 44, 94, 98, 117, 127, 134, 141, 146, 156, 161–2, 171, 178–84, 198–200, 203, 207
   intermodal 115, 188, 194

intersemiotic 136-7, 162
coupling 140-2, 158 (*see also* bonds)

dB (decibels) 129, 140, 152, 226
deixis 175
   deictic point 94
   deictic gestures 57, 94, 164, 169, 173, 177-8, 202 (*see also* paralinguistic deixis; pointing)
determiners 58, 162-3, 167, 175 (*see also* reference)
direction 100, 104, 109-10, 128, 164-5, 189
   spatiotemporal direction 29
discourse 16-17, 67-8, 74, 81-2, 84, 86-9, 99-100, 161-2, 178-83, 185-6, 192-4
discourse semantics 4, 10-12, 28, 68, 70, 91, 198
   discourse semantic systems 18, 29, 208
      appraisal 4, 14, 12, 15-16, 29, 33, 38, 54, 62, 117-18, 198
      connexion 12-14, 29, 32-3, 91, 112,
      ideation 4, 12-13, 29, 90, 92, 198, 208
      identification 4, 12, 16, 29, 38-9, 58, 161-2, 198, 208
      negotiation 12, 14-15, 29, 34, 38
      periodicity 4, 12, 16-17, 29, 38-9, 161-2, 179, 185-6, 191, 194, 198
disdain (*see* paralinguistic affect)
displeasure (*see* paralinguistic affect)
disquiet (*see* paralinguistic affect)
divergence 3, 112, 140
duration 68, 74, 124-5, 129, 133, 138, 176, 180, 183-4, 225

emblems 1-3, 34, 38, 41-3, 97, 123, 203-4, 209, 234
endophora (*see* recoverability)
engagement 37, 62, 115, 117, 143-4
   contraction 37
   expansion 37, 82, 143-5, 158, 183
   heteroglossia 143
   (*see* also appraisal)
ennui (*see* paralinguistic affect)
entities 10, 12, 29-32, 91-100, 102-6, 108-9, 112, 161-5, 167-8, 173, 175-6

activity entities 93
entity types 92
   (*see also* paralinguistic entities)
epilinguistic body language 22, 60 (*see also* semovergent paralanguage)
exchange structure 42
exophora (*see* recoverability)
expansion (*see* engagement)
expression plane 10
eyebrows (*see* body parts)
eyes (*see* body parts)

face (*see* body parts)
Facial Action Coding System (FACS) 120
facial affect (*see* paralinguistic affect)
fear (*see* paralinguistic affect)
figures 2, 5-6, 8-9, 11-14, 17-21, 40-3, 71-3, 80-2, 100-12, 117-21, 129-31, 133-5, 137-8, 141-5, 148-51, 163, 165-6, 185, 188-94, 197-200
   occurence figures 13, 101, 104, 106-10, 202
   presentational state figures 103
   state figures 13 (*see* state figure)
figures and entities 93, 112
foot 71-5
force and focus (*see* graduation; appraisal)
forearms (*see* body parts)
formants 227
frequency 17, 129, 194, 225-7
   fundamental frequency 68, 129, 225
   higher 228
   lower 228
frequency and energy 225-6

gaze 19, 27-8, 47-8, 51, 54, 60, 64, 141-3, 147, 149-50, 155-6, 179, 183
genre 17, 179, 181, 208
gesticulation 1-2
gestures 2-4, 18, 24, 33-5, 40-3, 48-9, 51, 54-60, 63-4, 91-6, 98-9, 102-12, 164, 178-9, 200-3
graduation (*see* appraisal)
grammatical metaphor 10

happiness (*see* affect; appraisal)
head (*see* body parts)
heteroglossia (*see* engagement)
homophora (*see* recoverability)

hyper-theme 86, 185, 187, 190–4 (*see also* theme; periodicity)
Hz (hertz) 68, 75–6, 80–1, 129, 140, 225–6

iconicity 93–4
ictus 70–4, 80
ideational meaning 2, 58, 61–2, 64, 88, 91, 99, 112, 184, 190, 199, 207
ideational paralanguage 29, 91–2, 112, 179, 202
ideational semovergence 91–113
ideational semovergent paralanguage 29
ideation systems 29
identification 4, 12, 16–17, 29, 38–9, 58, 128, 130, 132, 161–2, 164, 167, 171, 173–4, 176, 198
   identification system 162 (*see also* deixis; reference)
index finger (*see* body parts; paralinguistic deixis; pointing)
information flow 3, 38, 62, 161 (*see* periodicity)
instantiation 55, 207
intensification 35
interdisciplinarity 204–5
intermodality 44, 161, 205, 207–8, 210
intermodal relations 3, 20, 204, 207–8
interpersonal meaning 2, 57–8, 61–2, 82–4, 115, 149–50, 152–3, 156, 158–9, 161, 184, 199, 207
interpersonal paralanguage 29, 58, 115–59
   interpersonal semovergent paralanguage 33, 115, 117–18, 178
   interpersonal sonovergent paralanguage 115–16, 156
intersemiosis 120, 156
intonation 4, 9–10, 22, 24, 54, 57, 67, 88–9 (*see also* phonology)
isochrony 71–4

Legitimation Code Theory (LCT) 205, 251
lexicogrammar, 4, 10–11, 28, 51, 101, 181, 198
lips (*see* body parts)
loudness (*see* voice quality)

method of development 80
microfunctions 2–3, 6–9, 52, 55, 60–2
   early 52–3
   and emotions 52
   imaginative 54, 61
   instrumental 52, 54, 55, 60
   interactional 52, 54, 60
   personal 52, 54–6, 60
   regulatory 52, 60
   (*see also* protolanguage)
mime 54, 200–203
mimics 15, 35, 201, 203, 215, 222
misery (*see* paralinguistic affect; voice affect)
modalities 3–4, 9, 21–2, 60, 62, 119, 159, 204, 207–8, 210
modes and media 249
mood 6, 57, 62, 118–19, 121
   declarative 10
mood and modality 62
morphemes 70, 209
multimodality 57, 205, 210
multimodal studies 3, 205–6
multimodal texts 152, 180
muscle tension 33, 36, 122, 124–6, 152, 178

nasality (*see* paralinguistic affect; voice affect)
negotiation 14–15, 29, 38, 144, 158, 184
non-salient syllables 70–2, 86, 180

occurrence figures (*see* figures)
   occurrences 12–13, 29–32, 71, 74, 78, 91–2, 94–5, 101, 126, 165, 181
   concurring paralinguistic occurrences 110
   entitied occurrences 104–5
onomatopoeia 203–4
ontic relations 205–7
ontogenesis 18–19, 46, 63, 209
(*see also* protolanguage, transition)
orientation 62, 143, 147, 150, 155–6, 184, 189, 203
   back-to-back 62, 149
   face-to-face 62, 149
   oblique 62, 154
   side-by-side 62, 149
oscillating hand 147

pantomime 1–2
paradigmatic 4–6

paralanguage 1–5, 18–19, 22–30, 40–65, 67, 91, 93–5, 112–13, 115, 117, 144–7, 161–2, 165, 166–8, 170–1 73, 175–9, 181–5, 195–210
  (*see also* semovergent paralanguage *and* sonovergent paralanguage)
paralinguistic affect 34–5, 62, 122, 202
  facial affect 120–1, 123–5, 139–40, 142, 145
    cheer 119, 131–3, 138–40, 143
    disdain 121–2, 131, 139, 146
    displeasure 119
    disquiet 119
    ennui 119, 131, 133–5
    fear 118–22, 128, 135–7, 142, 152–4, 210
    happiness 52, 118–21, 141
    misery 119, 131, 133–5, 140, 153
  voice affect 120, 128–43, 149, 152–4, 157
    spirit: down: ennui 133–5
    spirit: down: misery 133–5
    spirit: up: affection 131–3
    spirit: up: cheer 131–2
    surprise 138–9
    system of voice affect 131
    threat: anger 16, 120–2, 128, 135, 137, 140, 152, 154–5, 157–8
    threat: anxiety 135–7
    threat: fear 135–7
paralinguistic beats 183–4, 190 (*see also* paralinguistic rhythm)
paralinguistic commitment 30
  paralinguistic deixis 20, 39, 161–79
  paralinguistic deixis system 169
    actual 166–8
    demarcation 174–7
    range 173–7
    self/other 166
    scope 173–4
    virtual 168–73
    virtual location 168, 172, 177–8
    virtual semiosis 168, 170–1, 177
  (*see also* pointing)
paralinguistic engagement 38, 115, 119, 143–5, 158, 165
paralinguistic entities 30–2, 93, 95–8, 100–1, 103–4, 146, 165, 175, 200
  depicted entities 97, 146, 184

specificity: shape 95, 104, 106, 176, 184
specificity: size 95
paralinguistic figures 100–2, 111, 200
  paralinguistic occurrence figures 101–2, 104–5, 108–9
  paralinguistic occurrences 30
  paralinguistic state figures 101–4
  non-entitied occurrences 105–7
paralinguistic graduation 115, 119, 124, 134, 145, 147, 178
paralinguistic focus 36–7, 146, 178
paralinguistic force 124–5, 146, 157
paralinguistic ideation 91–3, 176
paralinguistic orientation 142, 149–50, 154, 156
paralinguistic periodicity 161, 179, 185–6, 189, 194, 200
periodicity in language 4, 12, 16–17, 23, 29, 38–40, 161, 179, 194, 198
  (*see also* prominence; rhythm)
paralinguistic power 150–1, 155
paralinguistic prominence 194
paralinguistic proximity 147–8, 153, 156
paralinguistic rhythm 179
paralinguistic rhythm as beats 2, 4, 23, 25, 72–4, 146, 179–80, 186, 188
  silent beats 73–4, 169–70, 182, 190–3
  (*see also* rhythm)
paralinguistic systems 59, 65, 115, 145, 147, 159, 161, 164, 177, 179, 209, 211
  clause level theme 59, 175, 181, 187–8, 190, 192, 208
  hierarchy of periodicity 17, 179, 185–6, 191
  hyper-new 187, 193–4
  hyper-theme 187, 190–2
  macro-theme 185, 187, 191–2, 194
  method of development 194
  new 193
  pause 73–4
  periodicity 4, 12, 16–17, 23, 29, 38, 161, 194
  theme 190
  (*see* discourse semantic systems; paralinguistic periodicity)
periodic systems 89
phonemes 208–9, 232
phonemic 70

phonetics 67-9
phonology, 10-11, 23-8, 39-40, 42-3, 67-70, 96-100, 102-4, 106-10, 126-8, 132-40, 142-3, 145-8, 157, 167-8, 170-3, 175-8
  intonation 67
  phonological analysis xii, 23, 76-7, 88, 217-22, 224-5
  phonological foot / feet 20, 22-6, 71-5, 92-3, 96, 102, 106, 182, 189, 207, 214, 220
    foot boundaries 7
    silent feet 192
  phonological paragraphing 81
  prosodic phonology 4, 146, 179-8, 83, 194, 198, 200, 203
pitch 25-26, 67-8, 70-1, 74-7, 80-2, 85, 129, 180, 182, 225, 228
  pitch contours 68-69, 74-8, 81-3, 182, 184, 226
  pitch height 25-6, 38-40, 67-8, 74, 80-82
  pitch jumps 74, 85
  pitch level 67, 85, 129, 133-5, 138, 140
  pitch movement 18, 23-4, 48, 69-70, 81, 116, 182, 187
  pitch range 2, 81-2, 129, 134-5, 138, 236-7
  pitch variability 133
  variation in pitch duration 68, 77
pointing 2, 38, 41, 46, 57, 60, 164-6, 171-172, 198, 200, 202
  pointing gestures 18, 33, 38, 54, 56, 61, 94, 164-6, 173
  (*see also* paralinguistic deixis)
Praat 71-3, 75, 81-2, 126, 131-5, 139, 142, 157, 225-6
prelinguistic communication 45, 46-8, 63
  (*see also* protolanguage)
  protoconversation 47, 52, 64
pre-tonic syllables 75, 237 (*see* tonicity)
prominence 25, 70, 73, 78, 81-2, 86-7, 179, 181-4, 186, 188, 193-5 (*see also* salience)
prone position 37
properties 2, 13, 92
propositions 16, 84, 144, 146, 184
prosodic systems 89

protolanguage 18-19, 45, 49-55, 56-7, 59-64, 68-70, 88, 197
proto-graduation 56
protolanguage signs 48-9, 51-6
protolanguage system 50, 53
protolinguistic microfunctions (*see* microfunctions)
(*see also* transition phase)
proximity 19, 115, 147-8

recoverability strategies 163-4
  endophoric 164-5 (*see also* deixis)
  exophoric 164-5
  homophora 164
reference 16, 120, 162-4, 169, 180
  presenting reference 162
  presuming reference 163 (*see also* identification)
register 17, 179, 208, 210-11
remiss 70, 72, 88
representational meaning 2-3, 6, 8, 93, 179
restarts 87-88
rhythm 23, 25-6, 28, 67-8, 70-73, 80-2, 86, 88-9, 180-2, 198, 200, 207
  rhythm and intonation 4, 9, 18, 22, 24, 67, 181, 203
  rhythm and salience 70, 80, 86, 89
  (*see also* paralinguistic rhythm)
roughness (*see* paralinguistic affect; voice affect)

salience 70-4, 78, 80, 82, 86, 89, 117, 207, 237
  salient syllables 24-5, 71, 73-4, 86, 183(*see also* prominence)
  super-salience 80-1
security 52 (*see* protolanguage), 118-19
  (*see* affect)
segment of speech 130, 132-4, 226
semantics 8, 207
semiosis 3, 5-6, 8, 18-21, 44-6, 49, 62, 124, 168, 170-1, 197-8
semiotic entities 92-4, 99, 146, 162, 167, 169, 175, 184
semiotic systems 9, 18-19, 50, 56, 64, 67-8, 70, 88, 206-7
semiotic voice 67-89

semovergent / semovergence 28–42, 60–1, 156, 177, 179–81, 198–20, 207–8
sonovergent / sonovergence 22, 40–1, 60, 67, 179–81, 117, 189, 198–200, 203, 207, 211
shape (see paralinguistic entities) sign languages 1–2, 42, 46, 199, 200, 208–10
sign systems 19, 209
silence 40, 71, 74, 127, 141–2
silent beats (see paralinguistic rhythm)
size (see paralinguistic entities)
social context 88
social distance 62, 147–8
social relations 2–3, 8, 14–15, 115, 147, 159, 200, 205
social semiotics 1, 19, 67, 70, 76, 82, 94, 129, 144, 147, 159, 181, 206
somasis / somatic 3, 19–21, 24, 27–8, 40, 45, 47, 49, 97, 197–8
sound quality 18, 38, 129
sounds 18–19, 23–8, 47, 49, 51, 54, 68–70, 127, 129, 131, 179–81
specificity 42, 95–100
spectrogram 74–5, 129, 131–2, 134, 137–8, 157, 225–6, 228–9
speech function 10, 57, 62
state figures 13 (see also figures)
stratification 4–5, 9–11, 198
supine 36, 144–5, 165, 183–4
supine hand 27, 37, 173, 183 (see also body parts)
syllable 10, 70–8
synchronicity / synchrony 4, 21, 23, 28–9, 166–7, 180–1, 184, 189–90, 207–8
  intermodal synchronicity 180–2
syntagmatic relations 4–6
system and structure 5
Systemic Functional Linguistics (SFL) 3–5

tension (see voice quality)
textual meaning 2–3, 21–2, 58–9, 80–2, 86–7, 181, 184, 195, 199, 207, 209
textual metafunction 9, 61, 86–8
textual semovergent paralanguage 33, 38, 162, 178
theme (see periodicity)
  (see also hyper-theme, macro-theme periodicity)

tonality 23–4, 28, 71, 74, 77–80, 82, 86–7, 89, 194, 200, 207
  marked tonality 79–80, 87–8
tone 23–4, 51, 54–7, 64, 74–8, 80–5, 89, 116–17, 182, 184
  coordination ('listing') 84
  subordination 84
  tone choice 7, 60, 75–7, 80–1, 116–17, 182
  tone contours 234
  tone groups 23–4, 26–7, 30, 32–3, 38, 74–5, 77–80, 83–7, 125, 180–2, 184–8, 200–2, 207–8
  tone group boundary 7, 78
  tone system 57, 74–5, 77, 83–5
    compound tone 77, 85
    declarative 85
    falling 48, 54–5, 74–5, 83, 116, 158, 184
    falling-rising 75–6, 116
    high falling 85
    high level 54
    level-rise 75–6
    low falling 85
    rising 23, 55, 75–6, 81, 116, 142
    rising-falling 75–6, 116
    secondary 77, 85
    sharp fall-rise 85

tonic / tonicity 23–6, 28, 74–82, 87–8, 116–17, 183, 185, 187–8, 191
  marked tonicity 79–80
  minor/major tonic 77
  tonic syllable 28, 74–6, 78–80, 179, 182
transition phase 45, 55–8, 64
  mathetic/pragmatic distinction 57 (see also microfunctions, protolanguage)
trigger 120, 124, 127–8, 137–8, 141–3, 152

vectors 164, 166, 168, 173–174, 176, 179, 200 (see also paralinguistic deixis; pointing)
virtual (see paralinguistic deixis)
vibrato (see paralinguistic affect; voice affect)
vocalization 2, 47, 49, 51, 129
  segmental vocalization 57

vocal cord (*see* vocal fold)
vocal fold 68, 74
vocal tract 68
voice affect (*see* paralinguistic affect)
voice quality 38, 54–7, 64, 69–70, 128–38,
    140, 142, 153–5, 157, 197, 200,
    204, 225
  breathiness 68, 129, 132, 134–8, 140,
  creakiness 56, 68–9
  duration 129, 133, 138, 180
  intensity 68
  loudness 18, 54, 57, 68, 70, 82, 126,
    129, 133–6, 148–9, 151, 180
  nasality 68, 129, 137, 229

pitch level (*see* pitch)
pitch range (*see* pitch)
tempo 2, 18, 48, 57, 138
tension 57–8, 129, 134–7, 153–4, 226
roughness 129, 157, 226-7
vibrato 129, 132–8, 153–4, 226,
    228–9 (*see also* paralinguistic
    affect; voice affect)

waveform 74, 126, 129, 137, 225
waveform spectrogram 74, 129
waves of information 161 (*see*
    information flow; periodicity)

www.ingramcontent.com/pod-product-compliance
Lightning Source LLC
Chambersburg PA
CBHW062122300426
44115CB00012BA/1775